After nature is a timely account of fundamental constructs in English kinship at a moment when developments in reproductive technology are raising questions about the natural basis of kin relations. Kinship in this anthropological study is viewed in the context of contemporary cultural change, and the book is also a unique commentary on late twentieth-century English culture.

This essay on the English middle classes challenges the traditional separation of western kinship studies from study of the wider society. If contemporary society appears diverse, changing and fragmented, these same features also apply to people's ideas about kinship. Ideas of relatedness, nature and the biological constitution of persons are viewed in their cultural context, and the work offers new insight into late twentieth-century values of individualism and consumerism.

Central as kinship has been to the development of British social anthropology, this is the first attempt by an anthropologist to offer a cultural account of English kinship. Marilyn Strathern looks back at mid-century writings, both within anthropology and outside, and demonstrates continuities between middle-class folk models of kinship and anthropological kinship theory. She also shows how conceptualisations of change have enabled that past world to produce the present one. The values placed upon individual choice, as well as the vanishing of 'society' as a self-evident point of reference, are part of an evolving cultural explicitness about kinship and the naturalness of connections between persons. Thus the new reproductive technologies are seen to both indicate ways in which the natural basis of kin relations is being challenged and endorse the centrality of biology to late-twentieth-century views of procreation.

After nature

THE LEWIS HENRY MORGAN LECTURES 1989

presented at
The University of Rochester
Rochester, New York

Lewis Henry Morgan Lecture Series

Fred Eggan: *The American Indian: Perspectives for the Study of Social Change*

Ward, H. Goodenough: *Description and Comparison in Cultural Anthropology*

Robert J. Smith: *Japanese Society: Tradition, Self, and the Social Order*

Sally Falk Moore: *Social Facts and Fabrications: "Customary Law" on Kilimanjaro, 1880–1980*

Nancy Munn: *The Fame of Gawa: A Symbolic Study of Value Transformation in a Mussim (Papua New Guinea) Society*

Lawrence Rosen: *The Anthropology of Justice: Law as culture in Islamic Society*

Stanley Jeyaraja Tambiah: *Magic, Science, Religion, and the Scope of Rationality*

Maurice Bloch: *Prey into Hunter: The Politics of Religious Experience*

mai 23ᵈ Dynes Hall. Mrs S. & Wilkinson

Watercolour, 1817 or 1818

The watercolour (painted by Diana Sperling in 1817 or 1818) shows a conventionally attired couple (proprietor and servant) stepping through the half-open doors of the house (its choice interior visible) into the rain to improve the garden (with potted flowers). These relationships at once offer an allegory for the character of English kinship as one might think of it in 1989 or 1990 and are cancelled by it.

Reproduced by kind permission of Victor Gollancz Ltd, from *Mrs Hurst Dancing* by Diana Sperling, illustrations by Neville Ollerenshaw.

After nature: English kinship in the late twentieth century

MARILYN STRATHERN

Department of Social Anthropology
Manchester University

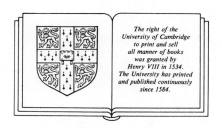

The right of the
University of Cambridge
to print and sell
all manner of books
was granted by
Henry VIII in 1534.
The University has printed
and published continuously
since 1584.

CAMBRIDGE UNIVERSITY PRESS

CAMBRIDGE

NEW YORK   PORT CHESTER   MELBOURNE   SYDNEY

Published by the Press Syndicate of the University of Cambridge
The Pitt Building, Trumpington Street, Cambridge CB2 1RP
40 West 20th Street, New York, NY 10011-4211, USA
10 Stamford Road, Oakleigh, Victoria 3166, Australia

© Cambridge University Press 1992

First published 1992

Printed in Great Britain at the University Press, Cambridge

Library of Congress cataloguing in publication data
Strathern, Marilyn.
After nature: English kinship in the late twentieth century/
Marilyn Strathern.
p.   cm. (The Lewis Henry Morgan lectures; 1989)
Includes bibliographical references.
1. Kinship–England.   2. England–Social conditions.   3. Kinship–Cross-cultural studies.
4. Ethnology–Philosophy.   I. Title.
II. Series.
GN585.G8S77   1992
306.83'094–dc20   91–3775
CIP
A catalogue record for this book is available from the British Library

ISBN 0 521 405254 hardback
ISBN 0 521 42680 4 paperback

For M.A.L.

Contents

Illustrations

Acknowledgement of sources

The author is grateful to the following for permission to use published material from the following sources in the illustrations:

Victor Gollancz Ltd; *Mrs Hurst Dancing*, by Diana Sperling, illustrations by Neville Ollerenshaw, Copyright 1981 (Frontispiece and Plate 12).

The Times Higher Education Supplement (Plate 1, Plate 17 and Plate 20).

International Thomson Publishing Services Ltd for Routledge: *Families and Their Relatives*, by Raymond Firth, Jane Hubert and Anthony Forge. Copyright 1969 (Plate 2).

John Murray (Publishers Ltd): *A Cartoon History of Architecture*, Osbert Lancaster. Copyright 1975 (Plate 3).

Manchester City Council (Plate 4).

Reed Publishing Services Ltd: *Signature* magazine (Plate 5 and Plate 18).

Pergamon Press PLC: *Made to Order: The Myth of Reproductive and Genetic Progress*, eds. Patricia Spallone and Deborah L Steinberg. Copyright 1987 (Plate 6).

Free Association Books: *Languages of Nature*, ed. Ludmilla Jordanova. Copyright 1986 (Plate 7).

Simon and Schuster for Macdonald Children's: *Delights and Warnings*, John and Gillian Beer. Copyright 1979 (Plate 8).

Dove Cottage Ltd, Westfield, New Jersey, USA (Plate 10).

Peter Waymark: *A History of Petts Wood*, Petts Wood Residents' Association (Plate 11 *left*).

J. Freeman for Molloy Homes, Levenshulme, Manchester (Plate 11 *right*).

Unwin Hyman Ltd: *The Two Paths*, John Ruskin (Plate 13).

John Ezard: *The Guardian Weekend Supplement* (Plate 15).

Collins Publishers: *Collins Dictionary of the English Language*, 2nd Edition, Copyright 1986 (Plate 16).

Neville Johnson Offices Ltd, Trafford Park, Manchester (Plate 18).

The Guardian News Service Ltd (Plate 19).

Camden Graphics Ltd and Fine Art Photographic Library Ltd: 'Mother and Child' by Noel Smith (Endpiece).

Foreword

Professor Marilyn Strathern delivered The Lewis Henry Morgan Lectures in 1989, with the general title 'After Nature: English Kinship in the Late Twentieth Century'. The four lectures were 'Diversity and Individuality'; 'Relatives: Analogies for a Plural Culture'; 'Persons: The Progress of a Polite Society'; and 'Greenhouse Effect'. They were delivered on 14, 16, 21 and 23 February and are here made available in a suitably modified form.

The volume continues work carried on by Professor Strathern for over twenty years, the development of which is to be found in several books and many articles. The scope of her efforts is very broad, ranging ethnographically from England to Papua New Guinea, and engaging a number of central theoretical issues. Anthropologists who may have been tempted to conclude that British anthropology has little new to say will surely, faced with her work, wish to think again. For while it is clear that she is firmly based in British social anthropology, Professor Strathern breaks new ground, and nowhere so clearly as here.

The present volume underscores the fascination – and the complexity – of what Professor Strathern is doing. Different readers of the manuscript have characterised it in various ways, though attempts to categorise it simply must eventually fail. This is work that does not fit neatly into accepted categories. Attempts to pigeonhole it serve only to obscure its implications.

Nevertheless it is important to recognize some of the key elements in what is offered. Professor Strathern's main concern is late twentieth-century English kinship, and her account is couched in cultural terms. In order to elucidate her material, much ethnographic data from elsewhere, particularly Melanesia, is set in relation to (and interaction with) the English data. As a result, we are presented with an exercise in comparison that is sophisticated, illuminating and powerful. Another integral part of the analysis is a demonstration of the ways in which English ideas about kinship are related to English ideas about other aspects of English society and how it works. The presentation of English kinship in combination with two carefully developed kinds of comparison – cross-cultural and internal to England – does more than illuminate English kinship. It indicates a need to rethink our ideas about it and about more general matters as well.

As the first cultural account of English kinship by a British anthropologist, this volume will attract the attention of anthropologists generally. Scholars in other disciplines who monitor developments in anthropology will also find it well worth consideration. Readers will find enlightenment and stimulation.

Whether as ethnography or as a fascinating example of complex theory (if these can be disambiguated), Professor Strathern's present work is a major contribution to our understanding of the world and of how to understand it.

Alfred Harris, Editor
The Lewis Henry Morgan Lectures

Preface

This is an exercise in cultural imagination – with respect both to its principal subject matter (English kinship) and to the discipline which is my enabling technology (social anthropology). True to the personifying idioms of each, I wish to demonstrate how ideas behave.

I must acknowledge inspiration from the few works of which it will be seen I make extensive use, not just for their materials but for their interpretations and analyses. They serve to demonstrate my interest in the procedures by which those with a concept of culture make 'culture' explicit to themselves. As a consequence, though, the reader should be warned about the status of primary information in this study. Observations about the English or about kinship are treated as ethnographically continuous with the secondary observations derived from the analytical and interpretive works. The arguments I cite from other scholars thus carry their own, and illustrative, burden of cultural evidence. As a result, the account can not pretend to a history or a sociology, though it incorporates what otherwise would comprise historical and sociological data; nor can it pretend to a history of ideas; and the apparent ascription of attitudes and beliefs to this or that set of persons should not be mistaken for a study of what people think or feel.

It has its own limitations. A problem that besets anthropologists-at-home is that the outcome may not even look like a cultural account. One has become used to mini-ethnographies or social histories or the sociologies of subcultures, whereas what I offer here is a methodological scandal by any of those standards. The difficulty lies, one might say, less in its distance from such genres than in its inevitable proximity to them. Or, to borrow from Paul Rabinow's introduction to *French Modern* (1989), 'while the whole may seem too complex, the parts may seem too simple'.

The original format of The Lewis Morgan Lectures is preserved in the four principal chapters. I owe the invitation to give the Lectures to Professor Alfred Harris and the Department of Social Anthropology at the University of Rochester. Those who have enjoyed the privilege in the past will know what I also owe them for their hospitality: I can only thank Grace and Alfred Harris for their especial kindness, and the Department for their stimulation. With an extension of time and critical attention that was a privilege in itself, members of the Anthropology Department and of Women's Studies at the University of Virginia also heard the full set of lectures.

I should add that the book was finished in June 1990. Since then the Warnock Report, to which several references are made, has become the basis of legislation, although I make no mention of this. There has also been a change in the British premiership. While it would have been in keeping to have retained the original text, this would have sounded odd, and I have made the appropriate alterations.

Several colleagues have read the manuscript, and they are thanked warmly for their comments and criticisms: Anthony Cohen, Frederick Damon, Jeanette Edwards, Sarah Franklin, Jane Haggis, Eric Hirsch, Frances Price, Nigel Rapport, Tim Swindlehurst and Nicholas Thomas, as are the Press's readers. Jean Ashton has also taken care of it in her own inimitable way. I should add that where 'n.d.' appears in the bibliography, I am grateful for permission to cite as yet unpublished work.

David Schneider is the anthropological father of this book, since it is both with and against his ideas on kinship that it is written; his reactions have been characteristically incisive and generous. Another colleague, Joyce Evans, is the mother of this book, since it is from her Englishness that I write; her love and knowledge of nineteenth- and twentieth-century literature have kept me culturally on track. She is also my mother in the literal sense, and my thanks are also filial.

Marilyn Strathern
Manchester
January 1989/June 1990

Prologue: making explicit

Visitors to England, the English are fond of telling themselves, are often struck by the space devoted to gardens and parks, so different from the civic plazas that grace continental Europe. Towns and cities are likely to be cramped, higgledy piggledy. But go into the suburbs with their lawns and flower-beds and you will sense an avenue architecture of its own kind, at once domestic (the semi-detached houses) and public (a common front of shrubs, hedges, fences). What might be regarded as typically English, however, is the product not only of the demands of a particular social class but of a particular period – from mid-Victorian town houses built as country homes to Edwardian villas at the very edges of the countryside and garden cities enclosing the idea of countryside within.

That is, of course, no revelation. On the contrary, the English also tell themselves about the particular periods they are heir to and the extent to which things have altered since. If it is no revelation, then one might wonder how the twin ideas of continuity and change coexist. How come that the one (change) seems as much in place as the other (continuity)?

For it is equally conventional to deny that the typical ever exists. When visitors to England remark, as they do, on rubbish in the streets of the metropolis or when the English abroad are treated as responsible for forest-stripping acid rain, the sense is of falling on changed times. In denying the typicality of particular characteristics, one may well deny that one can ever think of what is typical about the English. A vision of constant change displaces that of perpetual continuity; all appears transient and nothing stable. Change and continuity are thus played off against one another. Indeed, change can be visualised as a sequence of events that 'happens' to something that otherwise retains its identity, such as the English themselves, or the countryside: continuity makes change evident. It is in just such a coexistence of ideas that cultural epochs are formed. I wish to convey a sense of epoch.

The stable and the transient coexist in a manner that makes it possible to ask, with respect to almost anything, how much change has taken place. This is a very general, ordinary and otherwise unremarkable kind of question. It

1

seems to lead naturally to further questions about what should be conserved and what should be reformed. It also exerts a presence in certain academic ways of thinking, where the relationship between change and continuity is often spelled out with considerable explicitness. Let me illustrate the general idea through a particular example.

Take attitudes towards the natural world. When what varies seem to be the different meanings that different historical periods have put on it, or the different effects of diverse social practices, then 'nature' itself appears an enduring, even timeless, phenomenon. In Keith Thomas's (1984) detailed account of the dramatic changes that occurred in the idea of nature in England between 1500 and 1800, the reference point throughout remains the countryside and its plants and wild and domestic animals. This means, of course, that Alan Macfarlane (1987), with an equal order of detail, can trace a traditional love of nature back to medieval England and argue the reverse thesis: far from there having been radical change, one finds consistent antecedents to contemporary attitudes. His evidence includes the longstanding English obsession with gardening, and their habit of keeping animals as pets. The observations are not trivial. Macfarlane points to an intimate connection between these characteristics of the English and the individualism of their modern kinship system, a connection that, he claims, has roots in English society for as long as records go back. The cultural preconditions for later changes were always there. It is the extent of the continuity that is impressive, in his view, rather than the extent of change.

Whether or not there have been changes on the face of the countryside, or in ideas about the environment, the concept of nature thus remains a constant fact in the debate. One can therefore dispute as to whether activities and attitudes in relation to it have altered or have stayed the same over the course of time. The result is that change and continuity become measurable entities insofar as each appears to have had more or less effect on the same object. The one may be conceived as a quantifiable (how much, to what extent) constraint on the other.

Now an academic debate such as this, about the relative *amount* of change and continuity, is consonant with that mid-twentieth-century mode of scholarly theorising known as 'social constructionism'. The theory is that what is constructed is 'after' a fact. It is proved in the way people can be seen to fabricate their world and in the models they build of it, and offers a kind of autoproof, since it knows itself as a model also. In this theory that is also a model, values can be seen as constructions after social facts, or societies can be seen as constructions after natural facts. What becomes quantifiable is the amount of human activity ('construction') that has taken place. Implicit in the theory/model is the assumption that change is a mark of activity or endeavour whereas continuity somehow is not.

But I propose we disarm the antithesis between change and continuity of its quantifiable power. Instead of thinking what they measure, we might think how each depends on the other to demonstrate its effect. Magnifying one is to magnify both. I write with the hindsight that, over the span of an epoch, the English have brought the most radical changes on their heads by striving most vehemently to preserve a sense of continuity with the past. And have in the process revolutionised the very concept of nature to which they would probably prefer to be faithful.

The scholars' social–constructionist model of the world contains more than the idea that society is built up after, or out of, elements other than itself (natural entities such as reproductive individuals and primordial sentiments or units such as parental pairs and families). It also incorporates the idea that, in working upon and modifying the natural world, human artifice must at the same time remain true to its laws and to that extent imitate it. I suspect that this concatenation of ideas is borrowed from, as much as it describes, models more generally held. The academic debate to which I alluded, between the anthropologically minded historian (Thomas) and the historian–anthropologist (Macfarlane), leads us to an area where such models are to be found: kinship.

The anthropological study of kinship since mid-Victorian and Edwardian times, as well as the (indigenous) models held by others of the social class from which by and large the authors of such studies came, has drawn heavily on the idea that kinship systems are also after the facts, and specifically after certain well-known facts of nature.[1] The facts, it is held, are universal whereas ideas about kinship obviously vary. In this view, for instance, cultural dogmas differ in the extent to which they recognise biological connection, social classes in the extent to which they emphasise maternal and paternal roles, and historical periods in the emphasis given to family life. In short, societies or sections of society differ in the way they handle the same facts. This is an axiom or assumption that is as much part *of* English kinship thinking as it is of social constructionist theorising about it. I capitalise on the thought that making this implicit assumption explicit has already deprived it of its axiomatic and paradigmatic status.

The epoch in question covers a span of modern Western thought of particular interest to anthropology, following the hundred years or so after Lewis Henry Morgan's endeavours of the 1860s. Among other things, its practitioners were interested in quantification – not just in enumeration and statistical patterning but in whether whole cultures might have 'more' or 'less' culture (the yardsticks of civilisation), or groups evince 'more' or 'less' cohesion (indices of solidarity), or persons be symbolised as 'more' or 'less' close to nature (women's distance from social centrality). One might think of the modern epoch as pluralist, then, and its successor as postplural in character.

That there has been a succession and that this epoch is superseded is one of my themes. At least, I hope to show one of the ways in which such successions happen by contriving a postplural vantage point from which to look back to a modern one. The motive lies in a thwarted ambition.

For some time, it had been my ambition to write a counterpart to David Schneider's *American Kinship* (1968): a cultural account of English kinship. However, coming to the task more than two decades later was to realise that times had changed. The twin constructs on which Schneider was confident enough to premise his analysis of American kinship were not to be identified with such transparency. These were the order of Nature and the order of Law, the order of Law referring to human organisation, *viz*. Society or Culture. They had appeared to Schneider to constitute major dimensions of American thinking about kinship in the 1960s, and indeed were indigenous exemplifications of constructs on whose basis anthropology had developed its disciplinary force over the previous century. The social or cultural construction of kinship had always been a special instance of the general manner in which human beings constructed societies and cultures 'out of' nature. Indeed, the development of specifically anthropological models of human life had thus gone hand in hand with the elucidation of kinship systems. I believe this was equally true of British as it was of American anthropology.

Now I had deliberately wished to avoid a 'social' account in favour of a 'cultural' one. In the mid-twentieth century, these terms coded a significant difference between British and American anthropology. However, my cultural interest stemmed, I thought, not from a desire to Americanise my anthropology but from a desire to bring to light certain assumptions that seemed to inhere in British approaches to kinship.[2] The social anthropological models of kinship so well nurtured in Britain in the mid-century, and so illuminating in relation to non-Western societies, seemed after all to obscure rather than clarify things when it came to elucidating the English. I had in my mind an alternative cultural account because, whatever it was that gave this subtitle to Schneider's work, the twin constructs of Nature and Law were there to be unpacked as premises both of the indigenous English model and of the (British) anthropological studies that sought to describe it. I think in retrospect I had been interestingly naive; or rather, that I am (a cultural) exemplar of the processes that made me write this book.

It is widely the case in contemporary Britain that one's sense of time or change may also be sensed as the Americanisation of the English. Yet in my own case it is not just home-grown conceptualisations of kinship that have come to seem insufficient, *so too* do Schneider's motivating constructs. Neither seeing the English through models developed for non-Western systems, nor seeing them through that particular cultural model of American kinship, will quite do today. And these constructions appear insufficient for one simple reason. They are now visible from the point of view of their previously taken-for-granted assumptions.

The process that leads to the displacement of analytical models, an outcome of deliberate endeavour on the part of scholars, matches or is an analogy for similar processes in Western (Anglo-Euro-American) social life at large. In fact, anthropologists collapse this analogy when they claim (as they often do) that earlier anthropological accounts are informed by the general social and cultural precepts of their times. What was implicit, and not seen then, is thereby made explicit, and is seen now. Making things explicit I refer to as a practice of literalisation, that is, a mode of laying out the coordinates or conventional points of reference of what is otherwise taken for granted. One effect of literalisation is to realise that describing a process of construction is itself a construction of sorts. This is the autoproof of social constructionism.

Literalisation entails, so to speak, a half-movement; its complement is the recreation of what must be taken for granted and thus apprehended essentially or figuratively for its intrinsic qualities. But the constant opening out of the conventions upon which human endeavour is seen to rest has had such an emphatic place in Anglo-Euro-American discourse precisely for the emphasis given to the role of human construction in the making of society and culture. It is this *particular* investment in the efficacy of 'construction' that leads students of social life to make evident to themselves the basis of their own particular constructions.

Consider the revelations of change and continuity. What we might take as characteristically typical, a product of some continuous and taken-for-granted identity, may well be revealed as equally the product of specific historical times and thus of change. Such an opening out or literalisation of the typical as belonging to one particular period rather than another recreates in turn the taken-for-granted idea that it is, after all, historical periods that are distinctive by what typifies them.

There is one specific move towards literalisation whose effect I wish to make explicit: in the currently prevalent idea that nature and culture are both cultural constructions, the one term (culture) seems to consume the other (nature). We might put it that an antithesis between nature and culture as it might have shaped certain discourses in English life has become flattened; if so, it is flattened in a mode specific to the late twentieth century, and one that has indeed had an interesting effect as far as culture is concerned. This may be illustrated in the awkwardness of a recent critique of mine (Strathern 1988). My objection there was to the way the distinctions between Nature and Culture, Society and Individual, had in the past been attributed unthinkingly to the symbolic systems of certain non-Western peoples. The critique may well be justified, but I could not account for the uneasy status that culture retained in my own analysis. Culture in the sense of system or organisation was easy to make explicit as an analytical device; but the narrative was left taking for granted culture in the sense of a distinctiveness of style or imagery. Crudely, the conundrum is an outcome of an excess of sorts. The excess is that of cultural critique.

Culture exceeds itself (Nature vanishes) and, outcultivated, Culture is manifest as style. And an excess of individualism? Does Society also vanish; will the Individual become visible only in the exercise of an agency where all is choice? Excesses of style and choice may appear an obvious process of Americanisation from an 'English' point of view. Yet holding that view is equally a process of Anglicisation.

While much of what I say applies to Anglo-Euro-American or Western culture in general, such culture is only lived in specific forms. None of us lives generalised lives, generalise as we might about life as such, and I take English as one form. In any case, the English are adepts at literalisation – a penchant

---

Why do I prefer that we in Britain should take the route of expansion through diversification and differentiation? Most profoundly, because it seems to me to be the one which is natural to us. Historically, traditionally, Britain is a bottom-up, not a top-down society. We should build on our national genius, on what comes naturally to us. We do best when we avoid the abstract intellectual construct, the grand design. We do much, much better when the practical intelligence of the many is applied at the level where, in this case, the students are taught and the research is done. This is the way I hope British higher education will grow in the next quarter century.

---

1 *The Secretary of State for Education, 1989*
Extract from a speech by the Secretary of State for Education and Science, Kenneth Baker "Higher Education: the next 25 years". *The Times Higher Education Supplement.* 13 January 1989.
Reproduced by kind permission.

they share with Euro-Americans becomes a posture in their commitment to the ideals of empiricism and practical action. The stereotype of pragmatism[3] has an element of persuasion in it. They apparently love the literal-minded. Their fantasies are about 'the real world' – only clear away the assumptions and you will get to the truth; only clear away the constructions and you will get to the facts.

Making the implicit explicit is a mode of constructing knowledge which has been an engine for change for more than a hundred years. It has also produced an internal sense of complexity and diversity. But to make explicit *this* mode has its own effect: the outliteralisation of the literal-minded. I suspect something similar to this particular literalisating move has been behind the prevalent sense of a now that is after an event. This sense of being after an event, of being post-, defines the present epoch.

The single most significant event in question is the earlier modern epoch, when constructions were instead after a fact – the facts of reality, nature or procreation – and where human endeavour bore the imprint of a complex enterprise. This was the epoch that produced the scholars' social constructionism. Anthropology was the discipline that uncovered the quantity of enterprise in human endeavour everywhere. It is its own enterprise that is now made visible, and 'after' the facts has come to mean after the facts have ceased to be quantifiable. We know today that there are as many of them as we care to make. Hence this book is written from hindsight. It deals with the modern epoch from the vantage point of its displacement. The result is no more than a teleology that extends back from the present and in asking about how things appear in the late twentieth century attends only to their possible antecedents.

The following coordinates may be useful to the reader.[4] Modernists characterised English society as complex or plural, a product of long history and much change. The typical was timeless, and tradition or continuity implied homogeneity; change implied innovation, the introduction of foreign elements, heterogeneity, in short, diversity. Hindsight tells us that it was, of course, the sense of continuity which was subject to change, and all that was necessary to transform a tradition was to bring it into the present and give it a contemporary place. (The stylistic re-introduction of 'traditional' forms that constitutes postmodernism in art and architecture presents this as a revelation.) It was simply a matter of valuing one's already established values. In fact all that was necessary to transform ones' values was to value them in such a way as to make explicit (to oneself) their context or basis. In thereby making the implicit explicit, one took away that axiomatic status and created new taken-for-granted assumptions for excavation. With hindsight we can further see that, as a model of knowledge, such a practice offered a constantly receding horizon of what there was to know: one could seek to know more about something by investigating its context or the assumptions on which its assumptions were grounded.

That modern dimension of grounding or context in turn yielded a sense of perspective, the 'point of view' from which an entity was seen. One could always gain a new perspective by providing a new context for what was being observed. There were thus as many points of view as there were facets of social and cultural, including scientific, life. *This plurality was a given*, and complex society awarded itself the ability to superimpose perspectives (self-conscious 'constructions') upon a plurality inherent in the nature of things.

British anthropology participated in that literalising endeavour. Its claims to attention rested on the dual skills of putting things into (social and cultural) context, and in making implicit (cultural and social) assumptions explicit. It also claimed kinship as a particular domain of expertise and activity. Again with hindsight one can see that it nonetheless ran into problems when it came to dealing with kinship in its culture of origin: there was too intimate a connection between anthropological theories of kinship and indigenous constructs. The connection can be turned to use. In thinking about what English kinship was to become, I propose to use British anthropological kinship theory and English kin constructs as mutual perspectives on each other's modernisms. This necessarily deprives each of its perspectival completeness.

The processes by which the English produced a sense of complexity for themselves were alarmingly simple. But, like simple computer viruses, they could proliferate at speed through the social machinery. In showing the way literalisation constantly produced fresh perspectives, one has said all that need be said about the mechanism by which we once imagined ourselves in a complex world.

The effects were everywhere. The mechanism might be simple, but the products or results were innumerable. Thus when members of a complex society compared it with that of others, they could think of themselves both as producing 'more' individualistic individuals (more subjectivity), and as providing 'more' cultural and social contexts in which to act (more institutions).[5] In the account that follows, I give recent examples of simple proliferations of form – the shapes that ideas and values and idioms take. The material will appear inevitably disparate, out of scale even, an observation about kitchens in London illustrated by office designs in Manchester; an introduction to the field of English kinship [in Chapter One] offering observations drawn from quite disjunct levels. The immediate effect may suggest plurality taken to excess; but the disparateness is not quite what it seems. It is with postplural vision that the pluralism of the preceding epoch becomes evident.[6]

Illustrations have been selected widely but not at random. I have hoped both to make it evident that the observations that apply to kinship or to anthropological study are not applicable only to these domains and to draw in issues in the management of present-day political and social life from which neither kinship nor anthropology is isolated. At the same time I have also

hoped to suggest that such free-ranging access, such apparent freedom of
choice, in the end turns the sense of plurality into an artefact of access or
choice itself. An approximation to the insight, then, of what it might be like to
belong to a culture whose next imaginative leap is to think of itself as having
nothing to construct. It would not, after all, be after anything.

1

Individuality and diversity

To those who were bringing up families in the 1950s or 1960s, their children are already quite a long way down the road from dreams of garden cities, as they are from taking for granted a view of enclosed fields and hedgerows. Prairie farms can be found in southern England, and the rain that has kept the countryside with its own parks and gardens proverbially green prompts thoughts of a man-made pluvial. Despite such global manifestations of too much enterprise, however, the slogans of the self-named Enterprise Culture[1] assert that a natural and traditional individualism is being restored to the English. If so, its environment has changed. Today's is the individualism of zapping between television channels, of single-minded captivation by east Asian computer screens, of a world where social conditions are taken for cultural style and First World shoppers can consume the food of almost any country on earth. In 1964, I saw sugar cane and taro for the first time in the Papua New Guinea Highlands; twenty-five years on, I can choose African varieties of them in a suburban Safeway in Manchester. Meanwhile, there is talk of schemes to privatise city streets with security guards and residents' patrols – public areas are said to make the defence of domestic property too difficult.

It is tautologous to say that the change comes from microchips or consumer demand or urban decay: this is the change. And so is the form that late twentieth-century individualism takes. Such individualism as the English wish to award themselves is after all a new individualism. In any case, individual enterprise is regarded as containing an inherent momentum towards novelty.

In what sense, then, might we regard individualism as traditional if, as is also the case, it is the enterprise of individuals that is held up as a source of innovation, development and the transformation of tradition? The one abstraction (tradition) seems to work against and at once mask and expose the other (novelty). These are issues in the construction of ideas that are not to be settled by deciding 'how much' tradition or novelty is found at this moment or that. It is in order to approach the construction of ideas then, that I start with a field of phenomena in English culture that epitomises tradition under the

10

pressure of change. Kinship is my example. The period is roughly the modernism of the 1860s to 1960s, but the view is from now (cf. Hastrup n.d.). If I sometimes shift in tense, it is because the late twentieth century contains as much as it supersedes this earlier modernism. I speak of kinship; the English more readily refer to family and relatives.

Family relationships are conventionally taken as embodying primordial ties that somehow exist outside or beyond the technological and political machinations of the world, that suffer change rather than act as a force for change. Indeed, the enduring ties of kinship may be regarded as archetypically traditional in antithesis to the conditions of modern life. The wider the network and the more extensive the reach of kin relations or the more emphatic the solidarity of the family, the more traditional they seem. It is, however, possible both to accept that conceptualisation of tradition and to realise its contemporary force. Precisely because kinship is supposed to be about primordial relations, the fundamental facts it endorses have been intrinsic to the cultural enterprise built up after it. Ideas about what is natural, primordial and embedded in the verities of family life are thereby made relevant to the present, will be refashioned for the future. Where I turn to earlier historical periods, it will be to amplify how such ideas revolve on themselves – and revolutionise us in the process.

Facts of kinship

Pets and children

An antithesis between an extensive reach of kin relations and the enterprise of individuals is one that Macfarlane (1978) would project far back into the English past. There he finds quite habitual the denial of relationships and of kin claims beyond the narrowest span. Individualism is traditional for the English. Go back to the thirteenth century, even, and you will discover the English behaving in the same individualistic way we take as so typical of our own times. These connections led Macfarlane to conclude that the great historical divide (the origins of capitalism) was not such a divide after all, and indeed there was a reason why England was the first industrial nation of Europe. Thus he suggests that by 1500, and certainly by 1650, the pre-conditions for the modern view of nature were already established (1978: 97). But whereas his account would stress the continuity of ideas that are 'old' and run 'deep', or of proclivities that are curiously 'preserved', it is also an historical axiom (cf. Ranger and Hobsbawm 1983) that old ideas only endure insofar as they are reproduced in new forms; tradition is thereby reinvented in every change. Conversely we arrive at the other view, that new ideas can only emerge from their antecedents. It is tradition that changes: indeed, it is all that can.

That is, of course, a view implicated in the very claim (which is my claim) to hindsight. There is a similar view implicated in the claim to perceive connections. It is an anthropological axiom that however discrete they appear to be, entities are the product of relations; nothing is not embedded in some context or worldview that gives it its special shape. I propose to take the axiom literally, as though what applies to discrete concepts also applies to individual persons and that by relations we may also understand the 'relations' (one's relatives) of English kinship.

The English have a special emotion for dwelling on tradition, or for dwelling on what is just out of reach of enterprise: sentimentality. Their sentimentality for pets is a case in point. Macfarlane is taken with Thomas's idea of the link between keeping pets and 'a modern, atomistic, kinship system' (1987: 95). The link is that of emotional satisfaction – pets act as substitutes for children – and is one Macfarlane traces back into medieval times. He himself puts emotional attachment as a need that exists beyond or outside the relationships and, indeed, suggests it is a cause rather than a product of relationships coming into being. Such a need for surrogates is to be interpreted with respect to all the characteristics of English kinship that set it off from its European congeners, such as late marriage, low birth rate, isolated living units. Pets were regarded as luxuries, as alternative children, which in turn meant that the English came to regard children as luxuries also, as superior pets, and sentimentally accorded them a kind of uniqueness thereby. He cites (1986: 54ff) sixteenth- and seventeenth-century depictions of children indulged and petted as playthings.[2] And like pets, he intriguingly adds, in time 'they would leave their "owners": pets died, children left home and withdrew emotionally' (1986: 55).

It is thus a social relationship of a particular kind, namely between parents and children, which centrally evinces what he calls individualism. For much of the medieval period, and extending into early modern times, Macfarlane documents the concomitant independence of children from parents, the prevalence of wage labour and service, the contractual nature of inheritance, in short an individualistic system where private emotions were strong and 'formal kinship' weak (1987: 139). The individualism that these (social) arrangements nourished was exemplified in a sense of uniqueness often expressed as isolationism. It also had an elective nature, that is, was a matter of choice.

His own reach is generous: he traces the love of the countryside back to a Germanic preference that came through the three waves of Anglo/Saxon, Viking and Norman settlements of the country, and as something about the English that was still to surprise visitors in the nineteenth century. He quotes the Frenchman Taine and his comments on parks and gardens as a visitor to England in the 1860s:

> In my opinion these gardens reveal, better than any other work, the poetic dream in the English soul ... All their imagination, all their native inventiveness has gone into their parks ...

> [Of the then industrial town of Manchester Taine wrote that]

Here and in Liverpool, as in London, the English character can be seen in their way of building. The townsman does everything in his power to cease being a townsman, and tries to fit a country-house and a bit of country into a corner of the town. He feels the need to be in his own home, to be alone, king of his family and servants, and to have about him a bit of park or garden in which he can relax after his artificial business life. (Macfarlane 1987: 78, references deleted)

The individualism associated with a low birth rate, with a high value on each unique child and with keeping pets for surrogate emotional satisfaction was also to be seen in a cherishing of particular patches of the countryside – both the wild moors and mountains of the romantic aesthete and those pieces of private property which meant that 'the Englishman' could retire behind walls. Individualism became visible in professed solitude, and solitude was a condition in which wilderness was also to be appreciated. So where Thomas argues that a perceived separation of man from nature in the seventeenth and eighteenth centuries was the precondition for a new and individualistic attitude towards specific animals (quoted in Macfarlane 1987: 80), Macfarlane himself insists that such cultural traits were in evidence long before. Along with a market mentality and high mobility, they were part of 'a very ancient system' (1987: 137), *exemplified in the most intimate of relationships* when children could physically remove themselves from their parents and parents who wanted to be cared for by children had to enter into contracts with them.

It is less the claims to the historical continuity of individualism that I find interesting in Macfarlane's account than the contemporary rendering he gives of one of its forms. An individual in his view is a person who can set him or herself off from proximity to and relationships with others, and is thus created in being separated from the constraints of relationship itself.

Society is the Frenchman's meat and drink; to be left alone, the Englishman's. Hence it is that government of any kind irks him

wrote one Macneile Dixon (1938: 70) in the interwar years, a sentiment to which I shall have cause to return. What Macfarlane's observations add is that individualism was also to be found in the literal capacity of a person to move away from the society of others. Isolation was a physical (geographical) fact. And if separate households facilitated the individual's removal from the demands of prior relationships, then separation appears as a quantifiable fact! It ought to be possible to assess its degree or incidence by establishing how frequently children were able to set up on their own. This indeed is similar to the kind of questions often asked of historical material. Yet whether or not it is to be illuminated by enumeration, such a relationship between individualism and isolation is also one of analogy, and the analogy is an apparatus for signification.

Physical removal could stand for an exercise of independence. In the image of the child being sent away from home or breaking free from its parents was an invitation to imagine the individual person being set against the givens of his or her social situation, and against pre-existing relationships.

It is somewhat paradoxical, therefore, to regard individualism as a characteristic *of* certain relationships themselves. The evidence, as we have seen, is the way that parents and children might in the past have arranged contractual agreements with one another, or how like pets children may be the objects of their parents' special affection. To treat someone as 'special' is conceivably as much a relational device as to enter into an apparently impersonal contract with them: both reconstructions make one kind of relationship out of a relationship of another kind. What these particular possibilities have in common is the notion that the pre-existing character of relationships need not after all be taken for granted. The implicit status of the parent–child tie can be circumvented, and the relationship explicitly re-constructed to the greater or lesser private satisfaction of the individual parties.

English ideas about the value of individualism and the individuality of persons are not to be understood simply in terms of what they describe, namely by documenting people's solitude or resistance to taken-for-granted relationships – any more than ideas or concepts exist on their own! They coexist with others. The observer must consequently look at the management of relationships and at the relations between ideas. We might consider, then, how the particular social relationship of parent and child generates the image of the child not just as son or daughter but as a unique individual. Indeed, we might consider *the individuality of persons as the first fact of English kinship*.

Let me spell out the implications. Like continuity and change or tradition and novelty, society and individual may be construed in antithesis. Any one of these concepts may be thought of as an element or force or principle that has a governing or regulative effect on people's lives insofar as it competes with its pair in quantitative effect. Each pair of concepts thus seems to offer a totalising perspective on life. At the same time there are many such perspectives, for many such antitheses run through English culture. 'Tradi-tion' is similar to but not quite the same as and hence overlaps with the idea of 'continuity'; it is continuity seen from the point of view of what is regarded as characteristic or typical about something. The 'conventional' overlaps in turn with the idea of 'tradition'; it is tradition seen from the point of view of what is regarded as regulative in social life. Pairs of concepts may form a similar series. For instance, the idea of 'enterprise' working against the inert influence of 'culture' (tradition/continuity/convention) adds another perspective to what then appears as a string not of isolated concepts but of analogies. Finally a pair may well be composed of elements (enterprise/inertia) internally connected as though each were, so to speak, the other in a prior (inertia) or transformed (enterprise) state.

Think of these particular antitheses as though they modelled a reproductive process. The child that comes from its parents is not its parents. That the child is not its parents provides an image for thinking about the contrast between tradition versus novelty, relationships versus individuals; that the child comes from its parents prompts a counterinterpretation. Tradition innovates; relationships produce individuals.

Suppose these conceptualisations did indeed once constitute a reproductive, or procreative (after Yeatman 1983), model. The model would be both grounds for and an outcome of kinship thinking. Its implicit developmentalism makes generation appear irreversible: children seem further on in time from their parents; tradition comes 'before' change. We could thus say that relationships come 'before' persons. Parents already united in a relationship produce individual children. We might further say that their unity as one person presupposes the individuality of the child. Yet, in their children, parents (persons in a relationship) also produce other than themselves (individual persons). Individuality would thus be both a fact of and 'after' kinship.

Convention and choice

Individualism has its own quantification effect – persons are thought to exercise more or less individuality, by analogy with the amount of freedom one has to act in this or that manner. It is even measurable between parents and children, at least to the extent that the English regard children as more individualistic than parents. In the relationship between them, it seems that the parent can stand for the idea of relationship itself, cast in terms of given ties, obligation and responsibility, while the child demonstrates the capacity to grow away from relationships, as an independent person constructing his or her own reference points. Thus, as Janet Finch describes (1989: 53), the parent's duty to care for the helpless child is more of a certainty than the child's duty to care in later years for a helpless parent. However, it is quite possible to reverse the case, and stress the greater individuation of the parents (each representing a unique side of the family) by contrast with the child who belongs to both. The parent–child relationship in fact offers a two-way apparatus for imagining degrees of individuality.

It is a characteristic of the organisation of ideas that I describe that almost any perspective can be countermanded by another. Hence the view 'from the child' finds, so to speak, another version in the view 'from the parent'. The view from the child seems a specifically English echo of Macfarlane's seventeenth- and eighteenth-century observation 'that obligations, like emotion, flowed down [from parent to child]' in that, after the jurist Blackstone, 'natural affection descends more strongly than it ascends ' (1986: 82). The view from the parent has nineteenth-century antecedents in the uniqueness claimed for the parent–child relationship by virtue of its basis in the individual identities of each parent. This uniqueness became, for anthropology, an index for those kinship systems to which English was ultimately perceived to belong.

It was the American Morgan who, in classifying systems by their designations of kin persons, showed that the conventions of descriptive kin terminology were not universal but constituted a distinct type. The type was common to ancestral Aryan, Semitic and Uralian language groups, as he called them, the last a category that included Europeans and Muslim peoples of the biblical lands of the Near East, and thus in his view the ancestors of what we would call Western civilisation (Trautmann 1987: 133). Anthropologists who by and large reject the evolutionary model that lay behind Morgan's eventual sequencing of types nonetheless by and large accept the distinctiveness of descriptive terminologies.

A descriptive terminology acknowledges the uniqueness of a child's parents, being based upon the 'correct appreciation' (so he said) of the distinction between a lineal and a collateral connection. A child's individual parents are differentiated from other senior kin, as in the English designation of these as aunts and uncles. Descriptive systems contrast with those classificatory systems of kin terminologies from elsewhere in the world which confound these relations with others, and where parents and parents' siblings may be known by a single term.

Now originally, Morgan conceived the contrast as between those closer to and more distant from nature. The descriptive system was closer to the facts. Thus he characterised it as one that 'follows the actual streams of blood' (quoted by Trautmann 1987: 137). Indeed the draft opening chapter of *Systems of Consanguinity* referred to family relationships existing in nature independently of human creation. If genealogy was, in his view, a natural arrangement, then the genius of the descriptive terminology was that it implied true knowledge of the (universal) processes of parenthood and reproduction (cf. Schneider 1984: 98). The individuality of a child's particular mother and particular father was preserved in the distinctive kin terms.

Morgan was writing in the 1860s, about the time of Taine's observations on the English countryside. Adam Kuper (1988: 64–5) reminds us that Morgan was also a visitor to England, when he delivered copies of his *Systems* in 1871. He called on Maine, McLennan, Lubbock, Darwin and Huxley, and 'took the Lubbock–Tylor model [of social evolution] back to America'. British social anthropology was to become in turn heir to this American intervention (cf. Fortes 1969). However, parts of Morgan's theory were too much for some at the time. John McLennan's subsequent quarrel with Morgan included an attack on his explanation for classificatory terminologies, pointing to the absurdity of imagining that anyone might not recognise 'his' own individual mother. Ever since, anthropological debate has largely concerned the validity of Morgan's classificatory models; but we might turn that around and reclaim Morgan from a Western perspective. In the course of making his classificatory discovery evident, he had also made the uniqueness of parental identity the founding assumption of his analysis of that class of advanced, descriptive kinship terminologies which included those based on English language usage.

Whatever one might say about the formal properties of the terminology, perhaps the popularity of Morgan's scheme among anthropologists rests in the demonstration that the individuality of the parents visibly contributes to the uniqueness of the parent–child relationship as a whole. The contrast is with systems that do not afford such a sense of uniqueness. For the twentieth-century English, that contrast reappears as an internal feature of the relationship itself, in the same way, as I have suggested, that one party to the relationship can appear 'more' unique or individuated than the other.

The general point is indicated in the frequent interdigitation of kinship terms and personal names. It is as though the very use of kin terms in English has a classificatory cast to it, while personal names are held to be descriptive of the unique individual.[3] A kin term denotes a relationship and thus a perspective on the person from another's viewpoint. Of course, a contrast lies between kin terms themselves. Terms of reference for absent relatives appear more formal than the often familiar diminution of terms of address. But when a name is regarded as more informal or personal than a kin term, then all kin terms come to have generic connotations. Between names, there is a further contrast in the differentiation of surname and Christian name. These days one talks of first rather than Christian name and, for most people, the connotations of the baptised name as admitting the person to a community of souls is displaced by its personalising features (Firth, Hubert and Forge (1969: 304) equate the Christian name with 'personal name'). In that aspect, the first name is more personal, we might say, than the surname or family name.

Here lies a history within a history. Harold Nicolson, writing in 1955, comments thus on the twentieth-century revival of a fashion for first names which had prevailed briefly in certain circles at the turn of the eighteenth and nineteenth centuries:[4]

> In my own life-time ... the feeling about Christian names has [again] changed completely. My father would never have used the Christian name of any man or woman who was not a relation or whom he had not known for at least thirty years. My aunt called her husband by his surname until the day of his death. It was in the reign of Edward VII that the use of Christian names first became fashionable, and even then it was surrounded by all manner of precautions and restrictions. Today to address a man by his surname might appear distant, snobbish, old-fashioned and rather rude ... I am often amazed by the dexterity with which actors, band-leaders, merchants, clubmen and wireless-producers will remember to say 'Veronica' or 'Shirley' to women to whom they have not even been introduced. This engaging habit derives, I suppose, from the United States: from the belief cherished by the citizens of that Republic that all men, as all women, are created equal and that these gambits of intimacy form part of the pursuit of happiness. (Nicholson 1955: 273)

Note the consensus about the signification of such shifts, that among any circle of people the move from surnames to first names is a move from formality to informality; it parallels the decisions people make as to whether they use kin terms or names for their relatives. The latter is also interpreted as

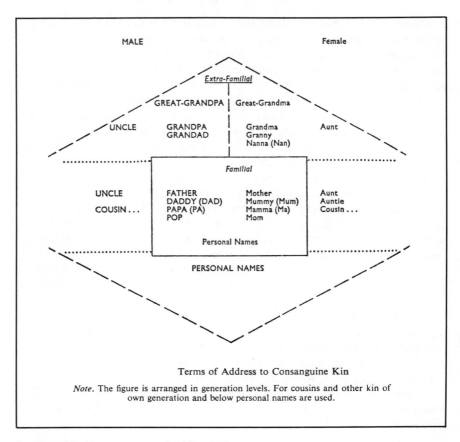

Terms of Address to Consanguine Kin

Note. The figure is arranged in generation levels. For cousins and other kin of own generation and below personal names are used.

2 *Terms of address to consanguine kin* c.*1960*
Reproduced by kind permission of Routledge, from *Families and Their Relatives, Kinship in a Middle-Class Sector of London*, by Raymond Firth, Jane Hubert and Anthony Forge, 1969.

a gesture towards informality, as down-playing the given role element in a relationship and up-playing the uniqueness of the interpersonal dimension.

What happens in everyday address is illuminating in this regard. Plate 2 is reproduced from a study of families in London begun by Raymond Firth and his colleagues some five years after Nicolson's observations (Firth, Hubert and Forge 1969: 302). (An accompanying diagram not reproduced here shows the rather different spread of terms used when people refer to kin in the presence of third parties.) The authors of the study remark that English terms of address were regularly replaced or supplemented by personal names provided, that is, the addressees were of a generation equal to or junior to ego. Only a tiny percentage (6 %) of their respondents in the early 1960s recorded using personal names to address parents (1969: 304–6).

An interesting aspect of the interplay between personal names and kin terms in intimate family life, then, lies in the asymmetry of reciprocal usage. Children are called by their personal names, parents and grand-parents by kin terms, while aunts and uncles are often known by a combination of kin term and personal name. Members of a junior generation are also assumed to be younger in age ('children' means both offspring and young persons). In some circles, it is an affectation to address someone as son or daughter face to face, while sister and brother as terms of address often carries joking overtones. In the principal contrast between generic kin terms (for parents) and individual personal names (for children), individuality seemingly belongs 'more' to the child than the parent.

It is parents who normally bestow these individual names. Although anyone can call themselves by what name they please, convention has it that your names are bestowed by the parents. So this individuation is established at birth. Parents produce a unique offspring; it is the parents' duty to name their child, anticipating the child's individuality in exercising their own. While there is no choice about giving the child a name, they can choose which name it is to be, and may even think they have invented a name – my own Marilyn being a case in point. The child may, of course, determine usage; I do not use my initial name. Friends, like kin, also reserve to themselves the right to vary the person's name as they please. Such practices can be taken as a particular example of a more general distinction between convention and choice. Within the parent–child relationship, I have asserted, that distinction is played out in terms of expectations that parents will implement convention – 'socialising' their children – while children will implement choice – making 'their own' lives; or between the roles in which persons find themselves and their freedom to act as individuals, to which a generation difference adds weight (cf. Strathern 1982: 80, 84).

A feature of contemporary kinship practice in the 1980s is a further shift in English terminological patterns, from habitual use of kin terms in addressing close senior kin to a choice between that and the personal name. Again, where formality as such is regarded as constraint, this is taken as a liberating informality. Using the first name to personalise the person named seems of a piece with the idea that to treat people as persons one must treat them as unique individuals. For the current trend towards apparent terminological reciprocity is frequently held to be an act of mutual individuation: in having the liberty to treat the parent as an individual person, the child is 'more' of an individual him/herself thereby. Yet calling a parent by a first name is not quite the same as calling the child by a first name. The child claims the greater liberty. Rather than establishing new conventions for relationships, then, the move is colloquially regarded as treating the parties to a relationship as individual persons *rather than* as relatives. That is, it is regarded as a negation of convention.

Now there is no inherent reason why calling a person Ann is more or less individuating than calling that person Mother (cf. Firth, Hubert and Forge 1969: 310).[5] The number of Anns in the world no doubt run in hundreds of thousands, while each person has only one mother. Indeed, Mary, a middle-class respondent in Firth's London study (Firth, Hubert and Forge 1969: 311) explained her small daughter's use of a kin term towards her thus: 'To her there is only one Mother, but there are two or three Mary's in our circle.' Another said that to use first names among kin was actually to introduce a distance, to make them feel less close. With respect to a circle of named individuals, then, the (generic) kin term can also work to a personalising effect. It singles out a specific tie. But much more than kin terms, names seem to add to the personalising move the significant factor of choice, itself an ingredient of informality.

That a move away from kin terms in address, or away from titles and surnames in other spheres, is imagined to be a move away from formality or convention perhaps derives part of its power from former habits of address. It was once the case that a superior was at liberty to address an inferior by the first name but not the other way round. In Morgan's time, servants as well as children will have been addressed personally, although the servant would have had to take regard of the rank order among the children. Employers might invent names for their servants. What lent this liberty importance, however, has long ceased to signify. Rank has been reconceptualised in terms of personal interaction, for the present choice appears simply between more or less formality. Formality still carries connotations of respect, but it has become a matter of individual style whether or not one implements that formality in intimate circles.

A practice once definitive of rank – calling someone by their first name – is now seen as a negation of rank. That is, one convention is challenged not by what is perceived as another convention, but by what the English perceive to be anti-convention. Underneath the convention, one discovers the 'real' person. Thus, to call a parent by a first name today is not necessarily a sign of insubordination or lack of respect. On the contrary, it may be encouraged by the parent as a positive indication that within the family everyone has the choice of being treated 'in their own right', as a person rather than simply as some role-player. They are all special, all as it were one another's pets. To borrow the words of a Canadian sociologist, the solidarity of the modern family depends on 'personal attachments' between individual members (Cheal 1988: 144). Convention is concealed in the anti-conventional effect of 'personal' expression. This bears on views of change and diversity.

Like certain kin obligations, time is seen to flow downward. It thereby contributes to the asymmetry in relations between parents and children, and to the contexts in which parents are regarded as acting more from convention, children more from their capacity for individual choice. Out of the fact and direction of generation, the antitheses between convention and choice or relationships and individuality acquire a temporal dimension. Convention, like tradition, seems to be antecedent, to 'come from' the past, while choice, like invention, seems to lie in the future. In kinship idiom, children are future to the parents' past. Increased variation and differentiation invariably lie ahead, a fragmented future as compared with the communal past. To be new is to be different. Time increases complexity; complexity in turn implies a multiplicity or plurality of viewpoints.

If modern people in the 1950s and 1960s did indeed see the future as full of more and more highly individualised persons, more heterogeneity, many analogies for the process were available to them. Change could be identified: 1. when convention was challenged, as in the shift from formality to informality in kin address; 2. when persons were able to exercise greater choice than before, as in what they wished to call another; 3. in increasing attention to individuality, so that when personal relationships overrode kinship oblig-ations, individual agency was seen to override stultifying givens of existence, manifested in the equation of physical with relational separateness; 4. in the consequent association between greater individuation and greater variation or differentiation, as in the notion that, as individuals, persons were singular in the sense of being unique and therefore innately variable; 5. in simple magnitude, in that with more things in the world – more individuals – increase itself indicated change; and so forth. In sum, the future was knowable by the infinite possibilities it held. Although any of these conditions might be imagined in reverse – more red tape, more constraints – such a reverse flow also appeared to go against what was apprehended as natural development. For the conditions could all be referred to the further supposition that over time things naturally evolve from simple to complex states.[6] Complexity displayed a variety and plurality of individual forms whose interconnections challenged any simple systematisation. Thus we arrive at the English view of the individualist who knew his/her own mind and made a life for him/herself, with the past thought of as relatively communal and homogeneous by contrast with a varied, heterogeneous future.

This proliferation of concepts, forming a string of associations between ideas that are not quite the same (continuity/tradition/convention: change/novelty/choice) supports the modern connection between the twin processes of differentiation and complexification. There were 'many' concepts in the same way that the world was full of 'many' things – so that even what appears the same (such as continuity/tradition) on closer inspection could be differentiated (continuity is a question of time, tradition one of form). This anticipated proliferation modelled the very comprehension of change. It also suggested that one's perspective was a matter of choice.

Ideas about increasing social complexity were concordant with ideas about increasing natural complexity (cf. Cohen 1985: 22). Time and variation became inextricably linked in this scheme, and the mid-twentieth-century habit of referring to contemporary society as 'complex' had just such a resonance. All I wish to bring into this well-known picture is the fact that the same sequence was reproduced in the context of family relationships, encapsulated in the widely held notion that as personal choice and autonomy became more important, kin conventions became less so. The diminishing importance of kinship over the generations appeared a reflex not just of increasing individuality but of increasing complexity in life at large. That the development was anticipated meant that such diminution was also intrinsic to the conceptualisation of kinship relations themselves.

Modernist complexity was perceived not so much as the complexity of involute and self-repeating patterns, of layer upon layer of textual exegesis or of the juxtaposing of mystical and mundane experience, as above all an effect or outcome of quantity. The more people there were, the more points of view, the more potential differences of perspective. This intimate connection between complexity and plurality rested on one presupposition. Proliferation led to complexity provided what increased was not homogeneity but heterogeneity. Complexity was thus held in place through a commitment to preserving diversity, underpinned by the notion that if what were reproduced were unique individuals, diversity would be the natural result. But insofar as diversity appeared to be in the nature of things, its naturalness also made it a precondition. This gave a fresh twist to the reproductive model.

As part of the supposed modelling of the reproductive process to which I referred earlier, I take *diversity as a second fact of modern kinship*. While individuals strive to exercise their ingenuity and individuality in the way they create their unique lives, they also remain faithful to a conceptualisation of a natural world as diverse and manifold. Individual partners come together to make (unified) relationships; yet as parents they ought at the same time to stand in an initial condition of natural differentiation from each other. In the relationships they build and elaborate upon, it is important that the prior diversity and individuality of the partners remain. Such relationships are 'after' individuality, even as human enterprise is modelled upon and in that sense 'after' nature with its own impetus to variation. If in order to reproduce persons must preserve natural diversity, then diversity would be both a fact of and have a priority 'before' kinship.

Diversity and the individual case

Such a reproductive model would have no purchase if the facts of kinship did not resonate with how people see and know the world. Let me exemplify the workings of the model in connection with one way in which the modern English reproduce and create knowledge afresh for themselves. Conceptualising a world full of individuality and diversity gave rise to certain 'questions'. My 'answer' offers an explanation or context for one particular question, from hindsight.

The question sounds obvious: to whom are my present remarks meant to apply?

Using myself as I have occasionally done offends the canons of generalisations: *qua* individual, that is, by virtue of my uniqueness, I have no
representative status. One would only draw so narrowly on one case by
showing some connection with individuals in the aggregate: generalisations
are fashioned from what a plurality of individuals share in common. Hence
one should really specify what replicable features form the reference point for
one's example. After all, I purport to be making general observations about
kinship, but where do I fit in – and to what area or region do the observations
refer? If the vast diversity of Western culture cannot be collapsed into a
homogeneity, the same is also true of Britain. There are class, geographical,
occupational and these days ethnic differences between the British, none of
which can be aligned in any simple way with 'the English'. In fact, the same is
also true of each individual, with his or her own life experiences. Whenever I
look at a social unit, including the individual person, and even if it is myself, it
seems as though I can only make sense of the isolated case by putting that unit
or person into their social or cultural context, and thus accounting for both
the specificity and replicability of its or his/her position. Obviously, this
qualification puts innumerable problems in the way of characterising
'English' kinship.

The problems evidently faced Schneider *apropos* 'America', and his exercise
has been criticised on this account. Sylvia Yanagisako (1978: 1985) shows that
a Japanese–American understanding of the relationship between Japanese
and American culture distinctively qualifies the way in which
Japanese–Americans interpret 'relatives' and 'persons', the apparently basic
elements of American kinship.[7] Anyone embarking on a study of English
kinship practices would certainly feel bound to specify the class background
of their study, and would expect to be dealing with class distinctive features.
Taine's Englishman is all very well in his country home, but we know that the
number of country homes per head of population has never been very great at
any time in England's history. We cannot conceive of *not* qualifying
generalisation by attention to the specific social and cultural background of
the individuals to whom it is meant to apply.

To what context, then, do I address myself? Habits, practices, norms,
nomenclature – anything the English might wish to say about 'English
kinship' (cf. Schneider's list, 1968: 14–18) seems subject to diversity. And to
what range of practices do I address myself? Individualism and diversity do
not seem on the face of it to have any specific place in the domain of kinship at
all. Moreover, I have not only invoked a high level of generality but have gone
beyond even 'the English' in implying that these or similar concepts also
belong to a field of Western ideas, while social scientists know that when they
look at specific institutions they find there is never any single Western type.

This has been Michael Anderson's (1980: 14) argument as far as the family
is concerned. Michèle Barrett and Mary McIntosh (1982) cite him to this effect
in their own characterisation of 'the anti-social family'.

Do we suggest that the family, recognizable in its different forms, is an essentially anti-social institution, or that this particular type of family is anti-social? In one sense there is a 'correct' answer to this question: *we must refer to a particular, historically and socially specific, form of family since no general or essential category can be derived analytically from the many varied arrangements commonly lumped together as the family* ... Michael Anderson, for instance, writes ... that 'the one unambiguous fact which has emerged in the last twenty years is that there can be no simple history of the Western family since the sixteenth century because there is not, nor ever has there been, a single family system. The West has always been characterized by diversity of family forms, by diversity of family functions and by diversity in attitudes to family relationships not only over time but at any one point in time. There is, except at the most trivial level, no Western family type' [Anderson 1980: 14]. (Barrett and McIntosh 1982: 81; my emphasis, original emphasis removed)

A related position is encapsulated in the opposite argument which they also cite – not that there are potentially many forms but only one (and see David Morgan 1985: 16ff).

Anderson's position ... is entirely denied by Peter Laslett. Far from endorsing the view that no single family form is characteristic of the West, Laslett maintains that, pending evidence to the contrary, we should assume that the nuclear form of the family prevails. He argues ... that *departures from this family form are merely the 'fortuitous outcomes'* of localized demographic, economic or personal factors. In his insistence that the extended family is no more than a sociological myth, Laslett puts forward the proposition that 'the present state of evidence forces us to assume that the family's organization was always and invariably nuclear, unless the contrary can be proved' [Laslett 1972: x, 73]. (1982:83, my emphasis)

Barrett and McIntosh's own conclusion, and one to which I shall return, is that the family is a contested concept. It is the place of diversity that is of immediate interest.

Diversity appears as an interference to generalisation; either there are 'many' types or else only 'one'. Once diversity is admitted, we can conceive it as starting with individual experience and proliferating through heterogeneous populations and organisations in a way that defies as much as it aids reduction. Social scientists are generally happy to settle for a middle range of diversity, such as class and ethnic background. Firth's study was not just addressed to families in London, but to middle-class families in two residential areas. Indeed, to reveal that in talking mainly about middle-class kinship values I am drawing on a privileged educational background, as well as a suburban upbringing in southern England, will perhaps make the reader feel on securer ground and might even allow me to use myself as an informant of sorts. My representative status would be evident.

But as far as the account as a whole is concerned I do not propose to defend my remarks on the grounds of their representativeness. They are intended to be exemplary. To repeat an earlier point: none of us leads generalised lives, only specific ones. One therefore always works through concrete instances, and encounters general ideas, values, norms, habits of conduct in particular forms. It is in this sense that I take 'English kinship' as a particular form of Western kinship. But my concern is not with a subculture of Western culture and the relationship is not one of part to whole. An exemplification is at once more than and less than its generalisable features.

It nonetheless appears necessary to specify what might be particular to the forms in which I render English kinship itself. I should be true to a specific version. As will become apparent (see Chapter Four), there are several reasons why I focus on middle-class usage, largely to do with the way the middle class enunciate and communicate what they regard as general social values. Yet particularity does not stop there. There are many middle-class ways of doing things, and southern suburbs are not the same as northern ones, and not all professionals are yuppies. The original question raises its head. What then is the middle class type? If English kinship is to be exemplified in its middle-class form, then it would seem that the middle class is to be exemplified in some particular education, regional and cultural style, a choice that invites us to consider further occupational and local variants; and so on.

When David Schneider and Raymond Smith (1973) attempted to grasp the diversity of American kinship, they did so by making middle-class kinship exemplary in a strong sense. Schneider's (1968) earlier study in Chicago in the 1960s had focused on a middle income population. Although this population evinced the cultural apparatus of 'American kinship', there were also marked divergences from what Schneider and Smith call 'lower-class' kinship practices, and the comparison is the subject of the joint monograph. They concluded that the middle-class values they had analysed – including emphasis put on the growing autonomy of the child and intra-familial individualism (cf. Firth, Hubert and Forge 1969: 460) – in fact encompassed lower-class values. Lower-class kinship did not comprise a separate subculture, but promoted values and attitudes specifically in reference to middle-class ones, which thus held a hegemonic status. Moreover, middle-class values were symbolically deferred to as ideal and generalisable (conventional), while lower-class values were taken to represent a particular and specific kind of struggle ('real life' choices) with the 'real world' of limited resources.

One contrast between middle- and lower-class kinship practices lay in the extent to which middle-class families emphasised competence in the management of social relations and applied rationality principles to decision-making (Schneider and Smith 1973: 114). They endorsed innovation, and were engaged on enterprises, including the 'making' of relationships, that is, reconstructing relationships through explicit affective and practical dimensions (as in love-making, cf. Varenne 1977: 188ff). Similar features have been highly relevant to middle-class English kinship; more than that, the middle class have been a vehicle for widespread and radical social change. However, I do not have the material to hand to contrast middle- and (what the English prefer to call) working-class kinship practices as far as the English are concerned. I cannot make the middle class exemplary in the hegemonic and encompassing sense that Schneider and Smith intended.

If there is a class dimension to my account, it addresses the opportunities for communication the middle class have made for themselves in terms of education and the dissemination of ideas through writing and reflection. This is the class that does not just advertise but analyses its own conventions. This is the class that makes its implicit practices explicit to itself. Here is the common background to the intimate connection between indigenous models of kinship and the way in which scholars over the century between the 1860s–1960s have described society and the nature of social relationships, especially the way in which anthropologists have approached and reflected on kinship systems themselves.

One could think, for instance, of the connection that George Stocking (1987: 200–2) makes *apropos* certain changing circumstances of middle-class family life in England from the 1850s onwards. The attention being paid to the possibility of divorce going through the courts rather than through Parliament can be related to the then current debate among anthropological scholars on matriarchal institutions. Thus he suggests that the argument of McLennan's *Primitive Marriage*, published in 1865, two years before the first Matrimonial Causes Act was passed, 'was conditioned by the contemporary concern with problems of human sexuality and by the processes of social change affecting the institution of human marriage' (Stocking 1987: 201).

That particular legislative practices in England raised in people's minds universal issues to do with human sexuality returns us to the relationship between the particular and the general as a cultural fact. The question of how one moves from individual cases to generalisations about systems is, so to speak, an indigenous one. Indeed the relationship is a problematic that has both informed the aims of descriptive practice and has seemed to prevent the elucidation of the perfect system. If overcoming imperfect description has driven scholarly practice for a century, it in turn has at once been fuelled by and sought resolution in a pluralist specification of quantity.

The specification has had two dimensions. Generalisation implies that collectivities are made up of units which can be enumerated. Society can thus be imagined as a plurality of particulars, as 'a collection of individuals' (cf. Schneider and Smith 1973: 21). However, there have always been competing models to this vision of society. Michael Carrithers (1985: 236) observes that 'a view of how individual human beings should interact face to face is not necessarily the same as a view of how they should interact in respect of a significant collectivity'. The latter, alternative, rendering evokes another quantification: the extent or degree to which a collectivity transcends its parts.

Under this second specification, individuals can only be defined in references to the whole. The question then becomes 'how much' of the transcendent whole is to be found in each. For if the former specification gives rise to enumeration and thus to quantity in the sense of the plurality or multiplicity of (singular) units that can be counted, then the latter gives rise to quantity by volume or weight. What can be traced back to Edward Tylor's 'culture-stage' or 'degree of culture', as Tim Ingold notes (1986: 44; cf. Stocking 1968), was already there in Morgan's notion of greater or lesser degrees of civilisation. It is also there in the historical dispute about whether more or less change/continuity can be observed, as well as in what I have deduced to be kinship assumptions about some people being in positions where they show more uniqueness or more individuality than others and who are in that sense 'more' of a person. Social scientists might no longer speak of grades of social development in an evolutionary idiom, but were still in the 1960s very concerned with the amount of choice or volume of freedom that individuals could exercise.

Whether or not this investment in specifying quantity is part of the middle-class pursuit of rationality as a utilitarian, competence-enhancing endeavour,[8] the specifications also make individuality and diversity into generalisable phenomena. They in turn resolve the phenomenon of individual difference into another phenomenon, the capacity to analyse. What becomes measurable is the *degree of applicability* of either the individual case or diverse examples to a generalised account of them. I give a brief illustration.

Stocking (1987: 200–1) suggests that it is from the 1860s that one finds the first hint of a number decline in the English middle-class family. The idea prevalent in the 1960s that 'the [middle class] family is small in size' (Fletcher 1962: 125) seems eminently quantifiable. If the reference point were the nuclear family based on the household, then one could look at changing household demography (by contrast with the past) or at comparative statistics (by contrast with the working class); either procedure assumes that what is to be enumerated are the numbers of individuals. What relatives live together? On the other hand, one could look at the degree to which family members cooperate or assist one another, a volume of behaviour measurable perhaps in terms of frequency of visits and amount of help (e.g. Young and Willmott 1957). How strong is the link between this or that kinsperson? Now both types of magnitude have a significant non-quantifiable dimension. The very idea that families evince one or other kind of 'size' is taken to be a general state of affairs. That is, the analytical proposition can be applied to all families, so that regardless of the particular measurements all are measurable.

In short, quantity (volume and enumeration) solves the problem of how to think of both individuality and diversity with respect to the general. One can measure the degree to which values are prevalent or how a society allows this or that through the behaviour of individual persons – as in showing the percentage of personal name usage for parents. Description based on such analysis encompasses both the representative and the unrepresentative. Conversely, any analytical type can be shown to have its counterpart in a particular (segment of) population. Only where the population cannot be specified does generality or representativeness make no sense. Hence

Anderson's sarcasm: there is no Western family type because, of course, there is no general Western population as such. There are only a mass of differences between people who imagine themselves as Westerners.

This self-evident proposition becomes in turn my own starting point. We are dealing with people who themselves make generalisations, who imagine they are part of larger collectivities, who act with reference to what they assume to be widespread norms and such like, and who are consequently preoccupied with what they *take* to be a relationship between the particular and the general. The English thus distinguish between phenomena whose own character includes the fact of their generality and those that seem characteristically atypical or individual. A version of this familiar to anthropologists is the question of how far 'symbols' are shared. It is not confined to the English. As Anthony Cohen (1986; 1987) has shown in his study of Whalsay in the Shetland Islands, the truth of the matter is that when people draw on certain symbolic usages they are drawing on constructs whose property includes the assumption that they are shared – it is they who generalise, and also thus (in the Whalsay case) evoke a community of sharing. Social scientists (including anthropologists) replicate people's accounts, and what we might call indigenous analysis, in attempting to measure the extent of the sharing: how many people hold this view; how strongly they hold it, and so on. Quantification presumes diversity as a given.

Now, as Yanagisako shows in Japanese–American attitudes towards tradition, kinship offers a field for the display of diversity. When thought of against other facets of life, kinship relationships are redolent of tradition and community; yet by the same token tracing genealogical connections back into the past, thinking about one's roots, can also diversify the past into innumerable 'different' and specific traditions.

Esther Goody and Christine Groothues (1982: 217) cite the judgement of the President of the High Court Family Division in 1972 concerning a Ghanaian girl being fostered by a professional English couple. Whereas her Ghanaian parents had intended to have her grow up with an educational advantage before returning to Ghana, the English couple pressed for adoption. One of the grounds was the length of time the girl had been with them. The judge felt obliged to offer some general remarks. His analysis of the situation was that a problem had been created by the West African practice of coming to Britain to study or work and then fostering out children, a problem insofar as the children were 'brought up in and learn our British ways of life. [For then] when a strong bond of attachment and love has been forged between the children and foster parents, the natural parents take them away.' In other words, in providing a home, the foster parents had accustomed the child to a specific way of life.

The specific family arrangements of the English couple are being contrasted with the failure of the Ghanaian parents (he said) to 'provide a home' for the child. From this perspective, the specific belongs to a general ('British') tradition and is held to represent shared values. But if home is where ways of life are transmitted, a further source of diversity becomes apparent. The specific can also become particular and non-representative.

Kin lives are private lives, the home is an intimate place, and every family has its own conventions. Whether or not they are shared with others of like class or region, or can be claimed for the nation, lives are lived according to specific domestic styles. If tradition is past style, style is present tradition; and in their styles, families are like so many individuals. Hence the judge's reference to particular attachments. While each family has the opportunity to recreate a general style or generic tradition ('class') in the way children are brought up, in becoming the focus of deliberate, decision-making transmission, such style may equally well be claimed as unique and innovative. The English point to the changes they have seen since the early twentieth century in household structure, rates of divorce, the meaning of adoption, patterns of care, state intervention, and so forth. In any case, couples do their particular thing. Certainly in relation to their own children, parents move on from what their parents did; each family quite appropriately creates its own modes, even as each parental couple produce in each child a new individual. In short, every 'home' (to use the judge's term) exemplifies the same, unique combination of possibilities.

The relationship between the particular and the general, the unique and the representative, belongs to an elementary mathematics that both differentiates oneness and plurality and sees each as a product of operations done on the other. Thus, like 'society' itself, kinship may carry the resonance of a tradition or a community made up of a collectivity of values or of individuals; their attributes contribute to its aggregate character (enumeration). At the same time, kinship may also appear as a transcendent order which allows for degrees of relatedness or solidarity or liberty and for relative strength in the 'expression' of values; it is like an organism which functions as a whole entity to determine the character of its parts (volume). This is true both of relatives (the number one knows, the extent of attachment) and of families (how large they are and how cohesive). 'The English' similarly appear as now aggregate, now organism.

Quantity is compelling. It offers a way of imagining the generalisations through which the English have analysed their own culture. But unless we completely take the actors' view, such indigenous analysis must be a subject of and not merely the means to study. It is particularly interesting for the natural limits it sets to comprehension. Recall the framing of the questions that if I wish to generalise about English culture then complexity – the pluralism of social forms – inevitably appears to interfere with my task. Diversity seems an inevitable fact of nature, self-evident when one thinks of human beings as themselves so many individuals. On its head, however, the problem is rather how the English make it self-evident that the world is plural, complex and full of individuals. Of what, then, and how is this pressing sense of heterogeneity composed?

Facts of nature

Who are the English?

Over the century between the 1860s and 1960s, 'the English' acquired certain definitive features, although they are ones that have, since the counter-emergence of ethnic politics in the 1970s and 1980s, been thrown into disarray. In that period of innocent ethnicity, the English were regarded both as a productive amalgam of diverse peoples and as a highly individualistic nation holding on to individualism as a transcendent characteristic of themselves. The aggregating concept stressed the 'melting pot' symbolism of hetero-geneity, the organic concept that of a redoubtable character that was only to be exemplified idiosyncratically in each individual English(man). The English were thus self-defined in an overlapping way as at once a people and a set of cultural characteristics. I exploit the ambiguity in my own account, and refer to the English as though they were identifiably both.

The following rendition sets out some definitions of a sort. In 1929, the Professor Dixon to whom I alluded gave a series of public lectures on the Englishman at University College London. He took the occasion as an invitation to expatiate on the distinctiveness of the English. We are treated to The English Character, The English Genius, The English People, the English Soul, The English Bible, and to cap it indubitably (cf. Brooker and Widdowson 1986: 119), 'Shakespeare the Englishman'. It is in his lecture on the English genius that Dixon claims the Englishman is typically an individualist (1938: 65). As a population of individualists, the English are also 'a many headed people' (1938: 71).

What is an individualist? our sage asks. 'He is a man more guided by his own opinions than by those he hears about him, not content to blindly follow the crowd, who desires to see things for himself, one in short who 'shoulders responsibility for his acts and judgements', with all the latter-day qualities of reliance and initiative (1938: 68–9). Indeed, rather than following the suggestions of others, he would by choice work 'in his own garden on his private plan' (1938: 67). By the same token, he is 'tolerant' of the habits of others. Dixon slides into a paean on diversity. Because of its respect for individuality, he argues, England has nurtured a multiplicity of spirits and opinions, and '[W]here in any society will you meet such a curiously varied, so parti-coloured mental tapestry' (1938: 72). This in turn leads to the celebration of the English as a hybrid people in terms of their origins; 'an astonishingly mixed blend', this 'glorious amalgam' (1938: 90) is the natural generator of manifold talent.

In the framing chapter on The English People, he quantifies the phenomenon.

> Kent, which stands with Norfolk and Suffolk highest on [the] roll of fame among English counties, although extremely prolific in the sixteenth and seventeenth centuries, decayed in the eighteenth, and wholly lost her genius-producing power in the nineteenth ... Thus a country or a county may lose, though we know not why, its mysterious vitality.
>
> The predominantly Saxon districts, Middlesex, Surrey, Sussex, Berkshire and Hampshire, stand low on the list of talent, comparing very unfavourably in this respect with Dorset and Somerset in the West, Buckinghamshire to the North, and Kent, Norfolk and Suffolk to the East. We observe, then that in the regions where the component elements are most numerous, where there is most mixed blood, the greatest ethnic complexity, genius or ability most frequently appears. The hybrids have it. Norfolk, Suffolk and Kent are the counties in which the mingling of races is greatest, and precisely these counties, and not the purely Saxon or purely Norse, are richest in talent. (1938: 108)

His book is about the generic Englishman, and 'his' genius in that sense; what the analysis then uncovers are the hybrid individuals (literally, the geniuses) whose qualification for being considered truly English lies in their talent and thus in their evident exercise of it. And if he can count up the number of counties who have produced geniuses by comparison with those that have not, he can also talk about Englishness itself as a matter of degree. In realising that the term is not susceptible to exact definition, he writes: 'Some of us in these islands are more, some less English, some of us, of course, in no sense English at all' (1938: 5).

The lectures celebrate the achievement of a period – particularly between 1880 and 1920 – when 'English' was being legitimated as a national culture (Colls and Dodd 1987). Nations did not just have characteristics or traits, they had cultures. In the later years of the nineteenth century, the new system of education was held in part responsible for the state of this freshly acknowledged nationhood (Dodd 1987: 3). The salient question became what attributes were to be taken as representative enough to be taught in schools, how a sense of being English might be conveyed. Among the traditions promoted in art, letters, music and architecture with which pupils became familiar was the ruralism of southern England (cf. Howkins 1987: 63).

Institutions such as 'English' as an educational curriculum or as an academic discipline taught at universities had to be invented: rural cottages and the countryside were there to be discovered. But they had to be discovered beyond the distress of the then agricultural depression, and were evoked above all in a particular form of past rurality, namely the Tudorism of Elizabeth's England (Howkins 1987: 70). As a style, Tudorism was eminently recoverable. Under the Henrys and Elizabeth, domestic dwellings had for the first time become significant both in number and in substance. Manor houses acquired a novel spaciousness and were built in the newly durable combinations of brickwork and half-timbering that meant even modest cottages might still be occupied three hundred years later. Like the Bard claimed by Dixon, and despite the Welsh origins of the name, Tudorism was at once visible in the landscape and indubitably English.

In retrospect, Englishness thus takes an architectural form, humorously conveyed by Osbert Lancaster's drawings of domestic interiors which first appeared in 1939. But under Lancaster's hand any one of a number of evocative forms serves: his sketchings evoke the diversity through which Englishness could *also* appear. Stockbrokers Tudor is flanked by Aldwych Farcical, Modernistic, Cultured Cottage and Vogue Regency.

> All over Europe the lights are going out, oil-lamps, gas-mantles, electroliers, olde Tudor lanthorns, standards and wall-brackets, and whether or not they go on again in our time, the present moment seems as good as any in which to contemplate the rooms they have illuminated in the past. For the history of the home provides the most intimate, and in some ways the most reliable, picture of the growth and development of European culture ... [F]or self-revelation, whether it be a Tudor villa on the by-pass or a bomb-proof chalet at Berchtesgaden, there's no place like home. (Lancaster 1953: Preface to 1st edn, 1939)

But although he Europeanises the context, it is clear that Lancaster is presenting an English version of European culture. On the word 'home' he comments:

> it serves, among other duties, to distinguish a psychological type – 'homeloving'; a high degree of discomfort – 'home comforts'; a standard of moral values – 'there's no place like it'; a noticeable lack of physical charm – 'homely'; and a radio programme of outstanding boredom – B.B.C. Home Service. But despite this tremendous adjectival expansion it still retains, beneath layer after layer of the treacliest sentiment, its original substantive meaning of the house in which one lives.
>
> On closer investigation one is able to isolate the proper application of the word 'home' still further, and properly confine it to the inside of one's house ... [T]he word implies a sphere over which the individual has complete control; hence its enormous popularity *in a land of rugged individualists*. And whereas the appearance of the interior of one's house is the outcome of one's own personal tastes, prejudices and bank balance, the outside in ninety-nine cases out of a hundred is the expression of the views on architecture of a speculative builder, a luxury flat magnate, or even occasionally an eighteenth-century country gentleman. (1953: 9, my emphasis, punctuation emended)

Of all the styles he brought to light, Stockbrokers Tudor became widely adopted as a self-description by those whose pretensions were thus so gently parodied.

My own disaffection from/affection for Stockbrokers Tudor lies in the southern English road in which I grew up. Its avenue of semi-detached houses, black and white frontages hinting at Tudorbethan gables, was built in the late 1920s; the houses were by no means as grand as the Osbert Lancaster interior suggests, though such houses and no doubt such people were round the

STOCKBROKERS TUDOR

" Four postes round my bed,
Oake beames overhead,
Olde rugges on ye floor,
No stockbroker could aske for more."

Sussex house-agents song.
(*Traditional, early twentieth century.*)

NOT even the first world war and its aftermath could sensibly diminish the antiquarian enthusiasm which had first gripped the English public early in Victoria's reign ; and the enormous advance in mass-production methods that took place during the inter-war period only served to increase the enormous output of handicrafts. The experience gained in aircraft and munition factories was soon being utilized in the manufacture of old oak beams, bottle-glass window-panes and wrought-iron Tudor lighting fixtures.

In interior decoration the cherished ideal, relentlessly and all too successfully pursued, was a glorified version of Anne Hathaway's cottage, with such modifications as were necessary to conform to transatlantic standards of plumbing. In construction the Tudor note was truly sounded : in the furnishing considerable deviations from strict period accuracy were permissible. Thus eighteenth-century four-posters, Regency samplers, and Victorian chintzes all soon came to be regarded as Tudor by adoption—at least in estate agency circles.

Soon certain classes of the community were in a position to pass their whole lives in one long Elizabethan day-dream ; spending their nights under high-pitched roofs and ancient eaves, their days in trekking from Tudor golf clubs to half-timbered cocktail bars, and their evenings in contemplating Mr. Laughton's robust interpretation of Henry VIII amid the Jacobean plasterwork of the Gloriana Palace.

3   *Stockbrokers Tudor, early twentieth century*
From the 1953 edition of *Homes Sweet Homes* by Osbert Lancaster, originally published in 1939.
Reproduced by kind permission of Osbert Lancaster, *A Cartoon History of Architecture*, and John Murray (Publishers) Ltd.

corner. The estate was thus under construction at the time when Dixon was delivering his lectures. Aspiring to a garden suburb, it had been carved out of an ancient woodland that once supplied Elizabeth I's successor with timber for his fleet, and some of whose remaining oaks carry individual preservation orders. Like many stately homes in England, the trees are no longer private property but part of everyone's past.

The Garden Suburb had sprung up in the wake of the garden city movement of the 1900s. One visionary model of the garden city, in the words of Ebenezer Howard, rested on making the distinction between town and country quite explicit. 'Town and country must be married and out of this joyous union will spring a new hope, a new life and a new civilization'; it was to be a marriage 'of rustic health and sanity and activity [and] of urban knowledge and urban technical facility, urban political co-operation' (quoted by Thorns 1973: 17). The very phenomenon to be avoided was the formless homogeneity of the old urban suburbs. The garden city promised a completely new urban form. But it was the garden suburb that spread with such popularity in the interwar years; and, neither urban nor rural, it was to collapse rather than sustain the distinction.

Let me return to one aspect of Dixon's rendition. This is the notion that diversity is a *natural* outcome of the mingling of different peoples, an amalgam which preserves its original vigour. Inter-mingling contains a genetic image of cross-fertilisation, though the difference between plant and animal imagery might give one pause. I suspect the hybrid that Dixon celebrates is to be thought of as rose rather than mule. Unlike the sterile mule, the cultivated rose with its Tudorbethan resonances grows healthily on a wild rootstock. Indeed, the vigorous programme of hybridisation developed by plant-breeders over the hundred years since the 1860s literally turned a modest Victorian shrub into the most prolific and diverse flowering bush in the English garden. Above all, in the range of roses called Hybrid Tea, according to my 1976 gardeners' manual, one finds both 'old favourites' and 'new exciting varieties'. New varieties appear each year. As Dixon intimated, infinite diversity is possible for the future.

1989, sixty years on, lies in Dixon's future. How fares the hybrid?

In the late twentieth century, the English are more conscious than ever of ethnic diversity. Yet the result does not seem to be an ever more heady amalgam. Or at least people do not readily assimilate latter day ethnic differentiation to that of the Celts and the Saxons and the Danes whose diversity, children were once taught at school, made up 'our island race'. Value was put on the mixing of ancestry where we now only seem able to see the proliferation and diversification itself. In the late twentieth century it has become doubtful who or what 'the English' are[9] – or indeed whether the term is usable at all. As a consequence, we might remark, former perceptions of quantity do indeed seem to have lost some of their power. Has something 'happened' then?

ETHNIC RECORD KEEPING & MONITORING

Manchester City Council believes in equal rights and opportunities for all its citizens. In its role as the largest local employer and an important provider of services, the Council knows it must work towards equal opportunities. Putting that policy into practice takes time and we need to see how much progress we are making.

Why these Proposals for Ethnic Record keeping and Monitoring?

Ethnic record keeping and monitoring make it possible to tell if Manchester's equal opportunity policy is working

MANCHESTER
——City Council——
Defending Jobs - Improving Services
EDUCATION COMMITTEE

What is Ethnic Record keeping?

The collecting of information about a person's ethnic group.

What is an Ethnic Group?

An ethnic group is one in which the members have a shared cultural background and identity. This does NOT mean country of birth or nationality.

How would Ethnic Record keeping be done?

Each person would be asked to say which group he or she feels they belong to by ticking a box.

For Example:

AFRICAN ☐		PAKISTANI ☐
AFRO CARIBBEAN ☐		MIDDLE EAST ☐
BANGLADESHI ☐		VIETNAMESE ☐
BLACK BRITISH ☐		OTHER BLACK PLEASE SPECIFY ☐
CHINESE ☐		IRISH ☐
EAST AFRICAN ASIAN ☐		WHITE BRITISH ☐
INDIAN ☐		OTHER WHITE PLEASE SPECIFY ☐

Would I have to give my Ethnic Origin?

Not if you don't want to. But the City Council hopes you will co-operate so we can check that the equal opportunities policy is being put into practice.

What is the Purpose of Record Keeping?

To make sure that all applicants for jobs and everyone who uses Council services are treated fairly and equally.

4   *Ethnic monitoring, 1987*
Manchester City Council's categories for a proposed ethnic monitoring scheme (1987). 'English' does not appear.

If I suggest something has happened, it is only to point to something that has been 'happening' all the time, namely the way people put value on what they value. When this takes the form of making the implicit explicit, then what was once taken for granted becomes an object of promotion, and less the cultural certainty it was. A cultural certainty to which I refer here is the association between the twin concepts of individuality and diversity. It was once a fact of nature that these went together.

Some part of the story as it was told in the period between the establishment of English as a national culture at the turn of the century and (say) 1960 went along lines like this. The English made variation, evinced in complexity and multiplicity, one of the vehicles for their sense of civilisation and enterprise. Variety was also reproductive variety. The greater the genetic diversity, the more rugged the offspring, and that was as true of culture as of peoples. If England formed the basis of a hybrid nation, it was a vigorous hybrid, created centuries ago by waves of conquerors each of whom added their genes and skills to the stock. Over England's history, the displacement of royal dynasties, the rise and fall of classes of merchants and industrialists, the absorption of small groups such as Flemings and Huguenots – 'additions to an already infinite complexity' (Dixon 1938: 100) – all sustained the imagery of constant infusions of 'new blood'.[10] The country's institutions were invigorated by cross-fertilisation. Each individual thereby contributed his/her unique portion without losing the transcendent characteristic of individuality; that was preserved in the singularity of 'the English' themselves.

That is a story that now belongs to the past. Uniqueness and variety have become *an aim of cultural practice*. Ethnic groups must be recognisably 'ethnic'. The constant production of new goods includes the reproduction of old ones, as the media promote fresh juxtapositions of familiar and exotic ways of living. Those late twentieth-century people who can afford it live in an infinitude of other people's variations, with the rider that many can be sampled, consumed, partaken of: bread done in the style of Vienna, of Poland, of Turkey. A consequence of this production of diversity is that 'real' (natural) diversity becomes elusive. Distinctions seem to collapse. The cognoscenti now know that Chinese food served in Manchester take-aways is Chinese food intended for English (?British) tastes; that novelty is specially created by specialists in creations; that giving your pet cat rabbit from a pink tin instead of lamb from a green one panders to a consumer demand for colour coding – variety is 'colourful'. Everywhere we see promotions and creations that seem to reference at whim this or that tradition. It is as though unique cultural forms must take after other unique cultural forms (Jameson 1985).

In the words of one 1980s journalist, Britain has become a wholesale imitation, of itself and of others imitating itself.

> There is apparently no Briton too incongruous or mis-shapen to sport a T-shirt proclaiming allegiance to Harvard, Yale or the Miami Dolphins. I even once saw a down-and-out under Charing Cross arches in baseball cap bearing the elegantly intertwined initials of the New York Yacht Club. (Wholesale imitation of a culture founded on wholesale imitation naturally produces some paradox. The 'Yuppie' style favoured by young bankers and brokers in Mrs. Thatcher's economic Wonderland is believed the epitome of hard-nosed, thrusting, fingerpopping New York. It is actually New York's rather confused parody of English 'classic elegance'.) (Philip Norman, *Weekend Guardian*, 10–11 December 1988)

Culture in turn somehow seems at once less than real and larger than life, in the same way as the relationship between English and British has become thoroughly ambiguous. This would be the view from the late twentieth century.

A sense of epoch has to be retrospective. At the time, everything feels as though it is in crisis. The present crisis is poignantly experienced in the sensation that there is much 'less' nature in the world today than there once was. Confidence about turning the world's natural resources to human benefit has given way to fear about their consumption. Teenagers talk about what it is right to eat. In the course of endless discussions about becoming vegetarian, I have heard reasons that appear on the surface similar to the sixteenth- and seventeenth-century hesitations over barbarous slaughter for the table that Thomas (1984: 293–4) records, although they are hardly based on the same theories of temperamental composition. It is not that animals should not eat other animals, I think, but that human beings are too easily systematic about it. The purposefulness of the domestic slaughter is 'unnatural'.

Animals rather than plants comprise a kind of proximate nature which may also be endowed with interests of their own (cf. Haraway 1985: 68). Whether through keeping pets in the house or filming wild creatures in their own habitats, the English can coopt them to preserve an essential sense of the diversity and plurality of natural life, a late twentieth-century sensitivity that belongs to a moment conscious of the numerical reduction of the world's species. Systematic destruction of England's own wildlife seems to have reached its peak at the end of the eighteenth century. By 1800 many species of bird that had been common centuries earlier were gone for ever and the countryside was already denuded of the small mammal life that had been hunted out or vermined out; fish that once swam in the Elizabethan Thames were polluted long before the coming of pesticides and chemical fertilisers (Thomas 1984: 274–6). The present crisis, however, is focused on the denuding of the planet.

I suspect there is too close a parallel between what is taken to affect natural life and what is taken to affect human life. Among other things, cultural diversity as such seems newly at risk. Societies are content to cocacolarise themselves; anyone's logo will do when costumes and customs are glossily preserved as the exotic face of adventurous multi-nationals.

A paradox becomes a commonplace: change is bringing about homogenisation. When it was a case of exporting constitutional reform or development schemes for health, education and standard of living, homogenisation had its justifiers. Uniform laws and universal rights were to be made available everywhere. But culture itself as a common export? The anthropologist at least has resisted the idea with his or her insistence on the individual integrity and plurality of cultures; the very idea of culture implied a distinctiveness of tradition and style. As long as the colonial encounter meant the clash of cultures or culture contact, there was the possibility that new forms would naturally yield unique and vigorous hybrids. Today, and to those that reflect on it, what seems to be traded everywhere is the 'same' heterogeneity: cultures borrow bits and pieces from one another, reassembling the old stock of styles.

SEPTEMBER 1988 VOLUME 2 ISSUE 9

Editor Mary Ratcliffe **Art Director** Graeme Murdoch
Publisher Marina Thaine **Production Manager** Caroline Emerton **Advertisement Director** Barry Hadden
■Signature is distributed exclusively to Members of Diners Club in the UK. It is published on behalf of Diners Club by Reed Publishing Services Ltd, 7-11 St John's Hill, London SW11 1TE, Tel: (01) 228-3344 Telex: 923115 REEDPS G Fax: (01) 350-1586 Part of Reed International PLC, Europe's largest publishers of travel, leisure and business magazines.
■The opinions expressed in Signature are not necessarily those of the Diners Club. For information and queries on Diners Club membership, please telephone: (0252) 516261 © Reed Publishing Services Ltd 1988
■**Printed:** Severn Valley Press **Originated:** Phoenix Scanner Graphics

Oyster House
is a pearl among restaurants. The popularity of this, the second Restaurant to be opened in the last two years, has been quite phenomenal.

with his undoubted knowledge of the fish trade, is the third generation of fishmongers and knows that top quality, fresh produce is of paramount importance. Oysters are flown into Heathrow twice a week from Ireland, crabs are despatched from Cornwall, live lobsters from Scotland and the wild salmon arrives direct from the Scottish rivers. There's quail, guinea fowl, wild duck, saddle of hare, fillet of venison, duckling from Norfolk and chicken from Surrey. Looking after the "drinks", has compiled an imaginative and extensive wine list.

Booking is advisable.

5 *Oyster House, 1988*
Reproduced by kind permission of Reed Publishing Services Ltd.

There is 'nothing new'; or rather there is 'too much' traffic. At least, such views and the nostalgia they evince for other times were standard in the middle-class press in 1989 and into 1990. They have a powerful counterpart in the future for kinship: the possibility that new forms of procreation will produce individuals not to enhance but at the expense of diversity.

Less nature, more technology

This is the nostalgia I call postplural. I do so to suggest that, self-evident as the anxieties may seem, they also stem from a prior and very specific (modern/pluralist) modelling of the world. If English ideas about reproductive process formed a model, it was not just for the making of persons but for the making of the future. Kinship delineated a developmental process that guaranteed diversity, the individuality of persons and the generation of future possibilities.

Hybrids were one element of the model. Out of a plurality of stocks was to come the singular characteristics of the English(man) who preserved diversity in a tolerance for all forms of life. In the language of the time, one could identify an English character. In the language of the gardeners' manual, 'one hundred and fifty years of hybridisation has given us the perfect [rose] plant'. If individuality were swamped, on the other hand, then hybrid could turn into mongrel, and The Society of Pure English, founded in 1913 (Dodd 1987: 15), saw only contamination in the blundering corruptions that contact with 'other-speaking races' produced. Here the purity of the individual form (in this case the English language) was jeopardised. Individual forms must also be kept separate.

The English sense of plurality was much indulged in the making of distinctions. Thus most thinkers on the subject have urged the readers of books and articles to keep separate the diverse meanings of 'nature'. With hindsight, however, it is intriguing to see how environment has been literally imagined as countryside, the life cycle of organisms as the habits of plants and animals, the taken-for-granted background to human enterprise as the so-called laws of the physical world, and so forth. In the same way, diversity has been literally imagined as a matter of genetic variation. Since the late 1970s, this last connection has acquired a new and pressing salience, and one that directly affects the cultural keepers of natural diversity, human beings themselves.

For a decade now, considerable publicity has been given to artificial parenthood, and particularly to the figure of the surrogate mother. In the image of the surrogate mother appears the possibility of splitting apart functions that in nature are contained in the one body, ovulation and gestation. The English reaction to the new reproductive technologies in general has predictably ranged from wonder to fear. For they appear to make within human reach other dreams/nightmares, such as cloning – the possibility of individuals reproducing themselves many times over – and genetic determination – that parents may be able to screen out or preselect certain attributes of the child for whom they wish.

The divergence of views can be summarised in the two positions stated during the Parliamentary debate on Enoch Powell's *The Unborn Children (Protection) Bill* in 1985. The debate raised general questions about medical research into human fertilisation; I quote from Naomi Pfeffer's 1987 essay.

One Member of Parliament stated the case as follows: 'The object of our interest in medical research into embryology and human fertilisation is to help humanity. It is to help those who are infertile and to help control infertility . . . The researchers are not monsters, but scientists. They are medical scientists working in response to a great human need. We should be proud of them. The infertile parents who have been helped are grateful to them' (House of Commons Debates, 1984–5, 73, column 654). Opposing this view, Pfeffer adds (1987: 81), 'are those who see these means of treating infertility as misguided and unethical because they see them as meddling with the secrets of life itself. This technology, they argue, "promises benefits perhaps, but [it] could end by destroying the essential humanity of man . . . The technology that promised a paradise now shows signs of delivering a hell" (*ibid.*, column 649)'.

Technology can also be understood as 'too much' culture; nonetheless as a source of anxiety in this field it seems a relatively new target. Anxieties over artificial insemination, for instance, have taken interestingly different forms over the last fifty years. I continue Pfeffer's account.

Artificial insemination (using donor semen) has been clinical practice as an infertility treatment in England since the late 1930s.[11] However, not until case details were later published in the *British Medical Journal* was it widely known. It then became a matter of public outcry, likened to 'human stud farming', a reference to the introduction of agricultural centres for cattle insemination in the early 1940s.

> An article published in the *Sunday Despatch* in November 1945 articulated many of the contemporary concerns about artificial insemination using donor semen. It warned that 'a super-race of test-tube babies will become the guardians of atom-bomb secrets . . . Fathers will be chosen by eugenic experts of the United Nations'. (1987: 93)

Different concerns surfaced during the 1950s. A divorce court had been asked whether artificial insemination by donor constituted adultery if a wife went ahead without her husband's consent. A committee of enquiry was set up in 1959.

> The social issue . . . was the question of legitimacy. As Lord Brabazon of Tara put it, 'When we come down to brass tacks, the whole thing revolves on whether the child should be a bastard or not'. Bastardy was perceived as a growing threat; since the Second World War the number of illegitimate births had been rising steadily . . . To many it appeared that the institution of the family, which they believed underpinned Western civilisation, was under threat. Children conceived through

donor semen represented a conscious effort to bring forth an illegitimate child within marriage ... artificial insemination would be used by the greedy and unscrupulous to defeat claims to titles and estates not rightly theirs. And not only was patrimony threatened; paternity itself was in jeopardy ... 'knowledge that there is uncertainty about the fatherhood of some is a potential threat to the security of all'.[12] (1987: 94, references omitted)

In the 1980s, however, the debates are less about the animality of the procedures than about the intrusion of technology into biological process, less about the lawfulness of a union than about the kind of contract the parties should make with each other, and less about the property claims to bastards than about rights to the products of one's body. Finally, they are less about the ownership and disposal of whole persons than about the ownership and disposal of reproductive cells.

Long established as procedures for artificial insemination might be, they find a new context in the 1982 committee chaired by Mary Warnock.

Handling human gametes [eggs and sperm] and embryos outside of the body raised the problem of moral responsibility and legal ownership. It is not surprising therefore to find that very many of the recommendations of the Warnock Report are about their ownership, supply and disposal. In many ways the Warnock Report recapitulates the anxieties about adoption of children current in the 1920s. Then adoption was not regulated by the law; it could be and was exploited as a source of cheap child labour ... Instead of a traffic in children, we have [today] a trade in human gametes and embryos, and in place of white-slave traders, in the public imagination are desperate infertile men and women and unscrupulous doctors and scientists. In this context, the reasons for the inclusion of artificial insemination using donor semen and surrogacy for consideration by the Committee chaired by Mary Warnock become clear; in both gametes are purchased either by doctors or through commercial agencies. (Pfeffer 1987; 95–6, emphasis removed)

The public mind, as reflected through the Warnock Committee, links artificial insemination to commercialism, to market manipulation and consumer choice.[13] And where those earlier anxieties touched on the implications for people's legal and social standing, the present anxiety concerns interference with natural relations. Civilisation is not so much under threat; Nature very much is.

Natural process is also about future potential. Hence clinically established procedures such as artificial insemination, and newer ones such as in vitro fertilisation, come to be put aside 'technologies' such as ectogenesis and parthenogenesis which are little more than imaginative extrapolations into the future. The Warnock Report (1985: 4) claims they all have in common 'the anxiety they [have] generated in the public mind'; the question is the kind of future one can expect. Hilary Rose expands the point.

Certainly beyond IVF and the actual or potential gene therapies lies a scientific and technological horizon along which are ranged other possible reproductive interventions: would it be possible to rear a foetus from fertilization to independent 'birth' entirely in vitro (ectogenesis)? To clone identikit copies of individuals from single cells or 'gene libraries'? To rear a human embryo in the uterus of a non-human creature or even make human-non-human hybrids? Or to provide a technique that would enable women to give birth without the need for sperm to fertilize their eggs (parthenogenesis, a form of cloning)? Could men have babies? These prospects and others form the stuff of science-fantasy dreams. (Rose 1987: 158)

Here the hybrid is no metaphor drawn from another domain (plant breeding), and does not describe cultivated characteristics. It refers to the literal possibility of producing human beings by graft.

Crossing human gametes with those of other species is at present technically impossible (Ferguson 1990: 24), and in any case unlikely to be developed for therapeutic purposes when transpecies genetic implants hold instead a realistic promise of development. Much of this thinking must remain in its science-fiction form, but it still remains thinking about the future. And the future has always been imagined as a matter of infinite possibilities. Thus Ferguson notes it is a possibility that the embryo may be manipulated 'so as to engineer into it additional genes which, for example, may not naturally occur in the human species' (1990: 14). Perhaps some of the apparently irrational fears such writers seek to allay are fears for the future of possibility itself.

If technological mastery were indeed gained over genetic makeup, the expressed fear is that the way would be open for eugenic programmes that would inevitably lead to preferences for particular types of persons. As the English are used to telling themselves, it is less the technology that is in doubt than how it will be used. Perhaps the prominence of the clone image in people's vision of the future encapsulates the anticipation that the exercise of choice in this regard would take away choice. The very idea of selecting for clones obviates the idea of selection itself. Choice would thus be shown up for something other than it seemed. More technology does not seem to compenesate for less nature.

Technology, for those who are afraid of it, is a kind of culture without people. Meanwhile one is at the mercy of people. The reduction of naturally produced genetic material, like reduction in the diversity of the world's species, is symbolised in the fantasy that if those with the power in fact get their hands on the appropriate technology, they would produce versions of themselves over and again and/or counter versions such as drones and slaves. A particular individual would be reproduced – but its multiplication would be the very opposite of individuation. Diversity without individuality; individuality without diversity.

I have referred to the modern English opinion that kinship diminishes in importance over the generations. Perhaps this has fed the present-day feelings of being at a point at which there is actually 'less' nature in the world than there used to be. And here we come to a confusion. In one sense it would seem that 'more' technology means 'more' culture. But if more culture creates choice that is no choice, then with the reduction of diversity there is also 'less' culture. The mathematics does not work. The perception that there is less nature in the world is thus *also* joined to the feeling that there is less culture, and less society for that matter – less community, less tradition, less convention. Tradition was traditionally perceived as under assault from the individual who exercised choice, from innovation, from change that made the world a more varied place to be in. It is now individuality that is under assault from the over-exercise of individual choice, from innovations that reduce variation.[14] 'More' choice seems less 'choice': with the engineering of genetic stock, the potential for long-term future variation may be reduced rather than enhanced. When diversity appears to depend literally on the vagaries of human individuals, it suddenly seems at risk; variation may not ensue.

In the modern epoch, kinship and family could play either nature to the individual's cultural creativity, or society to the individual's natural spirit of enterprise. But if that former symbolic order pitted natural givens against cultural choice, social convention against natural variation, then it no longer persuades. These perspectives will not play off against one another. The postplural nostalgia is for the simultaneous loss of convention *and* loss of choice.

At the root of current debate (for example, the several contributions to Stanworth's volume 1987; Magarey 1985; Spallone and Steinberg 1987; Dyson and Harris 1990)[15] is a profound issue about the shape not just the English but Westerners in general give to ideas. They have in the recent past used the idea of nature, including the idea of natural variation, as a vehicle for thinking about human organisation and its future potential. In its place is a late twentieth-century equivocation about the relationship between human and natural process. For every image of technological advance as increasing human potential lies a counter-image of profligate waste for trivial ends and of resource depletion. This includes Westerners' reproductive capacities. Artificial processes are seen to substitute for natural ones, and thus present themselves as 'interfering with nature' (Glover 1989: 18). What is interfered with is the very idea of a natural fact. Or, to put it another way, of the difference between natural and cultural ones.

Schneider's *American Kinship* depicted sexual intercourse as a core symbol: the diffuse enduring solidarity of close family relations was attributed to sharing substance through the act of procreation. Procreation was a natural fact of life. But that 'natural' image has lost its obviousness in a world where couples can seek assistance to beget offspring without intercourse. So too have the 'cultural' conventions of the union. The otherwise lawful connection of husband and wife may conceivably subsume a contract with a birthing mother or an agreement to obtain gametes by donation.

Yet change can always be denied. Some will seek comparisons with other cultures and other conventions, although the reassurance that these new modes are simply part of the manifold diversity of human ways of reproduction is, I shall suggest in the next chapter, misleading. Others who cast their minds back to the science-fiction writers of earlier this century, or even to Mary Shelley's Frankenstein, will say, as it is said of individualism, that these things have always been with us. Human beings have always fantasised about creating life; there have always been ways of dealing with infertility; there have always been those who deplored the spoiling of the countryside, as the English Lakeland poets protested with horror at the railways that were to bring tourists to their beloved spots (cf. Lowenthal 1990). It is, in fact, this very capacity to think one is perpetuating old ideas, simply doing again what has been done at other times and in other places, before, elsewhere, that is itself a profound engine for change.

Anthropologists have always had problems in the analysis of social change. Perhaps it is because social change sometimes comes about in a very simple way. As far as aspects of English culture are concerned, all that is required is what (middle class) people do all the time, namely that they do what they think can be done. Put into action, this becomes an effort to promote and implement current values.[16] Values are acted upon; implicit assumptions become explicit, and that includes rendering culturally visible what may be perceived as natural process.

This has been a conceptual enablement of change in the West since medieval times. Over the last century, it has also become a matter of rendering visible the cultural premises of the perceptions themselves. Thus what is made explicit is the basis not just of natural or moral but also social understandings of the world. The sense of new values, new ideas, new epochs, comes from the conscious effort to make evident the values and ideas people already hold. To feel contemporary time as a time of crisis is part of this: there is no going back. One cannot recapture the point before explicitness. Hence, as I remarked at the beginning, new ideas always come from old – but this is accomplished simply through putting current ideas into perspective, acting on and finding contexts or reasons for them. The resultant and constant relativising of 'our' understanding of 'ourselves' helps produce the sense that there appears to be less and less to be taken for granted and thus less nature in the world.

The modern English middle class have put effort into valuing their values, having ideas about their ideas, trying to typify their type of epoch. We might regard their curiosity as indeed a peculiarly 'Western' approach to knowledge. Since people simply value their values, it looks as though they are upholding their traditions. Yet it is that active promotion that takes them where they have never been before. Consider again the English concept of individualism and the individuality of persons.

The 1980s witnessed an interesting phenomenon. To a remarkable extent, British public discourse has become dominated by the metaphors and symbols of the government, by which I mean not a constitutional consciousness but the specific depiction of social and cultural life promoted by the political party in power. Its discourse generates a single powerful metaphor: that the way forward is also recovering traditional values. Tradition has become a reason for progress. The way forward is defined not as building a better society, for that smacks of the collective and state idioms against which the present ideology is constructed. For the way forward is a better life for individual persons, and that is to be achieved by promoting what is proclaimed as Britain's (England's) long lived 'individualism'. A return to Victorian Values is presented as at once evoking a decent, law-abiding citizenry, and as a retreat from state intervention interfering in individual choice and personal effort.[17] Rather, as a consequence, enterprise must be privatised, and the government has indeed privatised one of the country's foremost plant-breeding institutes along with its seed bank. Such a projection of the past into the future is beautifully exemplified in the elision with Contemporary American: recapturing traditional values will bring the bright future promised by (what English fantasise as) American enterprise. In the 1980s, English pubs have become heavy with reinstated Victorian decor in high streets dominated by over-lit fast-food outlets.

As a piece of history, of course, the 'return to Victorian values' is nonsense. But it ought to interest social scientists. A traditional value is claimed for England's (Britain's) true heritage, and individualism promoted and encouraged in the name of returning to tradition.

Not only is the individualism promoted so actively in the late twentieth century radically different from its counterpart of a century ago, it would not be conceivable with the intervening era which made the state an explicit instrument of public welfare. For the target of present political discourse is the tyranny of the collective. Indeed, the way in which the present 'individual' is construed comes directly from values and ideas that belong to that collectivist era. This is also true of many of the ways in which anthropologists have thought about the study of kinship.

Schneider was right to celebrate 1984 with a critique of the idea of kinship. His book is an attack on the unthinking manner in which generations of anthropologists have taken kinship to be the social or cultural construction of natural facts. But underlying the attack is the recognition that this is how kinship has been constructed in anthropology from the start, and indeed that this is its identity.

The anthropological construction of kinship as a domain of study was formed in a specific epoch. It came initially from the modernism of Morgan's era, from the 1860s onwards, but flowered in England in the middle decades of the twentieth century. This was the era when the anthropological task was to understand other people's cultures and societies, being thereby directed to their modes of collectivisation and public welfare. The concept of kinship as a set of principles by which people organised their fundamental relations epitomised the anthropological capacity to describe cultural production on the one hand and the way people made collective and social life known to themselves on the other. It was thus no accident that kinship played such a part in the making of British Social Anthropology, which – and however hybrid the origins of their practitioners – between 1910–1960 was basically

English anthropology. Kinship was above all seen to be concerned with what peoples did everywhere with the facts of human nature.

For the modern anthropologist the facts of kinship were simultaneously facts of nature and facts of culture and society. In this light, it is more than intriguing to look back on these mid-twentieth-century assumptions from a world that seems, if only from the ability for endless printout or in the timeless attributes of role-playing games, to post-date Society, and whose culture might no longer mould or modify nature but could be everything that is left once Nature has gone.

2

Analogies for a plural culture

Looking back almost ten years later, the British obstetrician who pioneered techniques of in vitro fertilisation and embryo transfer gave his motive as self-evident: 'It is a fact that there is a biological drive to reproduce', Patrick Steptoe said, and to thwart this drive would be harmful (quoted in Stanworth 1987: 15). The procedure involves fertilisation outside the body. The first person in England conceived this way was born in 1978; she was also celebrated in the press as the world's first.[1] Her birth has come to be regarded as cultural property – for it 'serves as a symbolic watershed' for a deeply felt debate about the new reproductive technologies in general (Rose 1987: 152).

It is, I suggest, a symbolic watershed for former reproductive models, and I interpret aspects of the debate in the reflected light of the model I have called modern. The debate turns on ideas about persons and relations that can no longer be taken for granted, and on this fact. While many women wish to have children, Michelle Stanworth comments (1987: 15), the views that have gathered round the issue do not simply reflect that wish; they institute their own vision of what is right and natural.

Displacing visions

Images in anticipation

The future orientation of the debate is provocative in itself. The last chapter touched on the ease with which discussion slides from the immediate accomplishment of embryologists to futuristic fears about genetic manipulation. Such leaps into the future accompany the scientisation of existing procedures. Diverse forms of assisted reproduction are classed as medical intervention, and medicine as science, 'science' providing the technology that enables otherwise childless persons to have children (cf. Doyal 1987; Spallone 1987). On the one hand technology is thus seen as enabling;[2] on the other hand intervention has become a symbol of interference. 'The Surrogate Mother has become ... the personification of anxieties about unpredictable technological and social developments' (Zipper and Sevenhuijsen 1987: 138).

47

Feminist reactions, on both sides of the Atlantic and on the continent as well as in Britain, have not been without their reflective irony (Petchesky 1980; Stolcke 1986). What to some had appeared earlier as utopian – the possibility of freeing women from their biological burden – now appears totalitarian. Far from being regarded as liberating women from their bodies, the new technologies may be taken to represent the supreme domination of them. The language of this debate matches violence with violence when motherhood is likened to female prostitution. 'Whereas in the beginning of this century the metaphor of the prostitute was a way of delineating decent heterosexual behaviour, cultural feminism now tends to use it as a way to create an overall feminist identity that denounces heterosexuality itself' (Zipper and Sevenhuijsen 1987: 125).

The concept of heterosexuality is sustained by a specific gender imagery which classifies a mother's body as axiomatically 'female'. The consequence is that any technological intervention is axiomatically 'male' – either in relation to the instruments themselves or in relation to male interests (cf. 'the woman' and 'the doctor' in Emily Martin's study of contemporary American attitudes (1987: Ch. 4)). From this perspective even the foetus can appear as intruder.

Ann Oakley (1987: 39) draws attention to findings which suggest that whereas some women may express disappointment with a girl at birth, during pregnancy it may be the discovery that they are harbouring a boy which they find disturbing. She quotes Barbara Rothman (1986: 144) as observing that it is one thing to have given birth to a son, quite another to be told that the foetus growing inside you is male. 'To have a male growing in a female body is to contain your own antithesis. It makes of the foetus not a continuation and extension of self, but an "other".' That the male foetus has a nature distinct from the mother is thus symbolised in its distinct masculinity. The assumption on which all this rests – that gender defines the whole person – thereby allows one to see the gender of the foetus as separate from that of the mother: the foetus becomes a miniature 'whole person' within the mother. The same assumption also implies that switching the gender might alter the mother's feelings of identity, as they are expressed here, but not the perception of the person. The body of the child is not the body of the mother, and its claims to an individual existence become as much its own claims to personhood as do hers.

The distinct identity of the child is also used by protagonists who may be of a very different political persuasion, those who desire to promote not female autonony but maternal bonding.

In the last decade, obstetrics has taken on a new and explicit responsibility, 'to bond mother and child' (Oakley 1987: 53). It came with the realisation that obstetricians had at their technical disposal a means to institutionalise this natural emotional bond, just as making fertilisation possible responded to the natural drive to reproduce. The means lay in being able to show the mother-to-be her unborn child via ultrasound imagery. Now virtually routine in pregnancy monitoring, diagnostic ultrasonography produces sonograms that can be reproduced as visual images. The ability to 'see' the foetus is felt to enhance the mother's impending sense of attachment to it – an experience widely confirmed by mothers themselves. This is the benign face of science, assisting in an apparently natural process, promoting the conditions under which 'nature' will happen (see Price 1990). The kind of emotions that can be expressed when the child is born is brought forward in time, a relationship is made out of a relationship. In short, what is being anticipated is the child as an individual person. It is when persons become visible as individuals that the English feel they 'relate' to one another. I expand the observation.

If there is a defect in natural functioning, then medical science is regarded as having a legitimate role to play in remedying it. What natural functioning might be defective in the extension of monitoring practices to the question of bonding? Maternal bonding refers to the *child*'s capacity to bond with its mother – yet it is for the mother that assistance is being provided. The remedy is anticipatory: lack of bonding is believed to put the child at risk of neglect or abuse, and encouragement of bonding is preventative action to protect the future child.[3] In other words, the mother is obliged to make herself into an entity that the child can bond with, and her own emotional development must provide it with an appropriate environment. If the mother shows a proper flow of emotions towards the child, the child will respond, while in the absence of such cues it may not. The flow of obligation and emotion is downwards: being able to 'see' the child cues the mother's emotions in order that the mother's emotions should be ready to cue the child when it is born. Indeed, the screen image which invites the mother's eye anticipates the eye contact that mothers are told is so important for their babies.

However positive the experience may be for mothers – and for fathers[4] – such procedures have also attracted outside critical comment. The ultrasound picture presented to the mother of the baby is *interpreted* as presenting her with her own self image as its 'mere' environment, her body appearing as its enabling technology or, in Oakley's phrase, support system. The mother seems visible only as an appendage to the foetus, in the same way as nutrients are simply regarded as resources. For the image has an existence beyond the social context of the clinic or the parents' responses: *someone else* looking at it sees not the parent–child relationship it may evoke for the parents, but only a picture of the (future) child.[5] On this interpretation, even the mother's presence as a support system may seem to have been screened out.

Rosalind Petchesky provides an American example. She analyses the influence of a report which claimed

> that early foetal ultrasound tests resulted in 'maternal bonding' and possibly 'fewer abortions' ... [for] upon viewing an ultrasound image of the foetus 'parents probably will experience a shock of recognition that the fetus belongs to them' and will *more than likely resolve 'ambivalent' pregnancies 'in favor of the fetus'*. Such 'parental *recognition of the fetal form*', they wrote, '*is a fundamental element in the*

later parent-child bond.' ... These assertions stimulated the imagination of Dr Bernard Nathanson and the National Right-to-Life Committee. The resulting video production was intended to reinforce the visual 'bonding' theory at the level of the clinic by bringing the live foetal image into everyone's living-rooms. (1987: 59, author's emphasis)

The video, *The Silent Scream*, purports to show a medical event, a real-time film of a twelve-week-old foetus being aborted:

> The most disturbing thing about how people receive *The Silent Scream*, and indeed all the dominant foetal imagery, is their apparent acceptance of the image itself as an accurate representation of a real foetus. The curled-up profile, with its enlarged head and fin-like arms, suspended in its balloon of amniotic fluid, is by now so familiar that not even most feminists question its authenticity ... ['Photographs' typically present the foetus as] solitary, dangling in the air (or in its sac) with nothing to connect it to any life-support system but 'a clearly defined umbilical cord'... From their beginning, such photographs have represented the foetus as primary and autonomous, the woman as absent or peripheral. (1987: 61–2)

She underlines the depiction of physical isolationism:

> In fact, every image of a foetus we are shown ... is viewed from the standpoint neither of the foetus nor of the pregnant woman but of the camera. The foetus as we know it is a fetish. Barbara Katz Rothman observes (1986: p. 114): 'The fetus in utero has become a metaphor for "man" in space, floating free, attached only by the umbilical cord to the spaceship. But where is the mother in that metaphor? She has become empty space.' Inside the futurizing spacesuit, however, lies a much older image. For the autonomous, free-floating foetus merely extends to gestation the Hobbesian view of born human beings as disconnected, solitary individuals. (1987: 63)

Yet if we go back to the rationale for making the video, at its heart is a concern for relationship: to make the parents, and especially the mother, feel positively towards the unborn child. In presenting an image of the foetus, the intention is to present a 'person', to make one see the person that is already there. An anthropologist might remark that one does not 'see' a person: a person is a subject who acts in the context of relationships. But I suspect that in this American view, there is also an English one. Culturally speaking, we can see the person when the person appears as an individual, and we see an individual when we see a body. The elation that mothers report when the ultrasound image is shown them – the sense of reassurance that it gives that the child is real, and the self-reporting that they do feel bonded with it – is real elation.

Here perhaps is a reason for the dissonance between such positive reports and much critical reaction, especially from feminists. The appeal to the personhood of the foetus takes place in a cultural context where relations are imagined as existing *between* individuals. What is claimed to be promoted is the bonding between child and mother, not that the mother contains the child nor indeed that the child contains the mother. At the same time, showing the child as a separate individual appears to exclude the parent. For the mother to see the child as an individual is to invite *her* response; but the image of the child in itself is not – in English cultural idiom – also an image of the mother. Hence, the counter-critique that the mother is displaced.[6] And hence the critique that creating an image of a foetus requires creating the foetus as an image.

Frances Price (1990) notes that from a clinician's point of view, ultra-sonography releases the foetus from the pregnant woman as a visible second patient for monitoring and therapy. I take this practice as an instance of the more general Western propensity towards making the implicit explicit. It is one that inevitably involves a shift of perspective.

Perhaps, then, the sense of maternal displacement on which observers (non-clinical rather than clinical and third parties rather than mothers) comment comes from the fact that, from an outside perspective, one image is being displaced by another. No doubt the child felt through the thickness of the mother's skin, or manifest in her reported nausea and weight change, can be imagined as though it were an object of vision. Yet live eye contact with the born child mobilises another field of perception: before ultrasound, eye contact with the child was a function of its physical separation from the mother, a displacement of earlier perceptions of bulk and movement. In the premature portrait of the unborn, what is displaced is the perception of the child mediated by alterations in the mother's physical state. At the same time it seems, very simply, just a matter of making what is otherwise hidden visible to the eye, since we 'know' the foetus is there, we are curious to prove the matter. It is there as a natural fact, and its perceptible body is evidence of that fact in singular, individual form.

Certain relationships are also natural, and that for the English is reason to value them. Maternal bonding confronts mothers as a necessity. Ultra-sonography can be regarded as a method for revealing the 'true nature' of the relationship as individual-to-individual contact. Indeed, we might character-ise scientific endeavour as a whole as an effort to enable us to apprehend our own natures.

I also take this as an instance of the abstract point made in Chapter One: the desire to make what we think is there known to ourselves leads the English to embrace the techniques that in apparently fortifying their values irrevocably changes them. The motive may be no more than the desire to be explicit about the source of values. In this case one wants to see what is not otherwise experienced through vision. The way this changes the nature of the experience is described, by some at least, as though the process were denigratory rather than enhancing of the mother as herself an individual person. For if what has literally happened is that one mode of perceiving the mother–child relation-ship has displaced another, it perhaps evokes an earlier displacement. This concerns the identity of the father.

It has always been a fact of nature for the English that while you can see maternity, it is much harder to 'see' paternity (e.g. Rowland 1987: 68–9). It is not just that the role that the father plays in conception and childbirth is thought to put men at a remove from paternal feelings but, it is held, the father's genetic tie must be a matter of inference. The father is naturally invisible. Paternity thus has to be symbolically or socially constructed (a picture made of it) in the way, it is held, that maternity is not. The necessity is supposed to be a primeval source of men's alleged greater interest in social life. Whole theories of social evolution were once built on the supposition that in primitive society, so-called, children would not know who their fathers were, and that civilisation has been a long process of making paternity explicit.[7] This was the supposition towards which, if we are to believe Thomas Trautmann (1987) (and see Kuper 1988: 59–60), Morgan was reluctantly pushed by his contemporaries. It would be ironic if the new techniques of image-making were thought to make maternity invisible. Certainly, when the 1980s debates on assisted reproduction dealt with the child's social origins, the question became not just who the real father is but (Warnock 1985: 37) who the real mother is.

These debates reveal analogies between certain values implicit in the way the English make kinship known to themselves. One lies in the very value given to making natural relationships explicit; kinship is to do with tracing natural ties. A second lies in the value given to a person's desire to reproduce, and reproduce themselves. Third is the idea that if something can be seen, it is real, and to uncover the normally hidden makes the latter especially 'real', formulations that may be contested in other domains but, in matters to do with procreation, carry an equation between what is seen, what is real and what is natural. Finally identity, like time and obligation, flows downward from parent to child; that is why who the real parent is matters.

The present epoch substantiates these values through an exaggerated attention to biological idiom. After all, it was not so very long ago that the 'natural child' was a stigma. The naturalness of the procreative act was not sufficient to establish real relations. There was also the issue, we might say, of the naturalness of social status. Reproducing one's own did not literally mean one's genetic material: one's own flesh and blood were family members and offspring legitimated through lawful marriage. Although illegitimate ('natural') children were consanguines, they did not reproduce their procreative parents socially. Schneider (1984: 103) quotes N. W. Thomas in 1906 on the point that in English law the father of an illegitimate child was not akin to it, despite the blood tie between them. It was thus improper for the offspring of illicit relations to go into public mourning for their parent (Wolfram 1987: 59). The fact of private grief was irrelevant: to claim kinship was a public (social) act.

If there were once, so to speak, a 'natural' conjoining of natural and social relations, it would be taken for granted that the paramount social reality was the legitimacy of the claims to kinship. But it is as though social legitimacy has since been displaced by the legitimacy of natural facts. This is an effect of a switch in what is made explicit. Increasing discourse on the role of 'social' construction in the conjoining of natural and social relations – of the artificiality of human enterprise – has given a different visibility to natural relations. They acquire a new priority or autonomy. And out of everything that might contribute to the substance of natural relations, genetics affords a complex map of inheritance and the transmission of traits. Genetic relations have thus come to stand for the naturalness of biological kinship – an assumption, we should note, that flourishes in the face of genetic 'engineering' and the deliberations of the Warnock Committee as to whether, in the case of surrogate motherhood, it is the genetic or the birthing mother who is the real mother.

The antecedents to this biologism were evident in the reproductive model of the modern epoch. For that model reproduced reality. English kin reckoning always distinguished between 'real' relatives and courtesy or fictional or step, and thus in some sense 'artificial', relatives. To call a number of people by the same term (e.g. uncle) invited the qualification of how one was 'actually' related to them. And mother meant a real mother, except when the term was used in deliberate metaphorical extension. Indeed, the very differentiation between literal and metaphoric meanings implied that the literal meaning was the one that matched reality. The question became what was taken for real. We could put it that the reality of a socially sanctioned relationship has since been displaced by the reality of a biologically conceived one. Today's problems are the ('natural') parents. For the ('social') child is bound to want to know, it is said, what its biological antecedents really are.

The language of realism had a further effect. The very fact that one could debate about 'who' was the real relative implied that individual persons were somehow prior to the relationship. The child was there, according to this view, as an outcome of the acts of other individuals whatever relation they might claim afterwards. From such a perspective, then, *individuals reproduce individuals*. This was the third fact of modern kinship.

Relationships, in this English model, were not reproduced in the act of procreation itself. For, however natural, relationships had to be made evident in a way that individuals did not. In this sense, individuals were regarded as real whereas all relationships had a conventional or artificial dimension to them. Thus whether one spoke of individual families or individual persons, as units they enjoyed an autonomous existence while the relations between them were open to negotiation. Units composed entities that 'made' relations. And when it came to perpetuating themselves, individuals did indeed have to produce 'real' individuals, that is, new ones: the individual person reproduced him or herself as *another* individual person.

Parents had to reproduce persons who were individual in themselves. In fact, this model guaranteed natural singularity insofar as the potential for variation was something each person carries in their genetic makeup.[8] While the study of genetics had borrowed the social terminology of inheritance and

is expanding the scope of genetic screening; diagnostic tests are being developed to identify genetically related "susceptibility" to certain diseases or genetically related "sensitivity" to toxins in the environment; DNA fingerprinting is an application of genetic screening being used in police work. (See *genetic monitoring*.)

genetic therapy The use of genetic engineering techniques to alter or replace "defective" genes. The techniques are experimental but researchers predict the technology can be used to prevent or treat certain genetic conditions.

genetics The science aimed at understanding what genes are and how they work. Today genetics comprises the study of a wide range of biological processes influenced by genes, including embryo development, metabolism, genetic disease, etc. Modern genetics began before the "gene" was actually discovered; it began as the branch of biology which deals with heredity and variation, and the origin of individual characteristics.

genome The complete set of genes of an organism or species.

GIFT, gamete intrafallopian transfer A variation of IVF in which collected eggs and sperm are injected into the woman's fallopian tube so that fertilization can take place there, instead of in the laboratory dish.

HCG, human chorionic gonadotropin A hormone used as a drug in infertility treatment. It is extracted from the urine of pregnant women. It triggers ovulation when administered as part of *HMG* therapy and *Clomid* therapy.

HMG, human menopausal gonadotropin A commercial preparation of two hormones (FSH and LH, follicle-stimulating hormone and luteinizing hormone) necessary for ovulation. It is extracted from the urine of newly menopausal women. HMG stimulates follicle development. It is extremely powerful and the risks include overstimulation of the woman's ovaries and enlargement of her ovaries.

intra-uterine culture, IUC A variation of IVF where the egg and sperm are placed in a tube filled with culture medium. The tubes are placed in a woman's vagina.

in vitro Literally, "in glass." It is used in science to describe biological processes which are made to occur outside the living body, in laboratory apparatus. Compare *in vivo*.

in vitro fertilization, IVF Joining of egg and sperm outside the female body. Egg and sperm are placed in a laboratory dish in a culture medium which contains nutrients and substances necessary for growth. It necessitates using other laboratory and medical procedures on women, that is, *in vitro* fertilization includes a number of other procedures, such as superovulation and embryo transfer. The risks to women and offspring are unknown.

in vivo Literally, "in life." It is used in science to describe biological processes which are observed occurring in their natural environment within the living organism. Compare *in vitro*.

laparoscopy Visual examination of a woman's ovaries (or other abdominal organs) by insertion of a light guide through a small incision in her abdominal wall. Her eggs can be removed during laparoscopy, by the insertion of a suction device and forceps for grasping the woman's ovary. It is a surgical procedure requiring anesthesia and the distension of her abdomen with a carbon dioxide gas mixture.

menstrual regulation or *menstrual extraction* A suction method of extracting a woman's uterine lining which is built up during her menstrual cycle. It is carried out within 14 days of the missed menstrual period, and can be used as an early abortion

6   *Glossary for the late twentieth century*
Reproduced by kind permission of Pergamon Press PLC from *Made to Order: The Myth of Reproductive and Genetic Progress*, edited by Patricia Spallone and Deborah L Steinberg.

succession (genes were transmitted over time like so much property or status), what was transmitted was significantly subject to random variation so that, outside identical twinning, each offspring appeared as a unique individual. This apparent piece of commonsense implied that a child was regarded as a new person, not an old one. The notion that individuals produced new individuals – novel combinations of themselves – was thus sustained by the idea that babies were new people, so that novelty was built into the passage of time and the sequence of generations.

But in what sense could one say that individuals thereby reproduced individuals when the English knew that a child was born of two parents? Whether it was the father who seems invisible or the mother, their invisibility was also a 'social construction'. For as far as the identity of the child's genetic inheritance was concerned, it was a natural fact that every person had two real parents. This fact was evident in the make-up of the body. And while it might be individuals who made relationships, the English always said it took two of them. If I suggest, then, that the reproductive model was not concerned with the reproduction of relationships, it must be from a perspective that distances my account.

To put the English at a distance

One anthropological reaction to the present debates has been to observe that there is nothing new in diverse social arrangements for assisting fertility – in any case, women have always helped one another. The naturalness of human ingenuity! But those easy parallels with other times or other cultures will not hold in situations where nature is not construed as the English construe it, for it follows that neither persons nor relations will be construed in the same way either. We may expect different analogies.

In order to bring out the particularity of the English case, I introduce some of the societies of Melanesia who entertain very non-English ideas about persons and relationships, and about time and number. They do not necessarily hold, for instance, that babies are new persons. Moreover, the way in which people imagine the process of conception may surprise us. The English might well regard the test-tube baby of 1978 as the world's first, and by their criteria of human accomplishment she is, as they may hold in equally high regard scientific photography, amniocentesis and devices for making the hidden foetus appear visually to the imagination. But consider for a moment how certain Melanesians construct images of the foetus.

In her 1986 Morgan Lectures, Nancy Munn drew on material from the Melanesian island of Gawa in the Massim – an archipelago off the eastern seaboard of Papua New Guinea dominated by matrilineal systems of kinship reckoning. These people deploy techniques for imagining foetuses external to the maternal body; in addition, they monitor their imaginings, because to them whether something is hidden or concealed affects its state of being. So they present images of a foetus in two ways, one of which is visually accessible, while the other has a hidden form which contrasts with the visible one.

I extrapolate here from Munn's (1986: 138ff) account of the connection between canoes, the human body and body decor.[9] The wooden materials are, she observes, metaphorically identified with internal bodily fluids. 'The most marked connection is ... between the red wood ... of the hull and blood, which is the body's maternal component and the essential medium from which Gawans say the fetus is formed' (1986: 138). The visual image of this medium is thus present all around in the red wood trees from which canoes are carved. While blood is the material out of which the fetus is made (1986: 140) and comes from the mother's body, its chief property in its interior location. It is the hull of a canoe which is compared to maternal blood, and the process of canoe-making emphasises the creation of a hollow container. So although Gawans say that the mother's blood coagulates within her to form the child, perhaps the canoe image in addition invites us to imagine the blood in the form of the interior maternal body itself. If so, its cavity would be filled by invisible persons-to-be. I suggest one might think of these as the as yet unborn children of a collectivity of kin.

Now the manner in which anthropologists have generally designated such collectivities of kin has been a source of much theorising. What is at issue is the way bodies of kin may be seen as the offspring of males ('brothers') or as in this case females ('sisters') and present themselves as a group thereby. Members of the former will seemingly trace descent through their fathers, of the latter through their mothers. However, here and in the discussion following, where a generic is required I propose to use the term 'clan' rather than 'descent group'. In the case of Gawa, the designation contradicts the author's specific usage. My reason, as will become apparent, is that descent is not the neutral term it seems to be.

On Gawa canoes are collectively owned by *dala*, small land-owning groups. *Dala* may be regarded as refractions of clans. However, the crews that sail in the canoes are varied. In fact it is mandatory that canoes circulate in affinal exchanges, so that the living persons borne by these containers are always more than simply members of a matrilineal clan unit – they also have an identity through affinal and paternal connections. It is these connections which make it travel between clans.

The canoe itself is thus likened to a (kin) group that itself contains a group (of members). While there are potentially many persons within, the entire vessel may be treated as a single person, and here of course one has to imagine that single vessel in the company of others when it sails. A canoe is sometimes called mother because of the produce it carries in its interior (1986: 147), and we have seen that Gawans make analogies between canoe and maternal body and foetus. I suggest we are invited to imagine the mother as containing 'mothers' (future members of the clan) or, equally, the canoe as a 'child' containing children. What one sees, however, is a body.

Body is made visible in the only way that vision works for Melanesians, perceived as a matter of exterior form. Perhaps the standing trees on *dala* soil are like so many external foetuses. If so, they are also like mothers: once the process of (canoe) creation begins then the particular body (the tree to be made into the canoe) will conceal other potential and undifferentiated foetuses within, while the outer body takes shape as a single visible foetus–child in the form of its mother. A canoe only ever 'appears' as a result of the actions which men perform on the outside of the hull. It is decorated (carved, painted and ornamented) on its exterior, with an outrigger made from a type of white wood associated with masculinity. The red wood is itself covered and thus concealed with whitewash, a new external form. The whole is highly anthropomorphised in Gawan thought (1986: 145), and once fully decorated may be likened to a beautiful young man.

Munn points out the close connection Gawans makes between these canoe-decorating activities and the father's actions in forming a foetus. Gawans insist that the child's facial features should look like the father's, or at least take after its paternal kin. This is a matrilineal system in which nothing is regarded as inherited from the father or transmitted by him during conception; rather we have to grasp, as Munn suggests (1986: 143), a sophisticated theory of visual imagery or aesthetics by which an external social orientation is implied in the way personal capacities are rendered visible. That is, the very process of making something visible is a social act that orients the entity (person, vessel) outwards towards those in whose eyes it appears.

The canoe's surface specifically evokes the facial appearance of the person which connects the person to his/her paternal clan. The father's features that show in a child's face indicate its potential for entering into external transactions with these kin, for whom the likeness acts as a kind of mnemonic. One Gawan woman said that the father's kin may go and visit his children after his death to look on the face that holds his memory (1986: 143). And what is remembered must be the acts of the father, his role so to speak in the canoe building. Hence a sea-going canoe is carved and decorated with the intent that the canoe will travel away from the land on which the trees grew in order to mobilise exchanges with others from other clans.

The relationship between the plurality of bodies, who fill up a canoe, and the conversion of the canoe into a single body, when conceived as an object from the outside, is recursive in Munn's (1986: 156) phrase. 'One' child so to speak is also 'many' children, depending on an internal or external perspective. Many trees grow on the one *dala* land, as a single tree may ferry its multiple produce abroad. It is therefore no paradox to say that one person – thought of as clan or canoe – contains many persons within. And analogous to all the other members of his or her kin group (*dala*/clan), the child is one among a plurality of forms. We might put it that the child is not of itself singular, for its maternal substance is intrinsically plural, the generalised potential of many children. The child *becomes* singular by virtue of the individual body its father's acts create, even as the internal plurality of the matrilineal clan is transformed into unity from the outside perspective of differently related affinal kin. As a consequence, the one entity (clan, person) also displays itself in diverse relationships, and thus manifests diverse forms of itself. The canoe is at once mother, child and young man.

When the external form is a body with a cavity within, what it contains may be kept invisible. That is, it constitutes a kind of negative space, to borrow a phrase from Debbora Battaglia (1990). Let me briefly touch on the deliberate conceptualisation of hidden forms.

Through a second set of images, Gawans draw analogies between garden growth and bodily reproduction (cf. Munn 1986: 296, n. 29). A garden forms a mass like a woman's body, may be said to give birth, and the members of a kin group may be referred to as its 'plantings'. Elsewhere in the Massim, explicit parallels are made between yams in the ground and the growing child in a woman's body; here it is crucial that what is contained remain hidden till the moment of birth, for only thus will it grow. Land must be heavy, Gawans say (1986: 86), in order to produce, and further aesthetic practices concern the respective heaviness of the land and lightness of the people who feed from it. Indeed, the equation between growth and what is hidden is so strong that Gawans prefer to contemplate food over consuming it. Food growing in the land satiates feelings of personal hunger; to consume food is to increase the possibility of future hunger. The invisible is not absent but hidden, and not accidentally but deliberately, to the point that people derive internal satisfaction, bodily satiation even, from imagining plentiful food still growing underground. The full garden is an undepleted version of the full belly, the more satisfying image.

Gawans are careful, then, about what they make visible. There is nothing inadvertent about the invisibility of the foetus, as there may be about the concealed paternity (even maternity) in English thinking. On the contrary, these Melanesians proceed by analogies which depict the productive effects of not being seen. In its contained condition, the hidden foetus grows, and what is contained acquires a surface only from an external perspective. It is surface features which the father visibly adorns, and thus draws the child's (visual) attention to himself or his kin.

Gawa also introduces what in English would be a quantitative paradox. If 'one' contains 'many' then one is as much a rendering of many as many are examples of one. To think of group members as a unity or collectivity is more than a matter of group inclusion. The condition of plurality, the multiplication of units such as yams in the ground or children in the clan, works to reveal the one – one garden, one clan contains them all, like the maternal body. The pluralism of a collectivity is contrasted not with singularity but with the pluralism of diversity.

Diversity is the capacity people display to make their own particular connections in such direction as they will, to extend themselves, as Munn argues, beyond the clan through transactions with external others. The capacity is generic (all children ideally have paternal features). The outcomes, however, are diverse and various relationships that can in no way be summated. Acts which take people off in particular directions – their individual contacts – can neither be added together nor reduced to unity; diversity cannot be quantified.

I asserted that in their analogies for complexity, the English make a simple equation between diversity and plurality – the more (individual) things there are in the world, the more difference (heterogeneity) there will be. The counterview I have imagined for Gawa is not simply a play on words. To underline the point I turn briefly to another English analogy for the proliferation of difference. If diversity is in turn strongly linked to the English idea of novelty, it is naturalised in the idea that children are born 'new' people. To the west of Gawa, the Trobriands, as analysed by Annette Weiner, furnish a counter-instance to this English supposition.

Trobriand babies are old people, not new ones. That is, they are ancestors re-appearing as spirit-children. In fact Trobrianders go to elaborate lengths in their mortuary ceremonies to divest the potential ancestral spirit of the paternal and affinal connections it made while alive in order for it to be reincarnated as matrilineal spirit (A. Weiner 1976: 120, 122–23). The reborn ancestor is a generic. One could say that children are born 'old' and have to make themselves 'new' (1983). Thus what their fathers do for them first they then do for themselves, creating afresh the diverse connections that establish their own social presence. But the innovation has to be effected – newness does not inhere in the newborn.

There are two points of contrast here with the English thinking described in the previous chapter. First, the English see plurality and diversity as interfering with the dimensions of a collective or shared life; hence the supposition that the diversity of English life naturally hinders generalisation about English kinship. The diverse personal paths that Massim people make for themselves, however, do not threaten their clan membership or in some sense confuse or confound it. On the contrary, the body of the group is made visible in being adorned with the exploits of its members. Second, the English commonly regard tradition as threatened by innovation, for by definition tradition continues until it is stopped;[10] and what stops it is innovation, since it is innovation that makes new things appear. The Massim premise seems rather that things do not appear unless people make them appear, and that must include old forms such as conventions and traditions. Indeed, that acts have occurred in the past is no guarantee that they will happen in the future: they must be made to happen. Gawan women, like their Trobriand counterparts, observe pregnancy taboos; magic and spells accompany canoe manufacture, and so on. Each action is at the same time a new action in that its outcome for the actor is always indeterminate. People thus work to make their conventions appear (as in reciting spells they have learned from others) and to make old entities appear (such as the child that is an ancestral spirit).

I have presented these Melanesian ideas as an aesthetic practice concerned with the reproduction of relations. It has interesting implications for concepts of plurality and diversity, and is a non-genetic view.

In this view, a child is not regarded as an autonomous yet random constellation of traits inherited from its parents. Rather, parental contributions are evinced in a relationship, as between internal cavity and external surface. The uniqueness of the child lies in the fact that it appears as its parents in another form. Through its own and the acts of others it embodies a new version of old persons. Parents in turn appear in their children, as on Sabarl Island (Battaglia 1985) where fathers are evident in the bodies of their children, until the children, conceptually pre-deceasing them, die. The 'father' (a cousin designated as such) also dies at the death of the child, but does not die till that moment. Continuity, then, does not have to show a sequence of likenesses: on the contrary, one form may give birth to a different form. And if continuity does not depend on the replication of likeness and similarity, it follows that diversity or variation is not itself an index of change. A variant form may be perceived as the analogue or version of another, as when the Gawan matriclan 'appears' in its canoes, in its mothers, in its foetuses, and in the ground in which the canoe/foetus/mother trees grow.

But what about the English sense of time as itself increasing the diversity and plurality of all the things in the world? The question will also return us to the idea of naturalness implied in the English distinction between real and artificial parents.

Let me briefly offer an example of kinship system not only patrilineal in character but also, if we are to believe the ethnographer, stridently masculinist in ethos (Godelier 1986). Baruya, from interior Papua New Guinea, are one among many Melanesian peoples who regard the foetus as a solid entity made from material provided by one parent alone. Baruya hold that the foetus, male or female, is internally composed of a male substance (semen) enclosed by an external female body. What a woman later transmits to her child, in the form of milk, is made in her by her husband[11] and can thus be seen as male substance in female form. Transmission seems an appropriate idiom here, though the mother's body acts as a crucial mediating vessel (transforming semen into the foetus/milk) for the passing on of such male substance, both before and after birth.

This being the case, one might note Peter Rivière's (1985) reflections on the Warnock report. He points out that the conceptual equation in English between social father and biological father is fundamental to the notion of the family. Since there is no clear division between social and biological parenting as is found in many other societies, he says, it is no surprise that the Committee hesitated in its recommendation that the DI child be only 'treated' as legitimate – it is not said to be legitimate (1985: 4). As we have seen, the

English division is between real and artificial parents. Insofar as the genetic father appears as the real father, artificial insemination by donor (DI) meant that the Warnock Committee had to establish the 'permitted' (artificial) paternity of the mother's husband. Rivière regards maternity as posing a very different problem. He argues that surrogate motherhood is rare in the ethnographic record, and suggests that there is no language in the world equipped to deal with the radical innovation that technology has introduced in separating conception from birth. Other cultures might make a distinction between 'biological' mother on the one hand and 'social' mother (nurturer) on the other. But now for the first time there is a new function: 'no human society has had to make allowance for this third function ... of the carrying mother who is not also the genetic mother' (1985: 5, after Warnock 1985: 37). For those with a theory of genetic reproduction, this must be true. But in Baruya, the carrying mother is not regarded as the parent whose substance forms the foetus.

When what is real is natural, then further splitting of natural function is radical and innovative. Western artifice intervenes where it never did before. Rivière thus observes that a 'distinction between genetic mother and carrying mother cannot arise in nature' (1985: 5). Again, for those with a theory of nature, this must be true. Baruya, for their part having no theory of nature seem to have no trouble in imagining a mother giving birth to a form that was not conceived from her own bodily tissue. In Baruya thinking, however, she is a surrogate not for another woman but for a man (her husband). But then women are imagined, one might say, as males in female form.[12] Gender is relative; girls, like boys, are composed of semen, and semen is a version of mother's milk.

The whole Warnock discussion is conducted in terms of the fit between genetic makeup, the recognition of real parenthood and the fact of birth. It would have us concentrate on the transmission of substance. However, to understand the Melanesian cases, a further element must be taken into account.

Each clan member on Gawa may be regarded as an icon of the clan; but each individual *person* is an icon of a *relationship*, and a microcosm of diverse relations. The person who appears composed of interior matrilineal fluid and paternal features on the surface encapsulates within him or her the relationships between mother and father, between matrilineal clanship and paternal ties. In the same way, the Baruya child, a 'male' body born out of a 'female' body, encapsulates the relationship between father and mother, between patrilineal clanship and maternal ties. Certainly the encasing body of the Baruya mother is not simply an empty vessel, symbolically discarded once the foetus has vacated it. Rather, I would suggest, the maternal body is everted (after Mosko 1985) at birth. The child born into its father's clan (a 'male' agnate nourished by 'female' substance, milk, the female manifestation of male semen) appears out of the maternal–foetal relationship (a 'female' form containing 'male' substance, semen, the male manifestation of female milk). In other words, the relationship between maternal body and foetus is retained in an everted mode as one between a clan and its members. Neither maternity nor paternity has a final effect here, and the child must be completed by the influence of the Sun and Moon (Godelier 1986: 53). These relationships are recapitulated over and again with great explicitness during ceremonies in which boys are made into fathers and girls into mothers.

If anything is transmitted, then, it is the relationship between the child's parents, and this has to be transformed if the child is to make relationships him or herself.

The paradox for us here is that the child 'contains' its parents, and must be turned into a parent containing its children. This is the essence of girls' marriage ceremonies and boys' initiations. In the latter case, I suggest that Baruya offer an image that doubles back on itself. If fathers give birth to sons, then sons must also be reborn as fathers. In the house that is their 'body' (1986: 34), the entire body of Baruya men assemble to induct younger members into sequences of a male cult which constitute various initiatory stages. Now adult men are spoken of as all sons of the Sun, children in the Sun's gaze. It is out of their collective activity that fathers will come, the newly adult men who will then be able to bear children themselves. The sons of the Sun thus give birth to 'new' sons, who are simultaneously born as 'fathers'. The collective body is sustained through a displacement of relationships.

These are analogies for temporal succession which make relations between the generations appear recursive in character. We might say that relationships reproduce relationships. I do not have to underline the contrast with the English formula that only fathers can beget sons, not the other way round, a view sustained by a concept of progressive time. It is not that the English cannot imagine time going back on itself – but that they cannot imagine relationships going back on themselves. For them the temporal sequencing of generations is irreversible. Indeed, the English are able to point to the 'biological' experiencing of temporality as vindicating a linear interpretation of it. The clinching argument is always the experience of body growth and decay. A life has a demonstrable beginning and end in this view, and biological time is irrefutable evidence of linearity.

Now a Melanesian might comment that the linear nature of time is proven only insofar as we imagine 'lives' as succeeding one another in irreversible sequence, with neither perpetual return nor generational replication. What must be explained for the English, then, is not just the manner in which they link plurality, diversity and novelty, but their ideas of irreversible generational succession and of a life having a specific duration.

The point is not trivial. The downward flow of time is also the downward flow of life. It is because of the downward flow of life, from ancestors to descendants, that so much weight is put on determining who the real parents are in the English case. This in turn has determined the way British social anthropologists have classified this kinship system by comparison with others.

Given the further fact that life seems to flow equally from both parents, English kinship reckoning has been invariably described in modernist parlance as cognatic or bilateral. This has been a principal comparative axis for contrast with the lineal modes of peoples such as the matrilineal inhabitants of the Massim or the patrilineal Baruya, who seem to privilege one parent over the other in the formation of kin groups. Kinship systems described as cognatic instead 'recognise' the duality of ties traced through each parent alike, since placing equal weight on both mother and father seems to reflect the facts of life. In part, the contrast thus repeats that between descriptive and classificatory terminologies. As it happens, cognatic reckoning has been claimed for some Melanesian societies. But cognatic systems in Melanesia are more Melanesian than they are English and, in the end, the classification obscures more than it clarifies. In putting the above contrast into the context of general issues to do with the perception of life, its beginning and its end, I wish to show that wherever it lies the particularity of the English kinship does not lie in its so-called cognatic mode.

Biological rhythms for a cognatic system?

The Warnock Committee refused to pass an opinion on when life might be deemed to have begun, or rather, 'when life or personhood begin to appear' (Warnock 1985: 60). The conflation with personhood is significant, and as far as the ethics of embryo experimentation are concerned, has seemed crucial. Janet Gallagher (1987) points out that in fact the duty to protect does not have to depend on whether or not the embryo is a person: the law protects all sorts of things that are not persons. However, in popular English reactions, the anticipation of personhood is important.[13] It is regarded as an issue that concerns the individual development of the embryo/foetus: personhood in this view is a developmental attribute of the individual, and emerges as a function of time.

Yet there is a skewing here. The English allow that life may have begun before they start regarding the embryo as a person (the embryo is 'alive' in a biological sense), but the cessation of the life of an adult does not obliterate personhood at all. Once a living creature has become a person, it always remains a person. Failing human memory may mean that he or she is only vaguely recalled, but the vagueness is regarded as a question of memory and not of the status of the person. The supposition is that if one could find out about one's forebears they would be discovered as complete individuals. That is, they could be plotted on a genealogy by name, dates of birth and death, exploits, occupation and all the rest of it. To talk vaguely of those who have died does not mean, as it might on the Trobriands, that the counterpart to the once living person now exists as amorphous spirit in the land of the dead. On the contrary, English who believe in a land of the dead believe that the counterparts to once living persons will be resuscitated as persons, though it will be good deeds and sins rather than occupation and social class that will signify on the day of judgement.

Persons are thus seen as more than the life that animates them. Death does not take away the identity or individuality of the person, who continues in people's memories and in records; thus dead kin are included in lists of relatives (Firth and Djamour 1956: 38). What death terminates are the active relationships the deceased enjoyed, in the same way as it terminates his or her enjoyment of life. Thus a marriage ends with the decease of a spouse – anticipated in the vows of the bride and groom who are united till parted by death (Wolfram 1987: 213). By virtue of the natural event (death), the surviving spouse is free to remarry. The effects of the earlier marriage, however, in the connections and children it created, remain unaltered.

From the point of view of the Trobriands and other societies in the Massim, this presents a curious reversal in the conceptualisation of personhood. There a person is defined and has identity through his or her social relationships, over the course of a lifetime augmenting such relationships through individual action. Death does not destroy them: people do. When a life ceases – when a person is no longer active in relation to others – then those related to the deceased must terminate or otherwise alter these relationships themselves. Unless that happens, the deceased continues to influence the living.

It is thus no accident that the Massim should be notorious for its treatment of widowhood. Until the relationship between spouses has been severed by human action, widows and widowers enter into a prolonged and onerous phase of 'negative marriage' in which their bodies are assimilated to those of the corpse. They are unmarried when this condition is ritually lifted. But it is not just the conjugal relationship that is subsequently undone – the future effects of the union may also have to be terminated, and thus all the relationships that were contingent with it. Death becomes the most significant moment for the redefinition of relationships, and by far the most important public ceremonials across this part of the world are devoted to mortuary rituals.[14] Life has no simple downward flow, and relationships do not have enduring consequences for the future. Survivors impose on themselves the obligation of terminating the relationships that made up the deceased's life. One effect of their so doing is to divest the deceased of his/her individuality; they also divest the deceased of a crucial dimension of personhood.

This is no empty metaphor. To the east of Gawa lies the island of Muyuw. There a person's death is accompanied by ceremonies at which the marriage of their own pre-deceased parents is undone (Damon 1989). They are unmarried in order that fresh marriages may take place in the generation following; for a subsequent generation to become parents, a previous generation is un-parented. The North Mekeo, on the Papua New Guinea coast, visualise a similar move. The composite of socially diverse substances (bloods) that a person derives from his or her grandparents has to be decomposed in order for him or her to marry, for marriage must bring about a composition of new substances (Mosko 1983, 1985). However, what happens at the time of marriage is a fictional or artificial anticipation of what will happen at death. 'It is at the final mortuary feast that each person and his or her surviving relatives are de-conceived once and for all' (1983: 30). This deconception is accomplished through rearranging the relationships implicated in the initial act of conception. It is as though ancestral spouses were returned to their own sibling groups. For exchanges undo the marital and affinal connections by which the deceased was brought into being, un-mixing as a result the bloods that were mixed in the deceased's own procreation. Foreign blood can be 'sent back' (1985: 177) from where it came.

More generally, persons embody their relationships with others and are the outcome of the acts of others. At death, the person that embodied those relationships can no longer serve as a living embodiment of them. They have to be re-embodied in others, and thus turn into, that is, reproduce, other relationships. Hence the Melanesian necessity to dissolve those specific relationships of parentage by which the person was procreated.

The English treatment of death reveals, by contrast, the idea that a person embodies a subjective self or agent. In terminating them, death freezes the relationships he or she enjoyed. The marriage that was made, the job taken, the style of life and above all parentage: subsequent generations might reclassify these according to their own interests, but there is no concept that the once living relationships have to be undone. They remain forever solidified in the record – which is why, of course, one can go to records to get information about them. Since the English regard the person enduring as a unique individual, the relationships in which he or she was enmeshed contribute to his or her individual life history. But the person is also distinguishable from them. It is precisely because individual agents are thus conceived to have an existence apart from their relationships that death can leave them as they were. Before returning to the issue of parentage, let us take further the English connection between time and quantity here.

Since persons are never de-individualised, the result is perpetual increase. In the same way as 'tracing back' people yields more and more ancestors, so with each generation more and more persons are born into the world. For however many Ann Evanses I were to find in the genealogical record, I would know that each name – if memory could be revived – was once attached to a separate person. That is equally true of all the Ann Evanses of the future. Names, like property, are passed on from one individual to another; they do not displace each other. To invert Lévi-Strauss's (1966: 195) observation of the Penan of Borneo: procreation is conceived not as the substitution of one being by another but as the addition of new beings to the entire stock of those who have ever existed.

The English passage of time therefore multiplies the number of persons in the world (Gellner 1964: 2). Indeed, each person embodies so to speak the plurality of time itself – its potential for punctuation into individual units. An associated notion is that there is always more time in the world, that is, as each day passes 'more' time has happened. This is registered not only through a knowledge of history, which punctuates this flow as a succession of events and periods, but through what is perceived as biological duration. Over a life span, a person is regarded as constantly adding to his or her number of days, weeks, years of life, an accomplishment engraved on tombstones. Conceiving the span of a person's life in the numerical passing of the years in turn encapsulates what the English imagine must also be true for the world: the world itself ages, gets older with each day. So it is not surprising that they are drawn into questions of when the universe began, and what its end might be like, for there are questions that can be asked of individual lives. The notion of a world growing older, having more history to it, in turn verifies the idea that the life of a person is of a specific duration. Individuals can then be plotted against the dating of the world: Jane Austen, 1775–1817; Lewis Henry Morgan: 1818–1881, and so forth.

A point of debate thus becomes 'when' death occurs. In much of Melanesia, the issue is decided by those around the deceased: the moment a person no longer embodies the relationships he or she has with others, or no longer embodies the spirit that animated him or her, marks the commencement of mourning. Signs of physical change are acted upon, but the signal is given by those in attendance.[15] The anguish of the English mode is that the signal has to be given by the dying person him or herself: it is terrible either to anticipate death or to discover it hours later.

The English regard dying as an autonomous process, something which happens *to* a person, for it takes away their life, as it irreversibly takes them away from others. But it does not take away their personhood as an individual. Mourning is a reaction to a death, not constitutive of it. Indeed, experts at reading the signals may have to be consulted when the manner of dying makes the timing of the end ambiguous. Since the signal is given by and thus read from the individual body, the capacity to keep certain organs functioning after others have ceased to do so generates controversy about which part of the person's dying constitutes 'real' death. Similarly, any suggestion that the person has not done his or her own dying raises a moral issue. This is not a question about will: voluntary death is equally problematic. It is a question about the individual (biological) body. Life is regarded as a condition of the natural body, and it is the body that must therefore register death. The person as an active subject is distinguishable from this embodiment, and to 'take one's own life' is as problematic as taking the lives of others.

Life, then, is seen as more than the person – as a force or principle that pervades the human world thought of as part of the natural world – and against which it is possible to offend. Punctuations of time are also punctuations of life. The span of years indicates that one has had one's share of it, has enjoyed 'a life'. Through moral precepts, ethical guidelines and legal statutes, society protects this diffuse principle against individual agents who would abuse it.

Each person not only marks off the accumulation of years (birthdays and anniversaries) but moves between stages, of greater and lesser duration, as so many mini-life spans. Transitions are conventionally troubling, and the English perceive problems in the development of the body. Adolescence conventionally epitomises the awkwardness of transition; physical maturation brings with it social privileges, but the match may not be a 'real' match, for rates of maturity differ. Defining when a person is old is equally problematic, compounded in the experience of the elderly who have a lifetime of ages they have passed through and which constitute their present. How old one feels is frequently reported by the elderly as a subjective reflex of their own vigour and liveliness (e.g. Jerrome 1989). Like adolescents, the becoming-old play off ambiguities in the supposed matching between chronological age and personal experience and capabilities, in their case not to hasten adulthood but to delay infantilisation. This is social infantilisation, the syndrome identified by gerontologists as the culture of old age care. It is heightened in the case of old people living in residential institutions, where loss of biological function brings loss of status as full persons (Hockey and James n.d.).[16]

From one perspective, a person is more than life; from another, life is more than a person. These perspectives overlap in their manifestation as 'a person's life', and it becomes possible for an individual to be more or less of a person and to evince more or less life. Such perspectival overlap is analogous to that encountered in an individual's distinction from and involvement in relationships.

Among everything that determines this English exercise of personhood and life, two principal factors are seen to be the capacities of the natural body, and the constraints and possibilities offered by the cultural and social world. These take effect in the living individual. It follows that a life cannot be affected by events after death – and although someone's acts may have consequences for the future, the future does not alter the acts themselves. Causes thus flow forward in time. Consequently a person may be regarded as influenced by many things that happened before he or she was born, for he or she is born into a world already full of events and relationships. Parents affect children's identity much more than children affect parents'. This downward or forward flow in time recurs as a question of individual development. As Judith Ennew observes (n.d.), childhood is thought to be the key to the adult's identity.

We return to parentage. The English question of 'when' life begins seems similar to that of 'who' one's parents are. This is a reason I think for Maurice Bloch's (1986) complaint about the emphasis British social anthropology has habitually placed on the determining role of birth as a criterion of status. Anthropologists of this tradition would point to societies such as Gawa or to

Baruya for examples of maternal or paternal parentage that give a person rights in a group lineally constituted with reference to the appropriate ancestors. Hence such groups have been designated 'descent groups', and the fuss that Muyuw or Mekeo make in their mortuary rituals is interpreted as a recognition of the disruption that death causes to the (downward) flow of life. Mortuary rites come to seem a variant of the practices of inheritance and succession familiar to the English transmission of identity (downward) between the generations.[17] The transmission of material assets such as property and immaterial assets such as culture itself seemingly compares with the transmission of rights of membership to descent groups. Since in this view membership of such groups flows from senior generation to junior, as holders bestow items of inheritance on their heirs, the release of property at death is bound to create the need for readjustment. Groups simply reconstitute themselves after death.

Bloch puts forward a counterview. He does so in relation to the Merina of Madagascar, Austronesian-speakers whose language belongs to the same family as that spoken by many peoples of the Massim. Where he retains the term descent, it is with a significant qualification.

Here, ties established at birth create what he terms 'biological kinship' of an interpersonal nature, but what is established at birth contrasts with the kinship of group membership (Bloch 1986: 38). If we call the latter 'descent', then it points less to birth status than to the blessings of the ancestors and a person's attachment to a specific tomb of the dead. Identity is variously established according to where the person is finally buried; the communal tomb summates an equation between 'descent' and ancestral locality, which contains all the tombs of all group members. The group so assembled in a final sense can only be assembled of the already buried. As a consequence, neither birth nor death but rather burial determines such status. This is true not only as a final classification of the deceased – corpses can be retrospectively regrouped (cf. 1986: 35) – but because where a parent is placed has implications for the attachments of the living. Such a suprabiological representation of parenthood overcomes 'the discontinuities created by biology', especially sexual difference, in Bloch's view (1987: 327).[18] Descent as an eternal and life-transcending condition, he argues, ignores the difference between men and women.

Now Bloch's account holds some interest insofar as the character of the tomb group is apparently cognatic. That is, it is composed of links through men and women alike, since one may be buried there because either one's father or one's mother was so buried. In effect, the sibling group is also reconstituted, although Merina may be buried with spouses on occasion. Merina practice bears a similarity to English habits of kinship reckoning in tracing connections through either parent; sexual difference in this regard is similarly ignored. However, the crucial issue in Merina is that the retrospective regrouping of corpses in the tomb asserts the continuity of these relationships *over and against* the sexual joining of the conjugal pair and the significance of conception. As Bloch pointed out earlier (1971: 170), the process involves the gradual depersonalisation of the dead. In effect, his argument is that (group) burial displaces the (individuating) act of procreation.

'In our own society', writes Fox (1967: 51) 'which lacks descent groups of any kind, we recognize all cognates as "kin".'[19] On the basis of the fact that ties are reckoned bilaterally, through both mother and father, the 'cognatic' system of the English has been held to be more like other cognatic kinship systems than they are like those whose descent groups have a lineal (patrilineal or matrilineal) character. Yet an unfortunate consequence of the terminology of cognatic kinship, so-called, lies precisely in the implication that the most interesting difference in the English case must be the absence of groups. It is this absence which in turn allegedly weakens the claim of English kinship to form 'a "constituent" unit of society' (Fox 1967: 166). Such perceived weakening or dilution of its potential encourages writers to go out of their way to apologise for the general insignificance of kinship in Western societies as far as public or social life is concerned.

One has to appreciate that where kin groups seemed to make up 'segments' of society, as in the case of matrilineal or patrilineal descent groups, so-called, the formation of and recruitment into such groups occupied much of the attention of mid-century British social anthropology. And it was because of the particular potential of lineal descent groups to form clear boundaries that they became an archetype. Meyer Fortes (1969: 287) summarised the position neatly: whereas 'unilineal descent groups' are defined genealogically, cognatic groups 'are open by genealogical reckoning and are closed by non-kinship boundaries'. They were imperfectly defined by kinship criteria alone, and their closure was problematic. From this view, the anomaly of cognatic 'groups' is apparently resolved in the English case where no-one tries to form groups out of the recognition of cognatic parentage.

I turn briefly to a Melanesian example of a society which by such anthropological criteria evinces cognatic kin reckoning. The ethnographer refers to 'personal kindreds' and to the absence of 'unilineal descent groups'. One would expect a radical contrast with the lineal Gawa or Baruya case, or with Muyuw and Mekeo for that matter.

In the Massim, one of the Melanesian corners of the Austronesian-speaking world, systems identified as cognatic have been rare. One such is the Molima of Fergusson Island, described by Ann Chowning (1989), virtually alone in a sea of matrilineal peoples. During a Molima person's lifetime, he or she nominally distinguishes 'mother's family' from 'father's family', but the living person treats kin on either side in much the same way.[20] At death, however, living kin differentiate themselves socially through their actions and thus with respect to diverse rights and duties towards the deceased. In fact, consanguines beyond an immediate circle effectively divide into two unlike categories, analogous to maternal and paternal sides. This distinction is deliberately created.

These post-mortuary realignments mainly concern the conduct of the funeral and associated rituals itself; kin categorise themselves according to whether they would trace a link with the deceased through a male or female tie. The two major classes are 'children of a deceased brother' (mourners) and 'children of a deceased sister' (workers). Not themselves kin terms, the categories create collective distinctions between kin. Mourners feast workers, who eat the mortuary food. It is the acts that people must do at death that thus make the difference. Difference is also made evident in terms of address, and Molima routinely refer to themselves by relatives who have died. The relationship is signalled in the term: thus one may address someone as 'man who has lost a brother', or 'parent of a dead child'. But the point of the mortuary division is that once a parent has died, the child acquires a different social relationship to the kin he traces through that parent from that which held when the parent was alive.

The necessity to rearrange relationships at death arises, as it does elsewhere in the Massim, because the once living person embodied not only his or her relationship with certain other relatives but their relations with one another. The living person, through acts and dispensations of interest, contained in him or herself a specific set of relations between paternal and maternal kin, or more widely those connected through males and through females. What was united in the reproduction (that is, procreation) of a living person must be undone at death.

I argue that the anthropologist's question of whether actions at birth or at death are determining of identity, or whether or not one can discern lineal reckoning, pale beside the fact that kin arrangements such as these effect a displacement of relationships over time (cf. Gillison 1987; 1991). The anthropologist's question of whether or not kinship organises persons into groups thus masks a prior issue: *whether or not parentage is a fixed point of reference for identity*. The analytical concept of 'descent' assumes that parentage is indeed fixed.

As far as the Massim is concerned, the differentiation of consanguines depends on a division of personal identity that may actually involve shedding parentage. Thus the way in which kin of the deceased in Molima divide according to whether they are related through a male or female connection undoes the procreative sexual partnership that reproduced him or her. A conjugal relationship is displaced by the new differentiation of brother and sister. Similarly, the foetal imagery of the people of Gawa or the Trobriand islands shows the child composed of a relationship between its two parents and thus between sets of kin who are affines to one another. Each trace their connection to it as the child of their 'brother' or the child of their 'sister'. Those affinal relationships are undone at death for the sake of a reproductive future on both sides. Consequently the deceased person must, in Mark Mosko's phrase, also be de-conceived. The point may be summarised more generally. As a person, the deceased has to be divested of what gave him or her social presence – these relationships – in order that (other) social presence(s) may continue to be embodied in others.

Life and death make a difference to the apprehension of social presence and of sociality itself. It is at death that the Trobriand person becomes pure clan spirit, the moment at which the person contains the clan (in its own spiritualised substance) even as the clan contains the person. But as a living and visible embodiment of the clan, the living person is like the living clan, enmeshed in relations with others: a group *plus* its connections. They are constitutive of its life, not extrinsic to it. The Gawan body is composed of internal matrilineal blood and its white external adornments and would not be complete without both. The foetus that is the canoe that is the *dala* is an image of the person (matriclan) moulded by external relationships. The image as such can be replicated in different versions; a male embodiment of it is a version of a female embodiment. In being thus diversified, one image is also displaced by another. The displacement is a deliberately achieved effect, not the incidental loss that comes from changing perspectives.

This is a reproductive model in which persons anticipate in the sense of being expectant of their own decomposition or deconception. And the lineal mode, we could say, simply anticipates or realises in advance what the cognatic Molima leave till after death. What differentiates the 'cognatic' Molima from the 'lineal' Gawa, Muyuw or Trobriands, then, seems the moment in life when paternal and maternal relatives are regrouped as the offspring of brothers and sisters, and thereby distinguished socially through their actions. For a crucial difference in sociality lies between those relationships or persons who 'produce', in Frederick Damon's terms, the visible body as it is extended in outward relationships, and those who to the contrary embody or contain and at death 'consume' it and thus endure beyond. Yet even that phrasing suggests that what is being imagined is an essential person to whom relations are extrinsic. I would put the Melanesian case as follows. It is not so much that the person moves among relationships but that relationships move the person. The living person cannot in fact be animated without the support of relationships, which is what gives him or her body. Body made visible both by his or her own acts and by the acts of others evinces the capacity for relationship. In that sense a person is equal to all the relationships that compose it, and in that sense they in turn are integral to his or her composition as a living body.

In their life-span imagery, the English are, I think, proposing something radically other. Their reproductive model is of non-recursive generation and of proliferation. For in the manner in which the child has received substance from its parents, temporal direction is fixed.

Now whether in Muyuw or Molima, those moments where maternal and paternal kin are equally visible are moments which celebrate both the composite nature of the personal/group body and its decomposition in the recreation of future parentage. From this perspective, the cognatic English can only be cognatic so-called. Division between maternal and paternal kin is unimportant for the English simply because division lies elsewhere – parentage is fixed and the burden of differentiation falls on the child. This fixing of parentage makes it appear that one looks 'upward' to ancestors (cf. Geertz and Geertz 1964), for the causes always flow from them, 'downwards' and irreversibly. It is less the difference (division) between male and female ties, then, than that *between child and parent* which is established at conception, and such a difference, coded in the make-up of the child's body, is never undone.

The Melanesian material serves as a commentary on the manner in which the English construe relations. More emphatically than that, it reveals cultural bias, in the sense that Richard Werbner (1990) takes the original formulation (Douglas 1978). It has been necessary to contrast conceptualisations of the beginning and end of life if only to show how life and death make a difference to the kind of sociality evinced in persons and relationships.

Let me summarise the contrast offered by the Massim in particular. The Massim person embodies a living composite of relationships, which at death are simultaneously separated and reabsorbed; the person, we might say, does not exist without the attendant relations that give him or her life. The English person is a part of life, while from another perspective life is also a part of him or her; what is true of life for the English is also true of society or relationships themselves, which are both more than and less than the whole person. Between these two cases lie different possibilities in the very way analogies are construed.

Overlapping views

Merographic connections

I have imagined a range of English constructs as components of a procreative model. We can think of it as a model for reproducing modernist futures. It presupposed that relationships produced (individual) persons and that (individual) diversity led to productive relationships, such that individuals created individuals. Difference was inherent in the nature of things, and entities either produced other than themselves or reproduced what was already different. We can now add a further dimension. The model became self-evident through the manner in which people construed analogies between different parts of social life or segments of the world. Connections could be made between parts in a way that sustained the individuality of each.

Consider: domains such as 'culture' and 'nature' appear to be linked by virtue of being at once similar and dissimilar. What makes the similarities is the effort to 'see' connections; what makes the dissimilarities is the 'recognition' of difference. Difference thereby becomes apparent from a simple fact of life: *it is a connection from another angle*. That is, what looks as though it is connected to one fact can also be connected to another. Culture and nature may be connected together as domains that run in analogous fashion insofar as each operates in a similar way according to laws of its own; at the same time, each is also connected to a whole other range of phenomena which differentiate them – the activities of human beings, for instance, by contrast with the physical properties of the universe. This second connection makes the partial nature of the analogy obvious. It presupposes that one thing differs from another insofar as it belongs to or is part of something else. I call this kind of connection, link or relationship *merographic*.

The term recalls but is not identical with mereology, the study of part–whole relations (cf. Thornton 1988).[21] I wish to refer not to part–whole relations, but to the English view that anything may be a part of something else, minimally part of a description in the act of describing of it. In this view, nothing is in fact ever simply part of a whole because another view, another perspective or domain, may redescribe it as 'part of something else'.[22] When that something else is perceived as a context or underlying assumption, the very grounds on which things appear become another perspective upon them. To return to one of my examples: culture belongs to the domain of human activity, and in that sense is universally part of it; but as an idea it may also be claimed as the specific construct of a specific era and thus (and to the contrary) also part of a particular culture at one point in time. Perspectives themselves are created in the redescriptions.

The ability to constantly re-describe something from another viewpoint thus produces a displacement effect of a particular kind. One entity is not substituted by another as a version of itself, as we might say Baruya fathers are versions of Baruya sons or the body of the Gawan matriclan can appear as the body of a canoe. Rather, the substitution connects the entity to a whole, other (distinct and unique) domain of phenomena. A different order of knowledge is introduced. So, for example, the ultrasound image of the unborn body brings the foetus into a social domain where individual persons have legal rights and the body of the mother is redescribed as a life-support system. Such a displacement is simultaneously a loss of perspective or loss of information: the new description makes maternity invisible.

The very desire to put facts 'into their context' is a merographic move. The context, by virtue of not being equivalent with the thing put into it, will 'illuminate' the thing from a particular angle (display one of its parts). This gives scholars some of the measures of quantity referred to in Chapter One: the idea that individual persons can be 'more' or 'less' individualistic, for instance, is measured by a dimension *other than* themselves (such as the context of their opportunities). In the same way, the notion of plurality – of the multiplicity of things – is derived not simply from the number of things in the world, but from the fact that any single entity can be differentiated from a similar entity by some axis other than their similarity (for example, individual

When we can feel assured that all the individuals of the same species, and all the closely allied species of most genera, have within a not very remote period descended from one parent, and have migrated from some one birthplace; and when we better know the many means of migration, then, by the light which geology now throws, and will continue to throw, on former changes of climate and of the level of the land, we shall surely be enabled to trace in an admirable manner the former migrations of the inhabitants of the whole world (Darwin, 1968, 457)

In this passage writer and reader are held in comradeship by that initiating 'we'; individuality and community are, equally, promised ('individuals', 'closely allied species', 'one parent', 'one birthplace'); continuity is assured 'the light which geology now throws, and will continue to throw'; affirmation and hope — something rhetorically both beyond and just short of certainty — are expressed: 'we shall surely be enabled to trace in an admirable manner', and history and fullest community are conjoined in 'the former migrations of the inhabitants of the whole world'. 'The inhabitants of the whole world' and their migrations include man, without setting him apart from all the other inhabitants of the whole world: animals, plants, fishes, insects — the whole of animate nature — become one moving and proliferating family.

7   *Darwin and the face of nature, 1959*
Extract from Gillian Beer "The Face of Nature": Anthropomorphic Elements in the language of *The Origin of Species*.
Reproduced by kind permission of Free Association Books from *languages of Nature*, edited by Ludmilla Jordanova.

persons are different not as units, for that makes them the same, but in the context of their histories over time).[23] We have also encountered a dramatic instance in the present chapter.

The contrast between the life that flows or unfolds in a ceaseless stream of events and the punctuated life that is full of different events is like the contrast between the life of the entire universe, or animal kingdom, and of the individual organism who exists as a particular segment of it. It looks as though social discontinuity is being mapped on to biological continuity (Ingold 1986: 160). But Ingold maintains that the contrast between duration and punctuation, as it is often treated in the anthropological literature, belongs much more to the way in which scholars conceptualise the relationship between individual and society than it does to theories of time. Thus, he argues, each organism can be regarded either as the embodiment of a life-process or as an entity with a specific configuration of elements.[24] Now if anthropologists have been less than sophisticated in these matters, perhaps it is because of the power of the indigenous model: the organism as a person, in the English view, conflates the two perspectives, and continuity and discontinuity can be imagined in either direction. Social continuity is also mapped on to biological discontinuity.

As a natural individual, the person only manifests for a while the larger life of the universe of living beings. In the same way, as life is larger than the individual who thereby embodies it for a while, and time is longer than the life span of any human being or historical period, society and culture are regarded as more extensive than the particular relations a person has or the values he or she promotes. Indeed, the English hold that society and culture only ever impose a limited range of possible relations and values upon any one individual who manifests their effect. Yet, as a person with a social identity, and as an agent who takes action, the individual endures in the historical record beyond the span of his or her own life. At the same time, then, the person is also more than the life he or she has enjoyed, and is more than simply the social relations and cultural values he or she manifests. Indeed it is possible for the individual's biographical or psychological complexity to seem more complex than any social system. These merographic connections between person-and-life or between individual-and-society thus resolve into a further analogy between the life that is both more and less than the person and society that is both more and less than the individual.

Such a formula allows us to redescribe some of the earlier arguments of this chapter. It will be recalled that I have questioned the concept of descent for the kin groups of certain Melanesian societies and the concept of cognatic kinship for the English case. Now a counter-objection could well be that I have overlooked a crucial distinction between radically different kin categorisations. Anthropologists have always posed society focused constructs, such as clan groups, against ego-focused kin constructs, such as personal kindreds, and the convention has dominated kinship studies for years. Thus Robin Fox adopts the contrast between ancestor-focused and ego-focused groups as a mnemonic for an obvious difference between two apparently self-evident facts, 'true of all kinship systems' (1967: 164): persons may share an ancestor whereas one individual never overlaps with another.[25] In this view, any group focused on an individual must be egocentric and cannot therefore be sociocentric. But whatever its analytical utility, the distinction is not as radical as it seems.

I suggest, in turn, that the possibility of such a classification is given in the indigenous (English) merographic connection between individual and society. One may switch perspectives from one entity to the other, so that the two perspectives seemingly encompass between them everything that might be said about social life.

The single Gawan matriclan, composed of persons unified in action, diversified in their exchanges with others, is replicated in their image of the single individual, who exists for both him or herself and his or her connections. It is not that the clan acts as a social 'group' and the individual acts in a personal or egocentric 'network'. Rather, social action in both cases takes the same aesthetic form (the social person is the individual *and* his or her relationships). In describing what is distinctive about English kinship, one will be describing instead just how anthropologists might have been persuaded to place so much weight on the difference between egocentric and sociocentric relations. For in respect of the English idea of the individual, relationships do appear extrinsic and society does appear to be a phenomenon of another order. An individual is a part of society, then, yet what makes an individual is not what makes society.

The popular supposition that kinship is only a 'part' of society rests on the fact that it is also a 'part' of biological process. Such parts are not equal to one another. The perspective that gives each of them its distinctive nature appears always as a different order of phenomena. Each order that encompasses the parts may be thought of as a whole, as the individual parts may also be thought of as wholes. But parts in this view do not make wholes.

The English imagine an inclusive series. Society is a part of life; kinship is a part of society; an individual person is a part of a kinship system. The series can be imagined in reverse. But it is also possible to conceive a reverse that does not retain the same serial inclusivity. A person is at once part of a kinship system, a part of society and a part of life, participating in all these fields 'in his or her own right'. In other words, these entities do not match completely on to one another. Whatever whole the person is, he or she is equal neither to a kinship system, nor to society nor to life. In turn, these domains must be regarded as constituted by parts that only from the perspective of their own individual identity (organisation or order) have a holistic character.[26] Thus the logic of the totality is not necessarily to be found in the logic of the parts, but in principles, forces, relations that exist beyond the parts. In English

THIS IS THE KEY

This is the Key of the Kingdom
In that Kingdom is a city;
In that city is a town;
In that town there is a street;
In that street there winds a lane;
In that lane there is a yard;
In that yard there is a house;
In that house there waits a room;
In that room an empty bed;
And on that bed a basket—
A Basket of Sweet Flowers:
    Of Flowers, of Flowers;
    A Basket of Sweet Flowers.

Flowers in a Basket;
Basket on the bed;
Bed in the chamber;
Chamber in the house;
House in the weedy yard;
Yard in the winding lane;
Lane in the broad street;
Street in the high town;
Town in the city;
City in the Kingdom—
This is the Key of the Kingdom;
    Of the Kingdom this is the Key.

8   *This is the Key, Traditional*
Reproduced by kind permission of Macdonald's Children's, from *Delights and Warnings*,
an anthology by John and Gillian Beer.

kinship thinking, persons connected through kinship are regarded as of a different order from the kinship that does the connecting.

The sense in which the English view the person as a whole is not as a kinsman but (the link is merographic) as a unique individual. It follows, in this view, that individuals are not in themselves relationships. Kin relationships are about how individual persons are connected to one another, yet not as whole individuals, only as kin, so that kin ties appear as but a part of that unitary entity, the individual person. Kinship connects unique individuals with the constant proviso that kin roles are only one among a constellation of roles. Each role comes from its own domain, in Schneider's terminology (1968: 58). Consequently, kin roles simply evoke a role-playing or relational 'part' of the individual person. If roles reproduce roles (playing daughter to mother) then to reproduce a whole individual must take a whole individual. Persons make themselves! This supposition is replicated in the very symbolisation of connection.

The parts that the English hold to be the source of interpersonal connections seem substantial enough: persons are literally and genetically composed of kinship substance in his or her very body. Yet genetics belongs (merographically) to the domain of biology, not social relations. Social relations are regarded as after the fact. Whether to legitimate or deny them, they 'recognise' the pre-existence of biological facts. Consequently, genetic connection does not embody social connection, though may be a reason for it. The idea, for instance, that families have 'two sides' (cf. Fox 1967: 173), mother's and father's, contributes to the so-called bilaterality of English kinship.[27] But while there is a concept that a person should have as part of their family experience both a mother and a father, there is in fact no concept that it is necessary for them to have both a mother's side and a father's side. The relationships are incidental, not intrinsic, to the child. Let us look briefly, then, at merographic connections in the representations of substance itself.

If the English are like Schneider's Americans, to whom sexual intercourse symbolises the close enduring solidarity that characterises relations between kin, then it looks as though a child born into a living circle of relatives is also appropriately born of an act of love. Regardless of the reputation of the ancient Greeks for having almost as many words for love as the Nuer have cattle names, the English tend to run these two forms of love together, which in the family context also takes on a third connotation, that of self-love. Love between family members is a kind of internalised love, a property almost, appropriately expressed in terms of a couple's desire to have children 'of their own'. Here the reproductive relationship between parents is assimilated to unity. Sexual intercourse indicates their merging.

> As a symbol of unity, or oneness, love is the union of the flesh, of opposites, male and female, man and woman. The unity of opposites is not only affirmed in the embrace, but also in the outcome of that union, the unity of blood, the child. For the child brings together and unifies in one person the different biogenetic substances of

both parents... At the same time, that unity or identity of flesh and blood, that oneness of material, stands for the unity of cognatic love. (Schneider 1968: 39)

Sybil Wolfram is emphatic on a similar point. An English marriage, she says (1987: 16–17), was never traditionally an alliance in the sense that is described for alliance systems in the anthropological corpus. Marriage creates a relationship between kin on both sides who become connected to each other, but the marriage does not consist in that alliance. It consists in the union of the spouses. Thus, she says, it was for long the case in English law that when two people married they became 'one flesh', one person. Indeed, among the reforms of the nineteenth century came the abolition of the correlative supposition that a wife was simply a 'part' of the husband's person (1987: 18). However, she observes that the attempt to put spouses on equal legal footing did not attack the doctrine of physical unity as such; a marriage that was not consummated could be annulled. Moreover, that merging of the spouses into one person was a self-sufficient act and marriage was not legally dissolvable because of childlessness.

This legal image of the husband–wife couple has since been dissolved, yet I surmise that it was simply dissolved into its elements. The modern English individual continues to be produced by individuals: the pair united as one person becomes regarded as a couple or pair of one persons (that is, two individual persons). When the contractual dimension of marriage is seen from the viewpoint of the substantive tasks involved, it is as though the spouses are engaged in a 'division of labour' (cf. Young and Wilmott 1973). If the tasks are made visible as the outcome of an artificial arrangement, the claims must in turn be made explicit because the assumption is that (in nature so to speak) either could do the entire job. Thus the English also conceive of one-parent families. A parent is potentially made up of an amalgam of roles – played out between a couple when either can do the work of the other. In some two-parent families, spouses negotiate with each other as though they were a pair of single parents.

If an individual can play parts from a number of kin roles, it is also true that if you look inside any one kinsperson, you find an individual. When a Melanesian looks inside a person (a relation), he or she finds other persons (relations). But such a relative is thereby composed of other relatives only insofar as the person takes on the task of attending to them. A flow of substance may be perceived as a reason for a counter-flow of gifts, thus producing a social relationship that contains the flow (Wagner 1977a). The Melanesian person thereby sustains the image of flowing substance through the wealth that is returned in the opposite direction, even as his or her descendants may return the flow (the substance) to him or her. What happens, then, in a culture where connections of substance are taken as a fact of nature and where social relationships cannot redirect them? How are the connections visualised?

Substance may be metaphorised as blood, and the connections created by the transmission of substance metaphorised as a flow. However, the blood that flows between English relatives is imagined as always flowing in one direction (downwards in irreversible time), so that what comes to rest in any single individual no longer moves. It will only be reactivated when he or she comes to procreate, and at that point flow is reconceptualised as a bestowal of parts or traits. The flow of blood is at once like a moving stream (and cannot travel backwards) and like a substance that can be infinitely divided into parts. Hence the 'dilution' of any one stream that comes from mixing, rendering any one individual an amalgam of blood. The procedures for working out their proportion are simple: one divides one's blood in half by parents, into quarters by grandparents, eights by great grandparents (cf. Wolfram 1987: 13). Born of a mother with two English parents and of a father with a Welsh and English parent makes me one quarter Welsh. But the actual 'flows' have been rendered invisible – one sees instead the traits each individual displays. Indeed, in popular belief, the parts that an individual person 'gets' from either mother or father may be thought of as parts of other ancestors that 'show' in descending generations.

What is visualised, then, is a transmission of substance proportionate to the individual recipient. The individual contains within her or him so much percentage of blood from this or that grandparent, an image I would call literalist. That is, it opens up a general metaphor – connections of substance are like the flow of blood – to a precision or specification that brings in further domains or perspectives, here ones that turn on quantity and on what can be seen. Popular understandings of biological science make the point.

The English always know there is more to see than falls within one's field of vision: one sees only ever a 'part' of what one could see. Hence the questions that pursue the metaphor or flow concern proportion and quantity. One does not act on the knowledge in such a way as to sustain or alter or redirect the flow, but rather acquires it as knowledge about what and how much one has within. Those internal elements in turn have an ultimate visibility, from another perspective. They can be seen as gene-carrying chromosomes visible under the microscope. Indeed it is as though such a vision were just waiting for the geneticist to map the genome. Yet the fact that each individual contains two sets of genes, inherited from the connecting of persons, replicated through the cells of the body, does not prompt an intrinsically relational metaphor. Connections of substance are imagined as intrinsically partial.

While bloods may be transmitted in proportion, what 'shows' is infinitely diverse. From a potential range only this or that trait or collection of traits gets passed on. For each parent passes on what are thought of as parts of his or her body (eye colour, tendency to obesity, personality, talent), and there are as many characteristics as may be seen in the making of an individual person. Thus parts are manifested in offspring less as a set of paired or opposed qualities than as a unique configuration of diverse particles, the random interaction of genetic substances.

So out of the coupling of parents and the pairing of chromosomes, we derive an image of a different order, of an individual who shows in her or himself a unique combination of heterogeneous particles. We stress the randomness and chancy outcome of this process. None of your phenomenal orchestration of maternal and paternal substance, no division into the red and white components of the body, nothing *in the individual* to indicate that the relationship between its parents took the form of anything more than a single act at the moment in time that started off its own and irreversible genetic clock.

Partial theories for a plural society
The connections imagined in English kinship can always turn into mero-graphic ones. Individuals produce individuals but relations do not produce relations. For those relations that produce individual persons reproduce entities that also belong to other domains of existence. The simple English idea that the individual person plays various roles by reference to various domains of which the roles are part, and which exist in turn as only a part of his or her whole identity, offers a (partial) model for social life in a self-consciously plural and complex world.

The single most significant feature of their studies of middle-class kinship in London upon which Firth, Hubert and Forge report is the factor of variability, the ground on which they choose examples to illustrate variation rather than typicality. 'Nearly every family had some circumstances which made it unique and introduced some complication into the pattern of relationships' (1969: 399). They are struck by the extent to which recognition of kin, both within the kin universe and with respect to effective contact, can be modified by the exercise of individual choice – whether an outcome of class distinctions or of the quality of the personal relationship. Variability exists as much within the relatively homogeneous section of the middle class as it does between classes. Indeed, other classes may be similar in this respect, and such variability was already a finding from an earlier study of a working-class neighbourhood (Firth and Djamour 1956: 60). It exists within as well as between families, a phenomenon not confined to the English counties. The question of the heterogeneity of social experience found within any one family, in the extended sense of a circle of relatives, was a point on which Colin Rosser and Christopher Harris (1965) opened their account of kinship in the Welsh town of Swansea.

There is an overlap of factors here. On the one hand people see themselves as exercising a degree of choice in whom they 'keep up with'; on the other hand they appear united and divided by social circumstances of class, demography and the like that lie beyond their control. The actors' perception of choice means that the manner in which relations are conducted can always be modified by some extraneous circumstance – such as geographical proximity or level of earnings or how one 'gets on'. The observer's perception of differing social circumstances, and the preferences people exercise in the way they organise family functions and the like, can lead (as it had led in the earlier study) to the conclusion that 'in the English kinship system no single emphasis seems to be outstanding enough to give its quality to the system as a whole' (Firth 1956: 18).

Towards the end of their account, Firth, Hubert and Forge reopen the question of whether English kinship forms a 'system'. They delimit a number of general features, and then introduce the topic of kin terminology.

> [W]hat stands out in this English system is the tendency all the way through to specify persons individually... In any formal context relatives must be properly pinpointed as individuals, with category label carefully qualified to bring out the personal aspect. In this sense the English kinship system can be called a *specifying system* as against the *categorizing systems* of many other, especially non-industrial, societies. But its specification is of individual persons, not statuses and roles. (1969: 451, original emphasis)

The analysis holds more generally.

Schneider's observation *apropos* American kinship is pertinent: 'The relative as a person is quite different from the distinctive features which define the person as a relative' (1968: 59). The individual person is 'a compound of a variety of different elements from different symbolic subsystems or domains' (1968: 59). The relative, on the other hand, is defined rather narrowly by reference to ties by blood or marriage, such ties forming a single symbolic domain. In fact, he later observes that the self-reported variety that appears to prevent any generalisations about American kinship at large (see Chapter One) belong not to this latter domain but to the system of person-centred definitions (1968: 112). In his view there is no variance as far as the distinctive features of kinship ideas are concerned; variance, a plurality of domains, is a characteristic of the person-centred system. In other words, he suggests a location for variability.

Diverse factors are seen to impinge on the relative *as a person*. Schneider introduces the concept of normativeness to account for the coherence of these plural domains as they are experienced by the individual person. The normative category 'father', for instance, contains components from the kinship domain, the age domain, the sex domain and other domains as well. For if what is appropriate or normative for a male upper-class person as a father is different from what is appropriate for a male middle-class person as a father, in his view the resultant variation in family form and behaviour is a matter of class and sex-role attributes, not of kinship thinking as such. Differences thus arise from variation in non-kinship components. Schneider and Smith (1973: 7) point to middle- and lower-class family forms in America as indicating 'differences at the normative level deriving from differences in the manner in which family structure articulates with other role systems'. The normative system, what makes the relative a person, is a cultural conglomerate (1973: 69).

Schneider and Smith take the individual person, or individualism, as a fact of American culture at large. I have suggested, however, that as far as describing the English is concerned, we might as usefully take the individual as a modern fact of kinship. Ideas about genetic transmission, the act of procreation or the unity of the conjugal union can at any time combine to merographic effect. English symbols of kin connection render the individual person at once an entity composed of parts and a part of other entities beyond him or her. The person as a relative is also a conglomerate.[28]

Conglomerates constitute mixes of parts from different domains, such that one kind of relationship coexists in conjunction with another of a different kind. The connection between 'child and mother' likened to 'an individual on a life-support system' captures the asymmetry. Indeed, the whole concept of human beings using enabling technology can be pressed into the service of merographic thinking. Neither entity defines the other: the person 'uses' or 'exploits' technology, as the technology 'determines' or 'allows' the person to do this or that.

Insofar as they are drawn from diverse domains, the components of conglomerates may be regarded as distinctive in nature and thus potentially unequal in their effect. Hence the symmetrical mode of reckoning kinship through both mother and father resolves into an asymmetry when either parent is thought of as themselves conglomerates of characteristics. Each combines in him or herself the effects of different domains of relationship. Thus the real father is a man who is both the genetic progenitor and the mother's husband; the real mother is both the genetic mother/birthing mother and the nurturer after birth. What defines one parent is not what defines the other (cf. Wolfram 1987: 209). And neither alone nor united do they completely define the child they produce. For all the identity parents bestow, it remains possible for individuals to reproduce 'real' individuals.

English kin relations do not make an individual person equal to his or her field of relations, let alone a universe of social relations. There is, in fact, no universe of relationships, any more than personal names or kin terms form universes. Thus they cannot be mapped on to each other. Far from one system of nomenclature being isomorphic with the other, as we saw in Chapter One there is a routine expectation that kin terms will shade into personal names. In the way that kin terms are qualified by personal names, and personal names by kin terms, neither therefore ever occupies a 'complete' social space. Either names or terms may classify or individuate, but that does not in English make them simple substitutes for each other. Instead they contribute to a plurality of perspectives from which persons can be seen.[29]

Thus is an infinitely plural world reproduced – full of persons only some of whom can be claimed as kin and with a range of kin only some of whom one gets to know as persons. A genealogy simply unfolds this diversity through time, making more and more individuals appear. Each life punctuates time itself into discrete spans – embodied in persons who have beginnings and ends – parts never equal to other parts. There are always too many, and other, different individuals to think about. Consequently, one's kin are part of a wider population, but not a part that is in any way equal to it: there is no closure to conceivable relationships.

What Fortes found disconcerting about cognatic groups, then, opened by kinship reckoning and closed by non-kinship boundaries, is an apt description of the perception of overlapping domains I have called merographic. Groups are a theoretical red herring; the very conceptualisation of relationships already manifests this indeterminacy. For no specification of relationships escapes qualification by criteria which seem to lie outside the relationships themselves. Hence, as far as the English are concerned, attempts to specify completeness in so-called cognatic kin term usage frequently fall foul of one of its distinguishing features. Randomness within the individual is the outcome of specific (parental) relations, yet indicates only his or her conglomerate nature – not a person whose multiple origins are potentially partible, but a location or place, so to speak, where different elements overlap. And like the random collection of genes that any one person contains within, there is a random element in whom one claims as kin. That outward gesture of randomness (whom one 'chooses' to claim) paradoxically has as its aim the creation of specific relations.

We return to an initial observation to be made of merographic connections, that although they precipitate a plural world of analogous contexts and domains, these domains are never sustained as exhaustive or total analogies. That is precisely because the domains are regarded as overlapping in certain 'places', in certain areas or institutions or persons, where they must appear only as parts (of other domains). Thus, one may speak of an economic or religious dimension to Western family life or, as Schneider did, to the effect of class or sex-role. 'The family' is equivalent neither to 'economic life' nor to 'the religious system', but is one of the places where the effects of both can be seen. Nor is economic life equal to the religious system, though they may share certain features of ideology and organisation and in the impact they have on the family (cf. Schneider 1969). The analogies between such domains remain partial, their fit incomplete, for none is conceptually reducible to a version of any of the others.

The proliferating capabilities of a plural society are revealed in its kinship practices, though that itself offers only one perspective among many. But there is a special reason why kinship evokes the conceptualisation of relations as merographic. I suggested that the merographic connections between persons-and-life, individual-and-society, resolve into analogies between life and society, or between the individual and person. They also evoke the further

SENSE AND SENSIBILITY

The young ladies arrived. Their appearance was by no means ungenteel or unfashionable ; their dress was very smart, their manners very civil. They were delighted with the house, and in raptures with the furniture ; and they happened to be so doatingly fond of children that Lady Middleton's good opinion was engaged in their favour before they had been an hour at the Park. She declared them to be very agreeable girls indeed, which, for her Ladyship, was enthusiastic admiration. Sir John's confidence in his own judgment rose with this animated praise, and he set off directly for the cottage, to tell the Miss Dashwoods of the Miss Steeles' arrival, and to assure them of their being the sweetest girls in the world. From such commendation as this, however, there was not much to be learned : Elinor well knew that the sweetest girls in the world were to be met with in every part of England, under every possible variation of form, face, temper, and understanding. Sir John wanted the whole family to walk to the Park directly, and look at his guests. Benevolent, philanthropic man ! It was painful to him even to keep a third cousin to himself.

'Do come now,' said he ; 'pray come—you must come—I declare ' you shall come. You can't think how you will like them. Lucy is monstrous pretty, and so good-humoured and agreeable ! The children are all hanging about her already, as if she was an old acquaintance. And they both long to see you of all things ; for they have heard at Exeter that you are the most beautiful creatures in the world, and I have told them it is all very true, and a great deal more. You will be delighted with them, I am sure. They have brought the whole coach full of playthings for the children. How can you be so cross as not to come ? Why, they are your cousins, you know, after a fashion. *You* are my cousins, and they are my wife's ; so you must be related.'

9 *Sense and Sensibility, 1811*

analogy between nature and culture. When the facts of kinship are simultaneously both facts of nature and facts of culture, this analogy in turn is revealed as a merographic connection. Kinship is, so to speak, the place of overlap.[30]

That such facts or domains overlap invites quantification – how much one or other has influence. Hence the possibility of anthropologists thinking, for instance, that descriptive kin terms are closer to nature than classificatory ones, or that cognatic kinship reckoning looks as though it is a truer representation of biological relationships than other systems. In this thinking, descriptive terminology appears to respect naturally occurring differences, as between lineal and collateral siblings, in the same way as cognatic reckoning appears to give equal weight to tracing connections through the two biological parents. I have tried to show that the conventions of English kinship also presuppose the natural existence of parents as individuals, and take this as an indubitable fact of parentage itself. Rivière comments on Warnock's credulity for imagining that registers of births are registers of genetic parenthood (1985: 4), but the compilers of genealogies no doubt work under exactly that presupposition.

In the 1960s, a heated debate sprang up between several anthropologists, British and American, about the relationship between biological facts and the social or genealogical categorisations of kinship relations. Ernest Gellner has recently reprinted three of his broadsides, initially written at about the time that Firth and his colleagues were embarking on their London study.

Gellner gives voice to the 'English' suppositions I have been trying to convey. Society, he states (1987: 184) 'can be seen as sets of relationships between people'. People thus pre-exist as entities between whom sociality exists like so many strands. And they exist in nature as discrete physical persons: 'it is a *given* fact (given to social studies by biology) that every [individual] person has two physical [individual] parents, one of each sex'; kinship terms are necessarily 'classifications relative to an individual' (1987: 172, 175, his emphasis). Hence, in large, 'kinship structure *means* the manner in which a pattern of physical relationships is made use of for social purposes' (1987: 170, his emphasis). After all, he points out, of all possible social relations, anthropologists decide which are kinship relations precisely because of their 'overlap' with 'physical kinship'. He continues:

> [kinship structure means] the way in which a physical criterion is used for the selection of members for a group and the ascription of rights, duties, etc. Of course, the available physical facts are used selectively, distorted (but systematically), with *some* irregularity, etc. But: the elements of the physical pattern are essentially simple and universal, whilst the social patterns imposed on it are highly diversified and complex. (1987: 170, original emphasis)

In order to analyse different systems, anthropologists must first be able to describe the physical reality which is their point of reference. The challenge therefore lies in how to devise an adequate descriptive language to cover various possibilities of biological relatedness. A prerequisite is that one must create 'unambiguous devices for picking out single individuals' (1987: 174). The ideal notation would thereby show the physical relations relevant to the society of study against which anthropologists could plot their social deployment. In passing, he says that of course this ideal notation of physical relations will require restrictions for it must be made nonsense, not just false, for a man to mate with a man or for a man to be his own offspring.

This makes one realise the extent to which the plural culture is, or was, committed to the idea that kinship is the social construction of natural facts. *Take nature out of the equation*, think of the Baruya of Melanesia, and one is thinking instead of a system premised on the idea that kinship is the social construction of social relations.[31] It comprises a set of analogies between relations *all* of which are social relations in some sense. That sons give birth to fathers is another way of thinking about the fact that fathers give birth to sons.[32] It is an imaginative possibility that in having procreative intercourse with a 'woman', a man is also having intercourse with a 'man', at least insofar as Baruya perceive a woman to be a male in female form, and vice versa. The nonsense, there, would be to imagine individual persons apart from the relations that constitute them.

Modern English views about the plurality and diversity of life, the novelty of time on the increase, and their connection to ideas about procreation – that babies are new rather than old persons and that parents reproduce individuals rather than relations – did indeed take the individual as a pre-existing unit. They thereby placed it in nature. But these ideas also turned on their own axis. If 'society' rather than the 'individual' were seen as part of nature, the concept of the individual would no longer appear as natural ground but would be revealed as itself a social construction.

The next chapter considers the power of the partial analogy between nature and society in English life. That axial turn is made possible by merographic connection – that a modernist could think equally of individuals as parts of nature, or as parts of society, as he or she could think of society as part of nature or nature as part of society. The aesthetic impetus towards either holism or atomism forever mobilised a plurality of perspectives. The coordinating perspective to which the English held through all this was contained in a hope for perspective itself. It carried with it the pluralistic impetus to quantification, the idea that by looking we would see more things and that the more we saw the more true to the nature of what we were looking at would be our knowledge. At some point we might even recognise our distinctive selves.

3

The progress of polite society

Some two hundred years ago, in 1789, a young widow married into the Sperling family. Her husband was the heir of the former High Sheriff of Essex, and she brought up her family at Dynes Hall, an estate of 500 acres including finely wooded parkland. The Sperlings were fur merchants of Swedish ancestry, the first émigré having been naturalised a century earlier, with dealings both in Northern Europe and across North America. By now acknowledged in county society, their rise into the ranks of the Essex gentry was signified by the purchase of the house which became their seat.[1]

The house had already been improved upon since its Elizabethan beginnings; the Sperlings' own chief improvements were outside – laying out drives, building new stables and furnishing ornamental water in the park. A generation later the middle girl of five children, Diana Sperling (her name shortened then as now to Di), began sketching life at Dynes Hall. Most of the scenes come from around the hall itself, but also include the Buckinghamshire home of the Von Hagens with whom they had connections through the marriage of her elder sister. The compiler of her sketches notes that, despite their recent origins, the Sperlings belonged to the middling gentry. 'The English squirearchy contained many thousand families of this kind, untitled but locally prominent, and collectively possessed of a large proportion of the country's land' (Mingay 1981: xi). Their family milieu evoked rank, proprietorship and the making of connections between similar prominent families.

Diana Sperling's sketches appear aimed to entertain. There are foxhunting episodes, several pictures of the family returning from dinner parties, and amusing inside scenes such as Mrs Sperling and her maid swatting flies, a reminder of the proximity of the home farm, like another comic sketch of her brother chasing a chicken around the yard to cure it of sickness. But the remarkable thing about the sketches is that more than three-quarters are out of doors: the family is set in scenes around the house – in the park – along the roads – and in one or two cases near the ornamental water whose outlook has been improved by a porticoed edifice. But the improvement and ornamentation of country life is observed with a wicked eye. In almost half of those outdoor scenes, someone's pretensions take a tumble, and quite literally. We are treated to people falling from their mounts, being unable to coax reluctant donkeys, getting stuck in the mud on the way to dinner, having to be carried through long wet grass, and carrying out geraniums when it is pouring with rain.

This last rather charming picture of her mother shows lowering skies (see Frontispiece). Mrs Sperling is holding an umbrella over herself and the servant who is carrying the pots of flowers with which to ornament the garden. They are literally going out, one might say, after nature. The glimpse through the open door shows that whatever aspect they are bent on improving, they already have a fine view of lawn and fields with woodland in the distance. Ironically intended or not, the sketcher enlarges the hallway enough to show that the family aspirations included a billiard table. Only the larger houses of the well-to-do boasted such bulky assets. As the compiler adds, having a billiard table might be fashionable but it was not always convenient.

It would be inept to say that pretensions to polite society are being mocked. The Sperlings are obviously very much part of society – always appearing suitably attired, for instance, and with the distinctive dress of servants scrupulously observed. Status is probably not in question, nor indeed the desirability of having a seat in the countryside. But the circumstances in which people find themselves give plenty of room for personal reverses of fortune, and while the improvement of nature is undertaken for its enhancing effect, the young sketcher observes that in the process one is likely to get muddy and wet.

Cultivation

Selecting language

The reader may ask what these people are doing in my account. Families like the Sperlings no longer exist; we regard them as having been overtaken by events, including the massive upheaval of industrialisation. – It probably would not even have crossed Mrs Sperling's mind as she tried to protect her servant, or at least the geraniums, that the rain would be carrying particles of soot from the then expanding towns. – After all, one of the most persistent adages of recent English culture seems to be that community life is vanishing, and the disappearance of the squirearchy becomes an example of it.

In this view, community is always in the past, and one of the kinds of community that has vanished is that of a supposedly closed, ordered society where everyone knew their place. Families do not observe the proprieties of rank any more, or at least not of the kind that characterised polite society in the early nineteenth century. The English of the mid-twentieth may, in fact, have fussed over who marries whom – Firth, Hubert and Forge (1969) note that for Londoners of the 1960s a contemplated marriage is the one point at which the respective social standing of the families becomes very much an issue (and cf. Strathern 1981). But we do not think we are bound by convention in quite the same way that our forebears were.

Indeed, it is common for the English to assume that before the twentieth century, everything was governed by convention, and everything since by release from convention, so that the epithet 'Victorian' may be used to signify convention itself. Exceptions prove the rule. Thus the court and city life of the regency period may be likened to the naughty twenties of our own century. The Sperling sketches, however, present us with daily, domestic scenes and unconventionality of a different kind. It is hard to see convention in Mrs Sperling being sketched while she was swatting flies. It looks as though Diana is being rather less than a dutiful daughter in drawing her mother rather than lending a hand.

If twentieth-century English have a perception of vanishing social orders and vanishing convention, all rolled up somehow in the idea that tradition belongs to the past, then it should be of some interest as to how the vanishing is done, as to what gets selected, as to what is chosen as the signal of a new modernity – or of the old tradition for that matter. The horses that dominated Diana Sperling's sketches have gone from the countryside: our stables are garages. Yet we still need pots for geraniums, and still associate families with houses, even to the detail of houses set about with gardens. Indeed, the late twentieth century has improved on the familial idiom in that it conflates the two; one now buys and sells 'homes'. In terms of the personal capital it locks up, trade in homes is one of the largest contemporary industries/services in the country. The buildings may evoke tradition, as Willmott and Young (1960: 10) describe for a London suburb in the late 1950s ('[a]ntiquity is always there in the estate agent's advertisements, even for the most modern of houses'), yet commerce as such is dissociated from the idea of tradition. No one regards the house trade as an old-fashioned business. We obviously hold on to the idea of convention and tradition, especially as we think there was 'more' of it in the past, but rather selectively see it in some things and not others.

By chance, an apposite example of selection has been described by Gillian Beer (1986). It concerns that proponent of natural selection himself, Charles Darwin, writing as he was a generation away from Diana Sperling. The interest of Darwin for our present purposes lies in the way he strove to mould the language he was using to express ideas about the evolution of life for which there was no imagery ready-made.

Among the images on which he drew were those of kinship. In order to talk about relations between natural species, he looked to relations between kin, referring for instance to 'genealogy' and 'affinity'. He was apparently quite deliberate about deploying such an analogy between the arrangement of social and of natural life.[2] Nature and society in this sense took after each other. At the same time, by extending the kinship idioms themselves, he was also extending the idea that human beings were akin to animal and other natural species. Human society could be grasped as a part of nature. In either case, the explicitness of the association implied an initial perception of difference between these domains. Beer notes the passage:

> As it is difficult to show the blood relationship between the numerous kindred of any ancient and noble family, even by the aid of a genealogical tree ... we can understand the extraordinary difficulty which naturalists have experienced in describing, without the aid of a diagram, the various affinities which they perceive between the many living and extinct members of the same great natural class. (Darwin, *The Origin of Species*, 1859, cited in Beer 1986: 221–2)

Darwin, she says, thus seems bent on a genealogical enterprise of a particular kind.

> Darwin sought to restore man to his kinship with all other forms of life ... an enterprise which seemed to accord with the surface ideals of his society and its literature. He sought the restoration of familial ties, the discovery of a lost inheritance, the restitution of pious memory ... The factor of irony ... is that all these themes, so familiar in the novels and dramas of the time, are here displaced from the class structure of his society. (Beer 1986: 222)

For the point is that he was using those images in a highly selective way. Where it had been taken for granted that genealogies were of interest to the highly ranked – as Darwin indicates in the above passage – he extends their meaning to quite different effect. His aim is to show affinity between species by degrees that record natural ancestry. In naturalising the connections at issue, he is able to democratise them.

Beer argues that Darwin thus laid the grounds for his great 'levelling' of man as akin to non-human creatures. He did so by divesting his language of its reference to social ranking and class:

> the emphasis on kinship changed the status of words such as 'inhabitants' or 'beings' into a far more egalitarian form: 'When I view all beings not as special creations, but as the lineal descendants of some few beings which lived long before the first bed of the Silurian system was deposited, they seem to me to become ennobled.' Lineage escapes from class and then from kind: 'We possess no pedigrees or armorial bearings; and we have to discover and trace the many diverging lines of descent in our natural genealogies, by characters of any kind which have long been inherited.' (Beer 1986: 222–3)

Man, Beer suggests, is the determining absence in Darwin's account of the origin of species. Consider his metaphor for organisation. 'The natural system is a genealogical arrangement', writes this contemporary of Morgan (cited in 1986: 231). Contained within such a supposition is a double move: in undoing the connotations of rank and status attached to the very fact of knowing one's pedigree, he puts in its place the assumption that *a genealogy is a recorder of natural relations*. It displays physical kinship in the chain of being. If there were once a sense in which only the aspiring had 'connections', now we all have connections and, as he put it, probably all the organic beings which have lived on this earth appear descended from one primordial type.

And what was being displaced? Was there a sense in which only the aspiring had connections? Darwin would not have had to travel very far in either time or space to think so. Despite his reference to nobility, the gentry and the middle classes of his parents' generation would suffice, and in the neighbourhood of his house in Kent where he did most of his writing. Kent, across the Thames from Essex, was also the original county of the Austens, though Jane Austen lived most of her life in another southern county, Hampshire.

I introduce the inevitable Miss Austen, a little younger than Mrs Sperling, a little older than Diana, and from a bookish rather than landed background, with intent. The geographical connections are, of course, artificial; they simply make evident the selective nature of my own narrative. But there is a further purpose. For while Jane Austen took for granted the idea that having connections was an attribute of social status, her sketches of family life incorporated a critical scrutiny of other assumptions. She professionalised, so to speak, the amateur humour of Diana Sperling's drawings. To have a pedigree is to be well bred; yet to have connections is to have managed one's life circumspectly, selected one's companions judiciously. People have to both behave according to and improve upon their own nature. Polite society thus regarded itself as the proper enhancement of nature. Yet the possibility of improper or, worse, vulgar claims raised the question of the criteria by which natural and social rank might coincide.

Her introduction needs a word of explanation. The facts and changes to which I have been alluding are not being presented as history. Indeed the cavalier selections offered here hardly add up to information, and my conventional, even old-fashioned, sense of period ignores contemporary work on the rise of the individual or on the concept of nature. However I am not concerned with 'when' individualism first appeared in European thought, nor indeed with what people in the nineteenth century 'really thought' about the natural world. My concern is to recover some of the contexts for the (cultural) mode or conventions through which ideas were presented. Thus we might regard the visual perspective in Diana Sperling's sketches as a medium of expression demonstrably available at certain periods and not others, as is also true of ultrasonography. Genealogies were available for Darwin to write with.

Yet the account may be misleading insofar as its own narrative mode offers concepts and ideas as though they were people's beliefs and feelings. To write that society is 'seen' this way or 'attitudes towards' rank changed like that suggests we are dealing with the perceptions of individual subjects, as in parallel vein I referred to Melanesian perceptions in Chapter Two. Such a presentation is of course a conventional twentieth-century literalism for conveying cultural idiom. This is consonant with the fact that although I deploy nineteenth-century materials in making the past present, it is contemporary preoccupations that will be exemplified. On the one hand tradition is relegated to a lost past; on the other hand late twentieth-century middle-class English also promote their continuity with a past that seems eminently recoverable. Thirty years ago, Willmott and Young sweepingly asserted that '[i]n England the new is only acceptable if it embodies the old' (1960: 11). Nostalgia has since become an enterprise of industrial proportions.

It would certainly be culturally inept to offer an account of English kinship that did not bring the past into the present. However, it will be seen that most of what is re-presented here comes through the language of twentieth-century commentators. Except in one or two instances, I have not gone back to the original materials. Rather, the latter-day perspective of this account is preserved. I draw on what mid and late twentieth-century writers have selected from the works of their predecessors, as though they were ethnographers and as though their interpretations provided ethnographic data on the present. The selections are also significant to the (retrospective) sense of periodisation itself.

The last chapter was concerned with the nature of English kinship at a time when kinship studies loomed large in British social anthropology, although I gave a description from a late twentieth-century perspective that could not have been composed at that time. This chapter extends the account as though earlier eras had produced those ideas. It thus suggests the kind of antecedents in English kinship that one might have discovered when kinship was still, as it was in the mid-century, the social or cultural construction of nature. At the same time, I must make the account leapfrog over itself in order to render equally evident the antecedents of late twentieth-century thinking. As a result, the selections are also teleologically oriented towards what English kinship was to become. They incline therefore both towards a delineation of the reproductive model of modern times and towards its subsequent dissolution. Instead of moving back and forth between English and Melanesia, one will be moving between different periods and discourses of 'English'. This apparent periodisation also acts to close off a flow of ideas: a happening is named as 'then'. Hence the always-present sense of contemporary life being somehow after the event.

Eliciting nature

The following sketch is drawn directly from Richard Handler's and Daniel Segal's recent book (1990). Its interest lies in their claim that Jane Austen manages her texts in such a way as to allow internal dialogues to create a debate. The debate is over the naturalness of social (in)equality, and thus over the relationship between 'nature' and 'society'. Assumptions about rank or degree and the character of social organisation – that people do divide into the equal and unequal – is not challenged; civil society is built upon nature and is proper and natural for human beings. But people are intensely preoccupied with what determines any particular individual's place. In Handler and Segal's view, Austen's concern with matchmaking goes to the heart of the matter.

Dove Cottage lovingly takes it's name from the simple family home in Grasmere of Dorothy and her beloved brother William Wordsworth, the poet.

In 1799 they came to Dove Cottage to "live in retirement" in the country, and Dorothy wrote in her celebrated Journal of hoeing the first row of peas, transplanting radishes and bringing back wild plants from the woods.

It is in the naturalistic spirit of the original Dove Cottage that we offer you pure and natural products, free from harmful preservatives, additives, flavourings and colours.

However, we carry our work a step farther. We know that it is no longer enough for products to be natural. To satisfy discerning customers they must also please both the palate and the eye. It is the joining of natural ingredients, exceptional taste and beautiful, original artist-designed packaging that makes Dove Cottage stand alone in today's crowded field of brand names.

We hope you enjoy the fruits of our labours.

—◆—

10   *Dove Cottage Carob Petals, 1989*
Reproduced by kind permission of Dove Cottage Ltd, Westfield, New Jersey, USA.

Matrimonial alliance is a point of practical action, a moment at which the assessment of status is embodied in personal conduct. In the idiom of the day, the question is the kind of connections one could summon.

However conventional the expression of behaviour, and however eloquent the external attributes of fine houses and convivial parties, people were known by how they behaved. The capacity to sustain connections of particular kinds, like the capacities to converse well or be good company, could only show in the individual person. And while the individual might actively cultivate the habits of polite society, the debatable question was the extent to which cultivation could displace natural breeding. Thus natural beauty is improved by human ingenuity only so long as 'awkward taste' does not obtrude as false adornment.

The characters and events as they appear in the novels offer conflicting assessments about what can be attributed to nature.

> [Sometimes] characters speak of nature as a model or guide for art, artifice, and judgement ... to be 'guided by nature' in one's judgement is to assess reality correctly. (Handler and Segal 1990: 19)

At the same time (1990: 22–3, footnote omitted):

> human reason – itself a part of nature – must follow the dictates of nature in order to improve nature and thereby to create civil society ... In civil society, then, human beings have transcended nature, but without violating natural principles or laws. And civil society is, in both a pragmatic and a moral sense, the proper state of human life ... People who attempt to deny that there is a properly civilized nature for human beings can only act unnaturally ... Similarly, the renunciation of selection, the choice to remain in a presocialized natural state ... is really a selection of the natural, and thus unnatural and immoral.

Elsewhere they observe how Austen queries the 'conceit of the belief in society's foundation in nature' (1985: 703). She questions the ostensible naturalness of social inequalities – the privilege accorded by birth order and so forth – not by appealing to any anterior condition but by remarking on the negotiability of the relationship between natural and social inequality. Good breeding reveals inherent differences in the manners of the genteel and the low, and itself encompasses a 'proper degree of consideration shown towards members of all social ranks' (1985: 700). They point out that Austen's characters disagree as to what the social order really is, for no final decision has to be made. Political writers of her day, by contrast, dogmatically and prescriptively laid such an order at the door of either society or nature.

Jane Austen is an unusual observer, then. We might observe in turn that her reflections also reveal prevailing assumptions. First, it is the individual person who is the site or place of this relationship between nature and society, whether one takes the external criterion of rising and falling fortunes or of the individual's internal capacity to act in a mannerly way. Second, the immediate social milieu in which the individual acts is a familial one (the authors evoke

Burke on the naturalness of property to be found in inheritance, Wollstone-craft on the unnaturalness of property dividing families). Finally, nature exists as a realm that receives the improving imprint of human actions and decisions. In their dialogues with one another, her characters make it clear that birth is not the sole determinant of a cultivated manner. What is civil or social is the proper *development* of nature, including the capacity to discern it in others. For '[w]hat is given to human beings in or by nature must be added to or improved by human means – in particular the exercise of human reason through proper choice' (1990: 20).

Now, by the end of the eighteenth century, the rhetoric of genealogies was already well established as a device by which those aspiring to (new) social heights could lay claim to (traditional) status.[3] But appeal to genealogies had to go hand in hand with proving current connections. And that meant scrutiny of the behaviour of individuals. One could be mistaken about the appearance of apparent worth. One could also be mistaken about another's assessment of one's own, and make erroneous inferences of intentions. Whether or not a person were a suitable marriage partner was the dramatic setting for much of Austen's analysis. For 'marriages ... should be made in harmony with the natures of the two parties, both their personal natures, and their families' natural social status ... [Since] marriage represents a claim to reproduce the natural order socially and the social order naturally' (1990: 39). Drama lay in how discernible either orders were.

In his or her essential person, the individual was held to evince the particular nature to be embellished or improved by the exercise of talent. Learning how to dance or converse in French enhanced the person, but only insofar as social standing was evinced in appropriate personal conduct, and thus in judicious (or injudicious) pragmatic action: the proper exercise of choice respected nature while going beyond it. Landscape was improved so long as the landscape gardening was in keeping with its natural character. As we have seen, such a character was also revealed in people's actions, including the connections they cultivated.

One certainly did not assume comparability of social status among everyone counted as a relative – distant relatives could be a problem. This vignette from *Sense and Sensibility* (published in 1811) is irresistible.

> In a morning's excursion to Exeter they [Sir John Middleton and Mrs Jennings, Lady Middleton's mother] had met with two young ladies whom Mrs Jennings had the satisfaction of discovering to be her relations, and this was enough for Sir John to invite them directly to the Park ... Lady Middleton was thrown into no little alarm, on the return of Sir John, by hearing that she was very soon to receive a visit from two girls whom she had never seen in her life, and of whose elegance – whose tolerable gentility even – she could have no proof, for the assurances of her husband and mother on that subject went for nothing at all. Their being her relations, too, made it so much the worse; and Mrs Jennings's attempts at consolation were, therefore, unfortunately founded when she advised her daughter not to care about their being so fashionable, because they were all cousins, and must put up with one

another. As it was impossible, however, now, to prevent their coming, Lady Middleton resigned herself to the idea of it with all the philosophy of a well-bred woman, contenting herself with merely giving her husband a gentle reprimand on the subject five or six times every day. (Austen 1917: 103)

Lady Middleton's resignation is underlined in the reaction of Elinor Dashwood, a neighbour who was also a relation, to whom Sir John Middleton further wishes to introduce the girls. To be better acquainted, Austen has Elinor think, was their inevitable lot.

The converse to such perceived inevitability was the degree to which one could choose to recognise one's relatives. This was not simply a matter of shedding junior lines from succession or inheritance: branches of kin might also become quite dissociated from one another through the circles in which they moved. Whatever demographic fortunes befell particular sets of kin, association and disassociation was regarded as the outcome of deliberate selection. If it were the capacity to make an appropriate choice of companions that evinced the quality of one's own (individual) nature, the great blessing – or curse – of this kinship convention was that in the end no single individual was irrevocably tied to the choices his or her relatives made.

Differentiation within the family was anticipated. It was built into the expectation that a couple would establish themselves in their own house apart from their parents. We might put it that a relationship internal to a coresidential unit was externalised: 'the developmental cycle of the household makes connections out of family relations' (1990: 34). Indeed, Handler and Segal emphasise the way in which relations with a newly settled daughter (or son) and son- (or daughter-)in-law became a 'connection': thus married siblings cultivated connections between one another's families. Brothers, sisters, children and grandchildren, parents and grandparents, as well as in-laws, immediate neighbours and those whom one visited, could all become part of one's circle of connections.[4]

It was, of course, necessary for the settling couple to have the means for an independent establishment, and much of the discussion in the novels about the suitability of a match is concerned with the pragmatics of money. In addition lay the consideration to which Jack Goody (1976) has drawn attention: the matching of like-status families by similar resources. Husband and wife both came to the marriage with their share, and one might say that the connections were connections of property. Yet precisely because a match rested on the supposition that persons of equivalent status should unite,[5] from the point of view of the diverse kin who could claim relationship it was the circles in which they moved, their choice of connection, that made people unequal. And it was individual persons who made connections. If at all possible, kin were also those whom one wished to know.

The term 'family' referred either to a line of descent or else to a household, including servants, guests, apprentices and so on. Insofar as connections were seen to be made between families, the family had the character of a given unit.

It was, above all, a unit in its pretensions to status, and in a way that potentially divided kin from kin. The authors note that for all the various connotations of the term, it did not include reference to all one's relatives in the twentieth-century sense. By no means all relatives were family. Although from one perspective a family was given, whereas connections were chosen, from another perspective one's family to some extent determined the reach of one's connections and one's connections the standing of one's family. Neither afforded a complete model of social position. Like the overlap between natural and social sensibility, the overlap between 'family' and 'connection' produced an individual person fully defined by neither alone.

The descent of a family name with an estate depended on the capacity to select relatives, that is, on making affinal connections. At the same time, landed families shed younger sons who had to move into other occupations. The outcome was that (social) rank differentiated kin from one another, the possibility of such differentiation being present even where property inheritance was not such an issue, as the new middle clases were to make apparent. Kinship convention meant that social inequality was perceived as possible, even inevitable, between those otherwise related. Perhaps this was the connotation that Darwin wished to divest from his democratising metaphors of descent and affinity.

Turning inside out

The very concept of rank underwent a kind of democratisation – it came to be 'class' that divided people, and the old classes to be divided by a new one. I refer to the middle class who were establishing themselves in Austen's time (Leonore Davidoff and Catherine Hall's study of the English middle class begins in 1780). In his classic essay on *Culture and Society*, Raymond Williams tells us that the phrase 'middle' or 'middling' class first became current in the 1790s (1961: 15). 'Industry', 'democracy' and 'art' also acquired their contemporary meanings in this period, according to his account, as did the concept 'culture' itself. While terms for the gentry and for the lower orders had long been in use, now the middle became visible – literally the category contained within or between these other terms. It provided a new perspective on society.

The middle classes differentiated themselves according to the assets they commanded: the building up and transmission of family fortunes is one of the themes of Davidoff and Hall's account. But there were also many families with income rather than fortunes, and whose children, far from inheriting duties on an estate, could be expected to find diverse occupations. One such family were the Taylors, who lived some miles away from the Sperling house in the Essex market town of Colchester.

Isaac and Ann Taylor married in 1781. Isaac's family had been goldsmiths, his father learning the new craft of copperplate engraving (Davidoff and Hall 1987: 61ff). He lived in a literate and religious milieu: his eldest brother edited a popular dictionary of the Bible and became the first secretary of the London Library, while his youngest was a successful publisher. Ann came from a family of minor gentry and clergy, and Isaac would have become a minister himself had illness not intervened, so that he carried on his father's engraving business by default; Ann's own father, having lost his patrimony in building speculation, worked as an estate agent. The Taylors moved several times – from London, to a small village in Suffolk, and then to Colchester in 1796, later to Ongar. They were non-conformists, and Isaac became a minister to a small Independent congregation. His income was supplemented by the writings of not only himself, but his wife and several of his children. In fact between them Taylor parents and children wrote and illustrated over seventy-three books. Many of these were aimed at young people, although Isaac's sons (one a draughtsman, one a publisher) also addressed themselves to theological, scientific and philosophical subjects. The parents had not really wished their daughters to become authors – professional literary work was precarious and inappropriate – and their early works were anonymous.

Here, then, we have a family whose (literary) tradition is also being carried on by default, as Isaac continued his father's business as a second best option. Its interest lies in Davidoff and Hall's claim that Isaac and Ann 'were representative of the new culture which enlivened the Essex and Suffolk countryside' (1987: 61). Culture is intended in a strong sense. 'The Taylors of Essex lived by producing cultural items: lectures, sermons, engravings, writing and publishing ideas about correct middle-class morality and behaviour' (1987: 51).

Nonconformist moralising of this period developed initially as something of an 'oppositional culture' (1987: 21), its face set against the perceived laxness of the gentry. Davidoff and Hall's analysis concerns the growing awareness of domesticity, its ideology of moderation and joy in small comforts and its promotion of the home hearth. William Cowper's explicit depiction of hearth and home had added a peaceful rural dimension. Jane Austen comments on his poetic enthusiasm for such scenes by making him a favourite of her enthusiastic Marianne (1917: 81), for his overt message stressed not public enthusiasm but inner commitment. His popularity was immense.

> Cowper's best-known poetry reflected on the calm minutiae of everyday life in the home, the garden, the fields and woods... Cowper's central themes were the humility, comfort and peace to be found in the whitewashed cottage. For generations of serious Christians born in the 1780s and 1790s, Cowper became the emblem of all their hopes and fears... [F]amilies of bankers, shopkeepers, manufacturers, farmers, tanners, brewers, millers and clergymen ... found succour and inspiration in Cowper, whether their politics were radical or conservative... He was reputed to be Jane Austen's favourite author. (Davidoff and Hall 1987: 157, references omitted)

But Cowper (who died in 1800) had already written, and we are talking of the generation (1820s–1830s) that took him up, and of a possible transformation of perspective. Cowper's depictions of the cosy domestic interior had been matched by the equal charms of the exterior: the garden round the cottage was 'Nature in her cultivated trim' which would be dressed to taste (1987: 166). From an era of landscape gardening, when estates were laid out to evince the taste of the landowner, here was an image of taste that had been miniaturised to the proportions of a country cottage. The reduced proportions are intriguing. They invite one to look within the house to the small family circle drawn round the fire. McNeil (1986: 197–8) comments that the generalised relationship between humanity and nature found in earlier poets of the eighteenth century was, in Cowper, 'transformed into the very personal interactions between individuals and nature'.

Here also perhaps lay the means by which a culture set against the ostentation of courtly excess could come to exaggerate itself (Boon 1982). Middle-class culture could not be promoted through the rhetoric of birth, nor through the artificialities it despised; it could not elevate family fortunes to noble estates. It addressed itself instead to small-scale connections, and to the social self-sufficiency of the domestic unit.

A conceit, of course, to animate a category ('culture') as though it had intentions, but perhaps we see here the development of a particular perspective on social independence. Handler and Segal (1990: 52, n. 6) suggest that the association of independence with choice, for instance, 'was not a new element introduced by an emergent middle class, but was an element of aristocratic life adopted [made explicit], and thereby changed, by the wider social order'. In Austen's circle, to be dependent upon another meant one was an inferior, so that 'the value attached to independence – the power to choose and select – is thought to characterize the highest, most civilized, form of human existence' (1990: 45). Independence was to be obtained with means, and with freedom from debt and from superiors who must be pleased. But such independence could be reappropriated (adopted) as self-sufficiency.

> Tensions over loyalties between the natal and marital family frequently surface even in small matters such as where the adult children would spend Christmas or family celebrations. It has been seen how each spouse's family and their own children could struggle for the services of a woman or the material support of a man. At times these intra-familial conflicts were exacerbated by differences in status and resources. When one branch of a family had made its way up the social ladder, poor or vulgar relations could be a handicap. Yet there are numerous examples of more prosperous or educated relatives giving kin a helping hand... Most men and women of the provincial middle class would have agreed that, indeed, 'Our Family is a Little World'. (Davidoff and Hall 1987: 356)

It is hardly new to say that the middle classes also appropriated the genteelness of demeanour that characterised upper-class good breeding, as they did the idea of good works towards those of lower ranks. In his classification of codes of manners, Nicolson called the period between 1770–1830 one of 'distilled civility' (1955: 204). However, it overlapped with what was to become a passion for 'respectability', reaching its zenith in the 1840s and 1850s. As he depressingly comments: 'by 1850 the whole of England had become middle class' (1955: 227), a revolution he puts down to the rapid increase in the numbers of families who regarded themselves as genteel. Piety became fashionable. Nicolson makes his own class prejudice evident: it is clear that he favours distilled civility as the 'English gentleman' era, and Austen's presence is an annoyance. He cannot conceal his irritation at her characters for spending passion on the meaningless subtleties of social status (actually the subject of his book), and can only accommodate them as harbingers of the new order of respectability.

Indeed, the process by which the new middle class culture of the mid-nineteenth century became visible has been the subject of endless English disquisition ever since, and one in which class prejudice has had a significant role to play. Thus scorn has been poured on the very notion of the category 'middle class' (Firth, Hubert and Forge 1969: 23), and my own vanity is transparent in the intellectual distance I contrive. Yet the middle class was not so much invented as reinvented. This returns us to the question of selection. When faced with changing attitudes or values or terminologies, we have to ask what it is of themselves – what of the 'already thought' so to speak – people are choosing to think about, and thereby making explicit. Hence the question of how a 'new' culture becomes visible and, in this nineteenth-century example, especially when it is a culture of moderation.

Suppose, like the emergence of the middle class itself, the centre of what was already there or within could be externalised as an object of thought.[6] And suppose the social field were already realised on a reduced scale. One would not then look to the outside world nor to polite society. Outward disposition would become reflected less in a spread of connections than in behaviour evincing one's own worth. Worth would have public currency not as taste but as a self-sufficiency of sorts.

That the job was to improve one's personal talents introduced a perspective of transformative force. In Cowper's case, these were talents given by God, and in that sense all were equal before God. But the middle classes subsequently made visible the improvement of those talents; it was they whose life style, with its emphatic domesticity, was to evince the peacefulness, skill and soul that lay within every one. They did this through miniaturising the act of cultivation, shrinking the social landscape to the interior person. It was therefore a supposed internal state of affairs that was explicitly externalised in people's works and deeds. No longer a question of finding a match between internal nature and the external expression of taste in one's connections or in the circles within which one moved or the society one cultivated, persons made

Scruby's dream.was a high class residential area with no tone-lowering terrace houses or bungalows. He wanted to stress the rural aspect of a suburb which was, nevertheless, only 13 miles and 22 minutes (on the fastest train) from London. The Reed and Hoad brochure referred to 'orderly roads, tree planted, wide grass verges, low stone walls. Hand-made tiles, giving every roof a mellowed appearance, most satisfying to those of artistic taste. Houses that, despite their widely differing styles, merge naturally into the green vistas of woodland that form their background. A sylvan town with birds, trees, flowers — a real country home that, thanks to the boundary of Petts Wood, will always remain country'.

11   *Amenities without and within*
Left: Petts Wood, Kent. Built in the early 1930s on an estate first opened up in 1928. Reproduced by kind permission of Peter Waymark from *A History of Petts Wood*.
Right: Manchester. An advertisement from 1988. Reproduced by kind permission of J. Freeman for Molloy Homes, Levenshulme, Manchester.

what lay within an explicit object of improvement. Civility acquired a new public face, 'morality': the behaviour of others was to be copied, or avoided, but in any case treated as examples for one's own.

Many of the ideas and forms that apparently distinguished the mid-nineteenth century were already in place in the early decades, there when Diana Sperling was sketching and Jane Austen writing, and a possible conceptual facility for the transformation of this polite society has already been noted. We saw how in Austen's novels every new household was modelled on an eversion of relations. The son or daughter who belonged (internally) to one establishment, on marrying founded a new establishment with which other family members now had (external) connections. This process was exaggerated in the case of the gentry, who built new houses or refurbished old ones to show it. The aesthetic outcome may well have been a reassuring perpetuation of status, a visual replication of well-maintained residences –

children appeared to be following the logic of patrimonial inheritance or the preservation of joint conjugal estates from one generation to the next – but that very perpetuation was also a perpetuation of the capacity for independence and personal choice.

Now replication took place on a significantly reduced scale. Enhancement was turned inside out as simplicity. Cottages were architecturally designed as popular forms of domestic building.[7] If those replicas of the country cottage shifted perspective, it was to create a world that had moved away from the search for some kind of isomorphism between internal and external worth, between family and connections, in which the improvements one did to 'nature' exemplified the capacity for self-improvement, in short that had moved from a sense in which nature was elicited from within. Now one *copied* the external form, the cottage, in order to depict an internal one imagined as domestic harmony. From outward form one could gauge inner grace, and individual exemplars were models to be imitated. In other words, what was contained within could actually be created or brought to conscious attention by correct outward behaviour. Moreover, the content of what was within became focused: not the minute gradations of politeness which varied with everyone – but the personal virtues redolent of good domestic organisation. The internal (what is within persons) has been literalised as an interior (residential) space.

I have laboured the analogy of domestic architecture (cf. La Fontaine 1988) because it seems as if the image of the secluded house/cottage accomplishes two things at once. It both miniaturises the 'size' of the family group within, and evokes a sense of intimate organisation (the simple cottager has few if any servants). What has become visibly internal to the family is its own arrangement or regulation. The long-established division between public and private is now attached to an image of the domestic family with respect to the world 'outside', and a reduced 'family' becomes a vehicle for conceptualising privacy.[8] If what was made visible to family members was its principles of regulation, the family could thus appear defined as much by the internal exercise of authority as by external comparisons with others.

Davidoff and Hall observe that residential segregation, and the expressed independence of the middle class from the values and aesthetic prototypes of the gentry, was realised in the separation of dwellings as units on their own. An explicit desire for privacy marked property boundaries with hedges and walls.

Humphrey Repton strikingly demonstrated the effect in his paper model of the space in front of his Essex 'cottage' where the view of shops, road and passing public was cut off by fencing, shrubbery and trees; a strong contrast to the communal squares and terraces of Georgian styles. The novel device of the semi-detached house, combining the privacy and economy of a smaller house with the appearance of one twice the size, was peculiar to suburban development. The inherent anti-urbanism of middle-class culture was reflected in the quintessential image of early nineteenth-century desirable housing, the *white cottage* with thatched roof and porch embowered with honeysuckle and roses. (1987: 361, references omitted, original emphasis)

During the boom of the first two decades of the nineteenth century, houses were built along roads or by parcelling up large gardens within old town centres, a pattern that set the scene for the mid-century. Residences were separated from both civic space and the workplace; social worth was conveyed as immediate outward appearance. Whereas the Sperlings' house had been set in a landscape that invited the ornamentation of its gardens, the garden round 'the cottage' was virtually attached to the dwelling itself. Roses and other plants came to ornament the dwelling, trailing round its door or closely clustered on its walls, an image whose details were revived in the Edwardian cottage garden. The cottage-and-garden appeared a free-standing entity, an individual dwelling. If persons were likewise imagined as individual dwelling

12   *Tudor cottage, 1816*
The watercolour is by Diana Sperling, captioned 'A cottage built by the Duchess of Bedford, in the style of Henry 7th's reign, September 1816.' It was built in 1810–11 by Humphrey and J Adey Repton. Architects provided owners with pattern books for such styles.
Reproduced by kind permission of Victor Gollancz Ltd, from *Mrs Hurst Dancing* by Diana Sperling, illustrations by Neville Ollerenshaw.

places, perhaps it is not surprising that Davidoff and Hall link the following shifts.

> Cowper ... envisaged ... an organic society, based on the land, in which there would be no substantial separation between production, reproduction and consumption. The household was to unite within it the separate but complementary activities of the two sexes. By the 1830s and 1840s such a vision was no longer appropriate or possible. Middle-class families were increasingly living ... in homes which were separated from work ...
>
> A second major shift had occurred by the 1830s and 1840s. The original inspiration for new patterns of behaviour in the home and family lay with the religious revival of the late eighteenth century ... Isaac and Ann Taylor and their generation were converted in their adult lives and had all the enthusiasm of the new discoverers of truth. However, for many of the writers of the later period, religion was a given part of their intellectual framework but no longer occupied centre stage. (1987: 181, reference omitted)

If religion did not have to be explicitly elicited neither did nature. And if one of the forms that nature took was the cultivated garden that clung visibly to the walls of the individual dwelling, then interior space could also be conceptualised as a garden – both the persons (especially children) that the house contained and the interior of those persons.

> Children *as* gardens was a favourite metaphor for writers on domesticity. Morality had to be sown, cultivated and deeply rooted against the winds of adversity and the weeds of vice eradicated, as a clergyman wrote in the juvenile magazine edited by Jane Taylor. The flower garden, in particular, was encouraged for girls. (Davidoff and Hall 1987: 373, reference omitted, original emphasis)

What was cultivated was held in that interior space, the individual mind and spirit: the plants growing *in* the garden, the children in the house, talents within the person. Nature thus provided the ground to the cultivation of the person. Like religion, it becomes a background to the exercise of talent. What was educated, drawn out, was the capacity for moral conduct evinced outwardly in respectable behaviour. External respectability displayed internal morality.

Which of course is what all those literary productions of the Taylors were about. They were, apparently, books of contemplation and reflection rather than dialogue. Their aim was to edify and instruct. Perhaps the most interesting development for our purposes, on Ann Taylor's part they included texts on motherhood.

> Both parents are seen as having awesome responsibilities, but the duties of the mother are given particular attention ... Ann Taylor was suggesting in the early nineteenth century the notion of professional motherhood which became more clearly articulated by the 1830s and 1840s ... This meant that wives and mothers should themselves be educated. How could they fulfil such important work without proper preparation, without attention to system, without organization and regularity? (1987: 175)

Here are matched two forms of domesticity. It was possible to achieve a resonance between an orderly, well-run and decent household and an orderly decent-thinking mind. The interior person appeared as a regulated and domesticated one. Mrs Taylor's daughter Jane was, among other things, editor of a religious youth magazine. When consulted about a young lady's education, she answered: 'The grand end which we ought to propose to ourselves in every intellectual study is *moral* improvement' (original emphasis; 1820, quoted 1987: 289). 'This included the domestic morality of inner family life. Contemporary educational movements went hand in hand with what a later generation would call the recognition of kinship roles as roles. The word 'duty' covered all: to oneself, to one's parents, to God. With religion the taken-for-granted idiom of middle-class culture, what was made explicit was the necessity to improve in the sense of educate, and educate in the sense of impressing upon persons their familial duties. Moreover, mothers were not just taking 'the moral and spiritual training' of their children as their 'most sacred duty' (1987: 340); they were *writing about* domestic duties – and in the 1830s and 1840s in full spate. It was one of the new evangelisms.

Education appears not as enhancement, an ornamentation eliciting a sense of scale, as windows were once placed to draw attention to the proportions of a building: it was an execution of inner will in which one's own matched the will of God, or one's parents. Hence the power of imitation. Mid-century public buildings attempted to capture the virtues of earlier ages, to imitate the exterior granduer of medieval cathedrals.

Consonant with the growing apart of public and private spaces, businesses also came to have a 'public' aspect. Banks, insurance companies and commercial enterprises of all kinds now created the civic centre of England's towns and cities. Private fortunes turned into public buildings; towering offices, like so many latter-day churches, were to displace the urban crescent or mall as the dominant image of urban space. Harking back to medieval imagery was no accident: if the (middle-class) English try to draw 'tradition' out of themselves, this became explicit in the 1860s, the moment at which the necessity for establishing a common culture in England is also being voiced.

At the same time as Darwin was democratising nature, Matthew Arnold was trying to democratise culture. Society as such could not be the direct object of democratisation, a point to which I shall return, for social difference provided the very images for improvement that a scale of perfection also required. Where Darwin naturalised once-ranked genealogies, then, in order to talk of the ennobling effect of perceiving a common kinship among all living species, Arnold drew on older aristocratic values in order to find an ennobling aim for the common culture of the English. Indeed, it is commonplace to observe that Arnold, a school inspector, did so in reaction to the narrowmindedness of the nonconformist schools he had to inspect. To him, the middle classes appeared under-educated philistines, and he did not conceal his distaste for their religious platitudes.

AND DESIGN   127

pomp and grace of Italy in her youth. For us there can be no more the throne of marble —for us there is no more the vault of gold—but for us there is the loftier and lovelier privilege of bringing the power and charm of art within the reach of the humble and the poor; and as the magnificence of past ages failed by its narrowness and its pride, ours may prevail and continue, by its universality and its lowliness.

94. And thus, between the picture of too laborious England, which we imagined as future, and the picture of too luxurious Italy, which we remember in the past, there may exist—there will exist, if we do our duty—an intermediate condition, neither oppressed by labour nor wasted in vanity—the condition of a peaceful and thoughtful temperance in aims, and acts, and arts.

95. We are about to enter upon a period of our world's history in which domestic life, aided by the arts of peace, will slowly, but at last entirely, supersede public life and the arts of war. For our own England, she will not, I believe, be blasted throughout with furnaces; nor will she be encumbered with

128   MODERN MANUFACTURE

palaces. I trust she will keep her green fields, her cottages, and her homes of middle life; but these ought to be, and I trust will be, enriched with a useful, truthful, substantial form of art. We want now no more feasts of the gods, nor martyrdoms of saints; we have no need of sensuality, no place for superstition, or for costly insolence. Let us have learned and faithful historical painting —touching and thoughtful representations of human nature, in dramatic painting; poetical and familiar renderings of natural objects and of landscape; and rational, deeply-felt realizations of the events which are the subjects of our religious faith. And let these things we want, as far as possible, be scattered abroad and made accessible to all men.

96. So also, in manufacture: we require work substantial rather than rich in make; and refined, rather than splendid in design. Your stuffs need not be such as would catch the eye of a duchess; but they should be such as may at once serve the need, and refine the taste, of a cottager. The prevailing error in English dress, especially among the lower orders, is a tendency to flimsiness

13   *Ruskin's Two Paths, 1859*
Extract from John Ruskin's *The Two Paths; Being Lectures on Art and its Application to Decoration and Manufacture Delivered in 1858–9.* In 1906 in its Thirty-sixth Thousand. Reproduced by kind permission of Unwin Hyman Ltd.

But it was not the aristocratic classes themselves that would provide such a focus. As they currently existed 'classes were the embodiment of our ordinary selves; to embody our best self we must create the state' (cited by Williams 1961: 130). Arnold made literal the parallels between regulation, culture and public life. In 1864 he wrote that 'to trust to the principle of supply and demand to do for us all we want in providing education is to lean upon a broken reed'. He believed that if schools were to be efficient they had to be subject to public regulation; only then could solid guarantees of quality be given (Scott 1988: 28). Of interest is what has happened to the individual person in this view. Williams (1961: 127, original emphasis) quotes from Arnold's *Culture and Anarchy* (1869).

Culture ... places human perfection in an *internal* condition ... [Yet] [p]erfection, as culture conceives it, is not possible while the individual remains isolated. The individual is required, under pain of being stunted and enfeebled in his own development if he disobeys, to carry others along with him in his march towards perfection, to be continually doing all he can to enlarge and increase the volume of the human stream sweeping thitherward.

This is another shift of perspective. For the Taylors, morality seems to have lain in externalising inner worth; following external prescriptions of duty was a matter of cultivation from within, and of copying good examples from without. Here, by contrast, is a perception that only as one in a collectivity can an individual progress in him or herself. Through the instrument of a culture in common, each will acquire that culture as itself an internal condition. Regulation, formerly an attribute of an interior condition, is presented as impinging from the outside. The social field is enlarged again, but as commonality rather than connection.

> In the end he saw no choice. 'For public establishments modern societies have to betake themselves to the State; that is to *themselves in their collection and corporate character.*' Arnold had no sympathy for the argument, as popular in 1860 as in 1980, that dependence on the state ... destroyed the self-reliance of those who benefited. Instead he believed that the failure to take collective action where individual action was impossible, inappropriate or self-defeating produced these very ills ... [For] he believed the state through education could combat the anarchy, the collapse of culture, which otherwise might be produced by the inevitable decay of the old aristocratic order ... So the middle classes were the key, not only to the preservation of culture but also to the peaceful transition to a democratic society. (Scott 1988: 28, original emphasis)

It is not fair, the writer continues, to reduce this argument to a simple-minded desire to make gentlemen of the Victorian middle classes. 'For he looked beyond the rule of the bourgeoisie to a mass age, a period when society would be ruled by its most numerous classes. Middle-class education was never an end in itself for Arnold; rather it was a means to the enlightenment of the whole people' (1988: 28). But how to conceptualise 'society' in common was going to require imagery of its own.

Arnold wrote, we are told, with the outcome of the French Revolution in mind; Trautmann (1987: 182) makes the same point for Arnold's (and Morgan's) contemporary, Henry Maine. Maine objected to 'Rousseau's belief that a perfect social order could be evolved from the unassisted consideration of the natural state' (1870: 89). In fact his *Ancient Law*, published in 1861, criticised two strands of political theory for their axiomatic assumptions about human nature, not only Rousseau's notion of a natural state of mankind but equally the competitive individualism of utilitarian thinking. The latter is far from a general condition of social life since it appears only in 'progressive societies' in their later stages; while the former is mere speculation that is used to evaluate proximity to or fall from an original perfection (Trautmann 1987: 181–2). Instead, different societies show a progressive development; for example, family obligation is dissolved and individual obligation takes its place. But in Maine's view, the individual person emerges quite crucially as *part* of a wider social reality: for the individual is manifest as 'the unit of which civil laws take account' (1870: 168).

Regulation and order are, so to speak, here externalised in the idea of a system of laws encompassing the individual person. The social order which thus exists beyond the individual is a collectivity presented to the person as the field of rights and duties by which he/she is defined. It now seems self-evident that human nature should be affected by the way such regulations are organised, and that social organisation will have its own specifiable features.[9] But procedures for such a specification – modes of description – still lay in the future, as did the twentieth-century concept of 'social organisation' itself.

Socialisation

Personifying society: management and the social order

At the time when Mrs Taylor's works were probably still being read – *Maternal Solicitude for a Daughter's Best Interests* (1814); *Practical Hints to Young Females on the Duties of a Wife, a Mother and a Mistress of a Family* (1815); *Reciprocal Duties of Parents and Children* (1818) (Davidoff and Hall 1987: 340; 494, n. 114) – a Dr Chavasse of Birmingham published his staggeringly popular *Advice to Mothers on the Management of their Offspring*. First appearing in 1840, it sold 460,000 copies. It was shortly followed by *Advice to Wives on the Management of Themselves during the Periods of Pregnancy, Labour and Suckling* (1843), as it was originally called, which sold 390,000. Not only was there a reading public avid for such advice, but their popularity endured. By the end of the century, the former had run into 15 editions, the latter to 14. Indeed, it was a copy of the 14th edition – no doubt much revised (Barnes 1898) – that my mother passed on to me saying it was still the most helpful thing she knew for its detail, lack of censoriousness and plain speaking on behalf of plain living.

Abstracted from the field of family morality, Chavasse's injunctions address the internal necessity of realising one is the keeper of one's own person. But a personal regime will succeed only if it follows the laws of the natural regime. Here nature is less the soil out of which individual souls will be cultivated than a regulative field that the individual organism ignores to its peril.

The motivating concept, one the later twentieth century has revived with such vigour, is management. In following such regimes, persons appear as managers of themselves. And although the word Chavasse most frequently uses is still duty, where the twentieth century might prefer role, the mother is clearly regarded as the incumbent of an office which requires her to observe certain procedures of conduct. This is the professionalisation of maternity.[10] Realising one's duty to the requirements of the office itself will make the difference between being a good and a bad mother, and the sanctions are natural ones. Those who deform their bodies through unsuitable dress or who live immoderately will suffer in their health, and the consequences may be particularly painful when the mother tries to breast feed her baby. Moreover, the mother runs the risk of meddlesome interference from the ignorant. 'Nature ... is generally best left alone' (1898: 261).

But what is this nature? In the section from which this judicious observation comes, Chavasse, or Barnes, a consulting physician to the British Lying-in Hospital who was responsible for the revisions to the 14th edition, is complaining about the quacking, interfering and fussing way in which nurses meddle in what should be left alone. The topic is breast problems and the advice is that in fact the baby is 'the best and only doctor the bosoms require' (1898: 260). Problems on the child's side do not come into it: the child is instead presented as a kind of natural expert. The other expert is, of course, the doctor, and there is a clear hierarchy of expertise here. Chavasse/Barnes says that it is the doctor's and not the nurse's province to direct treatment, while it is the nurse's duty to fully carry out such instructions. The source of the doctor's expertise in turn, it is implied, is his correct interpretation of nature, for nature – like the doctor – resents interference. Provided she is properly interpreted, she is the ultimate expert. 'Nature–beneficent Nature–if we will listen to her voice, will usually tell us *what to do* and *what not to do*' (1898: 262; author's emphasis). As he repeats elsewhere: Nature is the best doctor.

Along with this assumption about expertise goes an assumption that everything can be learned. There is nothing in the conduct of oneself, the running of one's household, the maintenance of health, that cannot be learned. Here writes a writer of books!

> If wives do not cook the dinner themselves, they should surely know how dinners ought to be cooked... Half the household miseries and three-fourths of the dyspepsia in England would, if cookery were better understood, be done away with! There are heaps of good cookery books in the market to teach a wife how a dinner should be cooked. She has only to *study* the subject thoroughly and the deed is done, to the great happiness and wellbeing of himself and of her husband. (Chavasse (Barnes) 1898: 77, original emphasis)

Education becomes a necessity. For since nature has to be interpreted, and there is plenty of room for the ignorant to otherwise pass on false learning, then the experts must be recognised.

The use of the expert in women's matters has been a source of recent feminist commentary,[11] and there is no need to labour the point. We might note, however, the further assumption that what is learnt is all of a piece. This is vividly imagined as showing in the health of the mother (and her child): all the rules she follows – the correct diet, ventilation of her house, exercise and so on – can be aggregated in the example of the healthy and happy matron. Her person will be the summation of all these observances. Orderliness is intrinsic to health, and management is the contribution individuals make to order. Personal management thus follows nature as the grand manager.

Chavasse/Barnes is running a polemic of sorts. Blue-stocking women he says make bad wives; better to cultivate her household duties than cultivate Latin or Greek, the crude rendering of an argument that neither began in the nineteenth century nor was to end with it (1898: 77). What goes unremarked is the need for cultivation. Cultivation is beginning to appear like the process twentieth-century people call socialisation; here it is the complete following of rules of conduct whose natural integration would be evident in the (healthy) body. Despite the standard of material resources required for their enactment, theoretically they applied to anyone. Yet the rules are not conceptualised as social rules, but as making explicit what 'experience' has taught about nature. In his view, too much social artifice is held actually to hinder nature's own path. The twentieth century was to produce the further idea that socialisation thought of as the inculcation of cultural values was the source of the very canons of health that Chavasse/Barnes took as self-evident. What he did not take as self-evident was the inculcation of rule itself. This was not a question of eliciting either the good manners that constituted polite society or the personal morality that ensured outward respectability. The regulative and systemic effect of following the rules as such had to be made explicit.

In Arnold's view, right behaviour must be collectivised for the good of everyman, for what was at issue was the management of social life itself. Where Chavasse hypostatised Nature, Arnold hypostatised Culture. Culture is right knowing and right doing, a process rather than a state, Williams suggests (1961: 134), but one with visible goals. Again there is an analogy between a regulative field and personal health. 'Culture, which is the study of perfection, leads us ... to conceive of true human perfection as a *harmonious* perfection, developing all sides of our humanity; and as a *general* perfection, developing all parts of our society' (from *Culture and Anarchy*, 1869; Williams 1961: 124, original emphasis). Culture, a study and a development, is an inspirational force which draws thought to itself. Indeed, Williams observes that the constant intonation of Culture in which Arnold indulged may have been responsible for the common English hostility to the word which developed after 1860, and which found the word itself artificial.

Nature had long been regarded as such a centripetal force.[12] The idea that either Nature or Culture should draw people's thoughts in an inspirational way towards themselves was an effect of personification. The twentieth century would no doubt add Society to the list. But society was not yet, despite Arnold's references to it, such an object of thought. In the mid–nineteenth century, an abstract concept of society existed in the sense of a self-evident condition of associative life – persons cannot exist outside of society in this sense, as Karl Marx declared at several points.[13] But what I have in mind are the devolved ways of thinking that twentieth-century people take for granted in their talk of principles of social organisation, as they do of ecology or of cultural values. These are all professional constructs.

I do not mean professional simply in terms of their disciplinary status in academia. What is significant in the twentieth-century formulations is the way the constructs depict domains each perceived as an autonomous field to be identified by its own internal regulation. If we wish we could thus say that the concepts involved have been 'naturalised'. They create their own contexts, whether these are thought of as domains akin to those under the operation of natural laws or akin to the variable outcomes of adaptation and selection.

That very phraseology of mine reveals the manner in which images of social and natural life illuminate one another. Thus one may say that it was through naturalising connections between species that Darwin was able to democratise the concept of descent. For other thinkers of his time, 'democracy' itself was problematic. But we should note his own initial reluctance to make direct reference to human society. Perhaps one problem was that, quite apart from perfection, the very images of regulation and order involved in the study of non-social phenomena drew on metaphors for human government: class as classification and class as social position. Order itself was a metaphor that also evoked social orders, even as Mrs Beeton's much quoted *Book of Household Management*, published between 1859–61, opened with the resounding evocation of commanders of armies and leaders of enterprise (the mistress of a house must remember she is responsible for the government of an establishment 'and that it is by her conduct that its whole internal policy is regulated' (Chapter 1)).

In reference to human affairs, then, the notion of social order perpetually recreated the connotations of rank and class that were its own metaphorical foundation. Arnold saw the possibility of transcendence in the state. 'But how to organize this authority, or to what hands to entrust the wielding of it?' (quoted in Williams 1961: 129). The organisation of existing society simply provided a model of entrenched and divisive interests, and this was the problem that lay in the path of conceptualising a social order that would be a common inspiration to all.

Imagining a contractual basis in the natural rights of men was not sufficient: it was the governing or regulative principles of social life and the accounting for social variability that required description. What was to happen, in fact, was a naturalisation of the concept of society itself. But that could only be effected through the further idea of society as some kind of self-regulating artefact, one that had been produced by human design but could not be reduced to it. It is most interesting, therefore, to see in the later nineteenth century valiant attempts to make human design the direct inspirational force of such an artefact.

Arnold was also running his own polemic – as in his diatribes against the vulgarity of wealth, and the petty adherence to differentiations of money and doctrine that blocked a sense of common purpose. But while that commonality could be imagined, any particular embodiment seemed to fall short of perfection. Thus nineteenth-century critics of wealth and greed could appeal to the general idea of social order, but *could not describe it in an ethnographic sense*. A mass society could be imagined, but not the form it would take. It is no surprise perhaps that the social experiments under way at the end of the century failed to realise the order of which these men dreamed. They could only imagine society in the generic. And one of the discoveries of the ethnography-to-be was that neither culture nor society ever existed in generic form – generic form could only be discerned by the experts, distilled from the comparative study of many societies, and represented in purpose-built models (cf. Langham 1981).

How then was the idea of a generic social order promulgated? One response was clear. Value, wealth and labour must be taken out of the jurisdiction of the laws of supply and demand, and related to the fulfilment of each person's part in the grand design of life.

> Such a fulfilment was only possible if society was regulated in terms of the general design: a society must regulate itself by attention to 'intrinsic values'... But a system of production geared only to the laws of supply and demand made regulation impossible, for it reduced men to available labour and thus made impossible any 'whole fulfilment' of their ultimate function as human beings. There could only be one right economy: that which led men to 'the joyful and right exertion of perfect life'. (Williams 1961: 148)[14]

So concludes John Ruskin, that persistent critic of the eagerness with which wealth is pursued. He observes the degradation of labour:

> We have much studied and much perfected, of late, the great civilized invention of the division of labour; only we have given it a false name. It is not, truly speaking, the labour that is divided; but the men:- Divided into mere segments of men – broken into small fragments and crumbs of life [from *Stones of Venice* II 1853]. (Williams 1961: 148)

It is not that men should not be organised but that they are ill organised. Here I run together Ruskin's terminology ('design', 'arrangement') and that of his twentieth-century commentator (Williams speaks of 'organisation'). 'The argument is a practical example of [Ruskin's] refusal to treat aesthetic questions in isolation: good design in industry, he argued, depended on the right organization of industry, and this in turn, through labour and consumption, on the right organization of society' (Williams 1961: 150). Both were to be measured by their faithfulness to natural form. Art practised for its own sake is in the end corrupt; 'whereas art, devoted humbly and self-forgetfully to the clear statement and record of the facts of the universe, is always helpful and beneficent to mankind' (1906 (1859): 16).

At an inaugural lecture delivered at the opening meeting of the Architectural Museum in South Kensington in 1858, Ruskin declared that no great school of art existed which had not had as its aim the representation of some natural fact – the human figure, the effect of colour and shade – as truly as possible. In relation to industrial design, the measure is the working man and his capacity for edification. One did not want thirteenth-century art or life back again, but one did wish for *a consciousness of design* that would reflect modern English life. As he further declared the following year (1859), design is not the offspring of idle fancy: it is the studied result of accumulated observation and delightful habit. Great art goes with a noble (elsewhere he says kingly) life. 'For in life as in art, there is first truth, the perception of the world as it is, and then the plan or design founded upon it' (1906: 47).

As well as town halls, museums and public libraries (Corrigan and Sayer 1985: 119–20), we have seen that those imposing commercial buildings going up in the civic centres of England were reminiscent of medieval churches, as factories and warehouses were reminiscent of grand stables or baronial halls. Williams reproduces excerpts from a speech (published in 1866) that Ruskin gave at the Bradford Town Hall. He had been invited to advise on the best style of building for a new exchange, yet this expert in style refuses to be drawn.

> I do not care about this Exchange, because you don't . . . You think you may as well have the right thing for your money . . . and you send for me, that I may tell you the leading fashion; and what is, in your shops, for the moment, the newest and sweetest thing in pinnacles . . . I can only at present suggest decorating its frieze with pendant purses; and making its pillars broad at the base, for the sticking of bills. (Williams 1961: 150, references omitted)

The reason is serious enough. It was because architecture was the expression of a whole way of life that the only appropriate style for their Exchange would be one built to the great Goddess of 'Getting-on'. Whether for tawdry or noble ends, that functional relationship was inevitable. At the same time, it did not reveal the true functionalism of Ruskin's ideal society for only that was truly organic.

> The basic idea of 'organic form' produced, in Ruskin's thinking about an ideal society, the familiar notion of a paternal State. He wished to see a rigid class-structure corresponding to his ideas of 'function'. It was the business of government, he argued, to produce, accumulate, and distribute real wealth, and to regulate and control its consumption . . . Democracy must be rejected; for its conception of the equality of men was not only untrue; it was also a disabling denial of order and 'function'. The ruling class must be the existing aristocracy, properly trained in its function . . . Below this ruling class, the basic form of society would be the 'guild' . . . [which] would regulate conditions of work and quality of product. Finally, at the base of this edifice would be a class whose business was the 'necessarily inferior labour' . . . The Commonwealth thus established would ensure 'felicitous fulfilment of function', and the 'joyful and right exertion of perfect life in man'! [from *Sesame and Lilies*, 1865]. (Williams 1961: 151–2)

Organism, design and function: what makes these ideas fanciful was not the imagined division of functions as such, but their unhappy concretisation in a class structure of aristocrats and craftsmen. It was a poor model for his humanising intent.

Latter-day commentators were also to find uncongenial the conflation of value with ornament, and in the largest sense art. Ruskin insisted that it was naive to imagine that one can borrow bits of decorations. They could only work as outward form if they bore some relation to the purposes of the edifice. Ornament and art are like aristocratic or craft taste, intimately part of social life. They cannot be arbitrarily extracted from it with any meaning, because society itself is an internally functioning whole. Art, then, is not simply a product of an aesthetic capability. The artist is one who *perceives* the organic, as opposed to mechanical, whole: 'the artist's goodness is also his "whole-ness", and the goodness of a society lies in its creation of the conditions for "wholeness of being"' (cited in Williams 1961: 144). When external form is 'mechanical', it is less than organically integrated, even as products geared to the laws of supply and demand make the fulfilment of human beings impossible. But these images of function and fulfilment are ambiguous. In his idiom, art embodies aspects of a universal, ideal truth (that is, natural facts). The organic society thereby facilitates the 'felicitous fulfilment of function' in living things.[15] Society, in short, has its own intrinsic order, which outward form reflects or expresses. Yet this was also true whether it was a perfect organism or not. Consequently, such forms could express greed and pettiness quite as much as perfection and beauty. Unlike Chavasse's generic Nature, society does not always know best. Unlike Arnold's generic Culture, the contemplation of society does not of itself invite a perfecting impulse.

From hindsight, one could say that one of Ruskin's problems was the ambiguous relationship between interior motivation and outward formation. Although Ruskin sees that other countries have diverse arts, he cannot conceive alternative modellings of social orders. He could say that the art of any country expounds its social and political virtues, but differences in virtue seem merely differences of wholeness and goodness.

Anthropologists were to accomplish exactly the task of how one might model and describe different social orders and the nature of their functioning wholes. Variability (social 'morphologies') became an expected result of differing adaptations. In fact, anthropologists would eventually find words for perceiving a 'functioning whole' as equally characteristic of the kinds of fragmented life which Ruskin found so wretched as in what was ostensibly organic and harmonious.[16] But for that, they needed an image of organisation or structure detached from place or class. Society had to be detached from culture.

Suppose this came in part from un-doing the idea of culture as refinement and adornment. Some indication lies perhaps in the following. Before the democratisation of the notion of society was realised, and thus the idea of an organic whole independent of specific cultural forms, 'form' and 'culture' were both popularised. I append two footnotes to this effect.

First, Ruskin's complaint to Bradford was that the building would fail either because the form of design was a borrowed idiom and did not reflect the social realities of the age or because it could reflect only corruption. 1914: Ruskin is dead. Here is Clive Bell, whose solution does not require the remoulding of social relations and who does not look to the conditions of work and craft. All you need is the form itself.

> You have only to look at almost any modern building to see masses of elaboration and detail that form no part of any real design and serve no useful purpose ... everywhere you will see huge blocks of ready-made decoration, pilasters and porticoes, friezes and façades, hoisted on cranes to hang from ferro-concrete walls ... Only where economy has banished the architect do we see masonry of any merit. The engineers, who have at least a scientific problem to solve, create, in factories and railway-bridges, our most creditable monuments. They at least are not ashamed of their construction ... We shall have no more architecture in Europe till architects understand that all these tawdry excrescences have got to be simplified away, till they make up their minds to express themselves in the materials of the age – steel, concrete, and glass – and to create in these admirable media vast, simple, and significant forms. (1928 (1914): 221–2)

Materials have their own significant shape. Remove the ornamentation to reveal their own functions, for this is what the form of the construction should express. A natural building one might say. What then remains of the relationship between Art and Society? Bell devotes a chapter to this question. Do not educate children, do not take them to galleries and museums, he admonished; experience has nothing to teach, let them find out for themselves. And find out what? The natural person.

> Can we save the artist that is in almost every child? At least we can offer some practical advice. Do not tamper with that direct emotional reaction to things which is the genius of children ... Therefore do not educate children to be anything or to feel anything; put them in the way of finding out what they want and what they are. (1928: 286–7)

The relationship between form and the expression of emotion is made explicit.

> There is nothing very wonderful or very novel about rag-time or tango, but to overlook any form of expression is a mistake, and to attack it is sheer silliness ... In those queer exasperated rhythms I find greater promise of a popular art than in revivals of folk-song and morris-dancing. At least they bear some relationship to the emotions of those who sing and dance them. *In so far as they are significant they are good* ... Not every man can keep a cutter, but every boy can buy a kite. In an age that is seeking new forms in which to express that emotion which can be expressed satisfactorily in form alone, the wise will look hopefully at any kind of dancing or singing that is at once unconventional and popular.
>
> So, let the people try to create form for themselves. (1928: 290, transposed, my emphasis)

Emotions reveal the person in natural state; hence perhaps the unremarked democratisation, the generic 'people'. But Bell was to be upstaged, for in finding out their emotions, people then began to 'do' them, to elaborate and ornament them and endow them with histories and pathologies of their own.

Bell comes close to prescriptive individualism. He could countenance boys flying their kites as them being themselves, but not when they were trailing after adults round a gallery! In fact, an innatist imagery pervades his sense of the artist, as in the exception he takes to the artifice of ruralism.

Second, then, this was also a time when national English culture was being defined in an explicitly rural idiom, with the revival of the folksong and Morris dancing that Bell detested. By 1914 it was well in place. As we have seen, the vision of the village green evoked a specifically southern English countryside in its thatched cottages and hedgerows. That the evocation of English rurality went hand in hand with a national cultural revival meant the discovery of the 'unlettered classes', 'the common people', not only surviving in the country-side but also preserving 'their own speech' and 'peasant music' (Howkins 1987: 72, quoting Cecil Sharp who began collecting folksongs in 1903). English culture was also English nature, at once countryside and character. Yet if culture was to be found in the popular arts of the countryside and its residents, it would disappear unless preserved. The countryside might be like an interior, but it was one vulnerable to degradation from the outside. A securer image could be found in those parts that were enclosed in garden cities or leafy suburbs.

We have come from the ornamentation of the landscape, an enhancement that elicited people's enhanced sensibilities, via the garden that is cultivated within, to the idea that the real countryside itself is to be enclosed for its preservation. Penetrated only by lovers of country ways, nature as country-side is now otherwise contained and hidden. It could, however, be appreciated in the deliberate encouragement of the proper flow of emotions towards it. This was a channelling of its inspirational force. For the middle classes, the countryside became an object of sentiment that was appropriately collective in character. Meanwhile, if the cottage, an abode of morality, has been re-discovered as the typical 'English' dwelling, it has also been rediscovered as the suburban house.

> Through children's books from Beatrix Potter onwards generations learned that home was a cottage and, if not a cottage, then the 'Janet-and-John' mock-Tudor of the inter-war suburb. This kind of house became infused with a domestic glow suggestive of an earlier and better world of decency and honesty. (Howkins 1987: 73)

Socialising persons: microcosms of the domesticating process

The personification of Nature had troubled Darwin. By contrast with Chavasse's apostrophes, he had been concerned with elucidating the concrete character of natural relations and their systemic connections. However she might be hypostatised, nature was not to be treated in the generic or abstract but must be made to show her profuse and particular characters. The general principles that made the natural world an entire domain of study had to be presented in their own terms.

Beer (1986: 229) offers Darwin's reflections on the phrase 'natural selection':

In the literal sense of the word, no doubt, natural selection is a misnomer; but whoever objected to chemists speaking of the elective affinities of the various elements? – and yet an acid cannot strictly be said to elect the base with which it will in preference combine. It has been said that I speak of natural selection as an active power or deity; but who objects to an author speaking of the attraction of gravity as ruling the movements of the planets . . . So again it is difficult to avoid personifying the word nature; but I mean by nature, only the aggregate action and product of many natural laws and by laws the sequence of events as ascertained by us. [*The Origin of Species*, 1859]

She comments that his grandfather Erasmus Darwin had already noted the ease with which personification takes place in English. With personification, as she says, enters intention.

Aggregate action and the sequence of events that appear as natural laws: this is the language of social life. Society in turn, I have suggested, came eventually to be conceived in a naturalistic idiom. This meant giving it a popular dimension, that is, discovering it as an attribute of people in general. A major problem for long lay in the apprehension of the profuse and particular character of social life as the affairs of persons of different rank and status. However, the new naturalism did not entail a corresponding view of nature as subject to cultivation and thus also exhibiting the fruits of polite society and its gradations. From our perspective, we might say rather that the idea of nature had been naturalised, in being given its character as a self-regulating system. This contributed to the process of professionalisation to which I referred earlier. By such a (newly) emergent sense of nature, then, a (newly) naturalised view of society in the late nineteenth century would mean describing social life both as the inevitable context for human life and as having (so to speak) a life of its own.

Early twentieth-century anthropology was to reconceptualise society in a double sense. First it elaborated the organic metaphor in explicitly naturalistic terms: functions could be related not simply to the overall fulfilment of human purpose and happiness in life, but to the working of the structure of social life itself.[17] The entire body appeared as a system. Second, people's motivations could be directed onto society as an object of contemplation; dance, songs and ceremonies could be understood as the collective expression of emotion towards the collective body. One could thus show how people represented society to themselves. This match solved Darwin's problem of misplaced intention. On the one hand lay a natural necessity in the workings of the social system; on the other hand, in perceiving their own society, people oriented their emotions towards it and intended its perpetuation. Or at least, such could be demonstrated for small-scale 'folk' societies, which appeared as popular creations.

These developments were not, of course, presented as a solution to Darwin's problem; only hindsight makes us see what Darwin seemed to 'lack' – as Fortes so observed of Tylor, twenty years or so Darwin's junior and concerned with culture as the vehicle for imagining stages of human development. 'What Tylor lacked was the idea of a social system' (Fortes 1969: 13).[18] More interesting perhaps from the present point of view, these developments involved not only changing views of nature but changing view of kinship. I refer here to the twentieth-century concern with socialisation, the idea that what parents produce is to be reproduced by society. It was an idea endorsed literally in the development of state education; metaphorically in the manner in which training from infancy onwards came to be regarded as the inculcation of specifically *social* values. The origin of these lay beyond the individual – not in his or her connections or in the example of others, but 'in society' itself. However personal or ostensibly untrammelled by convention ('do not take children round art galleries'), the values could be conceptualised as typical of a particular milieu, historical period or social stratum.

Society perceived in terms of its consequences for the development of the individual: we have here the delineation of a familiar reproductive model. Perhaps it was first conceived around 1860 or so, when the cultivation of nature was replaced by its own grounding naturalism, that is, by the apprehension of nature as a natural system. Given a concern with the reproduction ('inheritance') of organisms, one might suggest that evolutionary thinking also facilitated the equation of procreation and biology. The 'natural facts' of life were natural in the sense of belonging to the biology of the species. The early years of the twentieth century then moved into place those ideas of system and structure that allowed kinship to be imagined as the social construction of such natural facts. It seemed evident that kinship had its origin in the (biological) reproduction of persons.

No longer an obvious metaphor for the circles in which one moved, kinship came to be about reproduction rather than connection. In being moulded by convention thus, individuals were socially constructed, we might say, rather than well connected. The further idea that individualism itself was a social construction, a cultural invention, emerged from the way culture was reattached to society. Societies were seen as having their own distinct cultures, and cherished values (such as individualism in Western society) to be distinctive of these cultures. Hence, in latter day usage, one could talk as equally of 'cultural construction'.

Significant for the subsequent perception of system and structure was that turn of the century discovery of form. Those public buildings, ecclesiastical copies of earlier virtues, came to seem ugly. The decorations and intricate ornamentation that tell us which age is being imitated appeared as meddling artifice: but what is a building stripped of its artificiality? Function came to have its own form (structure). As we have seen, the children of the nineteenth century appeared in retrospect as overtrained. Bell, writing in 1914, begged for a return to the simplicity of uneducated perception, as aesthetic practice struggled with the lineaments of colours and blocks for their own sake: form is the thing. Form in this sense appeared self-regulated.

If a perceived stripping of imitation were necessary to the appreciation of the structure and function of social life, a separate place had to be found for culture. The English found it in their Englishness. The turn of the century had witnessed a pluralisation of the idea of culture – anticipating Boas's American presentation of anthropology as the study of cultures. Indeed, a gulf separated Boas's perception of multiple cultural traditions from Tylor's earlier idea of culture as a stage of development. Tylor too was dead, as was Arnold's view of culture as 'the pursuit of our total perfection' by getting to know 'the best which has been thought and said in the world' (quoted by Williams 1961: 124), thereby extending elite values to the common man. A generation later culture had acquired an ethnic dimension, to use an epithet from the late twentieth century, what it is that already holds men in common.

At home, 'Englishness' was specifically promoted. A new *collective* promulgation of culture as national culture (Doyle 1986: 91) thereby reattached culture to the notion of society. The English Association founded in 1907 'applied itself to the advancement of the new English [language and literature] within the national culture' (1986: 102). Indeed, this was an era of associations and organisations, of public interest expressed in a plurality of collective, corporate forms. Eric Wolf's (1988: 754) aphorism is apt: when Society becomes the Nation, it is seen as incarnated in a project. The national or ethnic view of culture in turn realised a vision of the world as plural in its many cultures, full of different traditions. All traditions are seen as culture transmitted and thus reproduced, and 'education' becomes a metaphor for what is acquired generally by people. What they all acquire is in turn revealed to be what they have in common, a proposition which seems to have enjoyed a long life in anthropological thinking. When what is already common and innate ('Englishness') is made visible, it must become an object (as national culture was) of deliberate cultivation. So the culture that belonged to many also in that sense lay outside the individual person. Insofar as culture was a collective and thus extended object of thought, it had to be at once impressed and imposed on the minds of individuals.

As British social anthropologists tell themselves, their tradition in fact diverged from American insofar as it did not pursue Boas's ethnic vision of plurality and of the patterning of cultural personalities. What preoccupied the British was the transmission of society itself – the rules and relationships that made up social life. This meant being able to specify social organisation or social order as an entity with distinctive attributes. Specific (not generic) social orders could then be compared, yielding generalisations through the comparison of different structural forms. The fact of organisation or regulation was taken for granted; the question was analysing the distinctive features it took in different societies.

Here British anthropology had borrowed from the French. The discovery of social morphology went hand in hand with the revelation of society as simultaneously an external object of people's thought and as a phenomenon that existed outside of and imposed upon the individual. This solved another problem: the source of morality. Thus it was possible to refer, in Durkheim's words, to 'different forms of external constraint [and] the different forms of moral authority corresponding to them'.[19] More than that, Durkheim's inspirational formula that society was constituted in collective sentiment led to the idea of persons individually attaching emotions to the collectivity of which they were a part. They apprehended themselves as members of groups.

Perhaps what made structural form or morphology a compelling image was the way that British anthropologists rendered it visible. A structure could be approached as a mechanism for eliciting emotions from persons. But it did not simply pattern the emotional interactions between persons: it itself was an object of sentiment. Consequently one could describe how various observances and customs encouraged people to experience a flow of emotions towards their own social forms. Ceremonial expression enabled sentiment to be transmitted from one generation to another.

A. R. Radcliffe-Brown finished writing his account of *The Andaman Islanders* in 1914. It opened with 'The Social Organisation' as 'the customs and institutions' by which the people of these islands 'regulate the conduct of persons one to another' (1964: 22). His principal object was to demonstrate the function of such practices and customs. On the one hand, '[t]he knowledge of what to do and what to avoid is what constitutes the tradition of the society, to which every individual is required to conform' (1964: 386); on the other hand, the individual is made aware of his own attachment to this entity, for rites and ceremonies serve 'to keep alive in the mind of the individual a certain system of sentiments necessary for the regulation of conduct in conformity to the needs of the society' (1964: 275). Thus, he gave as an example, through the activation of social sentiments in connection with rules governing food the child is 'taught his *relation to the society*' (1964: 277, my emphasis).

In the late 1930s and 1940s, British social anthropologists who kept company with Radcliffe-Brown, and who came to give the local discipline its name, advanced this idea with much refinement. It was not so much 'society' in the abstract which encouraged a flow of emotions towards it, but specific structures such as descent groups.[20] Structural forms were made manifest in social institutions. Moreover, their rules and organisational procedures did not simply encourage a generic sense of collectivity: they promoted specific sentiments in turn, such as political solidarity, the religious veneration of ancestors, and fears and anxieties about witchcraft or insubordination. Indeed, social organisation, its structure, its groups, and its categorical boundaries, could be presented to the observer as a kind of external orchestration of the diverse sentiments that an individual person might experience. Indeed, it came to seem very obvious in the 1950s and 1960s that social classification itself presented individuals with emotional as well as cognitive problems/solutions. In describing social structure one was also describing how people 'felt', their 'attitudes' and values. It was assumed that they were oriented not only to the existence of social life but to desiring its perpetuation.

Collective society thus conceived stood over and against its constituent members who arranged themselves according to its laws and rules. The aggregate was more than the sum of its parts: as a 'system', it displayed properties of its own. These properties were not to be derived from recalling the value of a vanished aristocracy or the promotion of crafts and guilds; in this thinking, order acquired its own autonomy. The needs society evinced, or the sentiments evoked from individuals, contributed to the preservation or perpetuation of specific structural principles. In its demands and as the foundation of organisation, structure like society was at once personified and naturalised.[21]

With considerable persuasiveness, Radcliffe-Brown made explicit his vision of social structure in the institutions that seemed indigenously to deal with this very issue; *viz*. the recruitment and continuity of kin groups. Kinship systems might be 'made and re-made by man' (1952: 62) but what rendered them systemic in this view was a property of their own requirements as systems. On the one hand, then, the concept of social structure was made concrete (personified) in the image of groups peopled by persons; on the other hand, relations between those persons were seen to operate according to abstract structural principles[22] and systemic necessity (naturalised). Duty became one such systemic necessity. Thus he asserted, in quasi-legal terminology, that where 'there is a duty there is a rule that a person should behave in a certain way' (1950: 11), and the claim of a duty from another could be regarded as a 'right'. Relationships conceived in terms of rights and duties appeared self-regulating ('reciprocal').

The self-regulation of the system became imaginable and could thus be described in the way persons were linked in their obligations to one another. Indeed, this proposition lay at the heart of his description of a kinship system as 'a network of social relations which constitutes part of that total network of social relations which is the social structure' (1950: 13). Culture became an expressive mode. Polite behaviour or etiquette comprised those conventional rules 'which express some important aspect of the relation between two persons' (1950: 11). Not just society or groups but relationships too were brought to consciousness as objects of sentiment. In every aspect, the individual person had to be socialised into his/her relational field.

Socialisation meant more than learning the arts of life or modes of good conduct. Individuals had to be made aware of 'the society' on which they depended. That one would wish to sustain it (society) seemed as un-problematic as the 1925 virtues which that adviser of parents, Truby King, saw in the regulation of childhood habits. Parents must be aware of what they are doing. 'Granted good organic foundations, truth and honour can be built into the edifice [the baby] as it grows' (quoted by Lewis and O'Brien 1987: 28).

If I have suggested that the theories of kinship which British social anthropologists were to develop with such conviction in the first half of the twentieth century had antecedents in aspects of English kinship, it was in practices *as they were made conscious* in reflection and thought. My examples have been from English people writing (or drawing) – largely a prerogative of first the gentry, then the middle class and finally of the articulate products of universal education. Kinship practices were part of the way middle-class English came to formulate those much broader connections known in the twentieth century as the relationship between the individual and society.[23] If Austen's characters really did debate the fit between natural and social worth, and the kind of persons that their connections and relations revealed, a hundred years later it was 'the relationship' that an individual had 'with society' that held centre stage. The problem was then where to locate consciousness.[24]

Education could be treated as a privileged source of knowledge about (among other things) society itself. Tallensi parents in Ghana might produce recruits for the lineage;[25] English parents produced recruits for schools. Their disciplinary regimes instituted the methods and rules by which domains of life could be known, and imparted the practice and requirements of social roles. The object of education in turn was the individual person. And what the individual person thus evinced was the effectiveness of the socialising process – not simply in following rules but in articulating his or her own relationship with society. That effectiveness was in turn modulated by the life choices that lay ahead. Running in perpetual antithesis to the conceptualisation of society in twentieth-century anthropology was a question mark over the status of the person as an individual agent. We could summarise it thus.

Writings that mid-century British social anthropologists addressed to non-Western systems took society as an already naturalised entity: it was visible through its intrinsic characteristics of social organisation, rule and sentiment. Society as a network of relationships between persons incorporated *a self-evident model of its own regulation.*

Radcliffe-Brown had distinguished the person, as a complex of social relations and thus given by a constellation of 'places' in the social structure, from the individual as biological organism. 'Persons' were technically the components of society (1952: 194), but the very sense of uniqueness that marked off the individual came to be seen by anthropologists in general as a social artefact, and Radcliffe-Brown's distinction was not sustained. Rather, the individual person was held to be the entity that was socialised, and existed in response to the demands of collective life and its values, moulded by convention. The individual was socialised, we might say, into playing the role of individual. Socialisation thereby subsumed the absorption of cultural values, including those of individualism.

No-one thought that society really acted like an agent with a will of its own. But a corporation or a group of individuals could project an awareness of itself. Indeed, to be a corporation meant to act as 'one person'. Group organisation became regarded as social organisation's quintessential 'organisation' – an idea entertained with such conviction in the theoretical writings of some anthropologists that first Edmund Leach and then the school known as the transactionalists saw themselves as iconoclasts in restoring the individual to view. Here was the mid-twentieth-century debate: how could an individual both be a product of society and culture and act *qua* individual according to interests not completely defined by society and culture? For by the time the transactionalists of the 1960s wished to consider this figure, we have seen that they were faced with an entity conceived in the anthropological literature as itself a social and cultural construction. The individual had to be re-naturalised, that is, 'given back' its innate consciousness as a unique subject.

The naturalised individual was reconceived as a person in terms of 'personal' criteria, of which the ability to exercise choice became crucial. The goal of subjective judgement that made Mrs Taylor's Christian readers perform moral acts as they went about their daily lives now had to be given back to the product *of* collective morality. Against the impression that individuals seemed produced only by the conditions of society, and as reproducing those conditions, was placed another self-evident fact of nature: as persons, individuals were also conscious agents, and in a way a system could never be. In this 'naturalising' move it was persons who were, we might say, re-personified. Individual persons came to appear most evident in their autobiographies, in their private lives and idiosyncratic histories, and in their expressions of self-interest as well as in their emotional states (cf. Lutz 1986: 298).

It is apposite to return briefly to the conclusion of Munn's account of the Melanesian Gawa. In discussing the way in which people anticipate the future effects of their actions, she writes (1986: 273) that 'experience is being formulated in terms of a model of choice'; the dialectic of choosing regularly 'locates the capacity to produce value directly within the actor's will'. Familiar as this might sound, the depiction of choice in fact sits rather awkwardly athwart common English understandings. As she makes clear, Gawans imagine for themselves not so much an ever-receding plurality of options, but the sharply divergent effects of positive results on the one hand and negative ones on the other. Value is produced, Munn argues, by rendering the self in terms of the favourable or unfavourable attitudes of others. All acts have negative as well as positive potential, for the potential inheres in the radical divergence between paths taken and not taken. While a native English-speaker might apprehend the necessity of warding off unfortunate consequences, she or he would probably find it less easy to understand the human will in terms of the Gawan insistence that one should take steps to block the effect on the future of choices not taken. Like the necessity to terminate at death the relationships in which a deceased person was enmeshed (blocking their future effects), it is further necessary to deal with the fact that one's relationships may suffer the consequences of actions brought about by someone one has ignored or simply by one's own inaction (Munn 1990). Gawans attempt to block the relational implications of negative futures by 'finishing' the forward continuity of emotions such as anger or resentment.

Chapter Two depicted mid-twentieth-century English kinship as a model for the reproduction of individuals and suggested a contrast with the Melanesian interest in the reproduction of relations. As individuals, persons in the English model do not symbolise whole social entities and cannot be isomorphic with a collectivity or a span of relationships. Rather, individuals are held to exist as parts of numerous different systems – a part of the kinship system, part of a naming system, part of society – and do not replicate in total any one systemic configuration. I referred to the conceptualisation as merographic. We are now in a position, I think, to give this merographically conceptualised English person its aesthetic or iconic dimension.

If the modern person is a microcosm of anything, it is of *the socialising or domesticating process* itself. The person registers the effect of culture on nature, society on the individual, and is in this sense convention (partially) embodied but never of course convention (fully) realised. Rather, the individual person is constituted by the impact of different systems, including its own self as an autonomous bio-psycho-physical organism. In short, and in this aesthetic, a person is a constellation of 'roles' rather than relationships. She or he plays different roles off against one another, for in mid-twentieth-century parlance roles are worn rather like the hats of an earlier era.

In this modern view, then, roles and conventions exist apart from the individual. They do not exist already within the individual person, to be drawn out, because that place is taken up by the (personalised) self, by the unique personality, its emotions and motivations. Thus the capacity to be a parent is not uncovered in the child because, far more important, what must be realised is the child's differentiating uniqueness.

This in turn affects the way the child's role is conceived. Social science has given back to popular parlance the idea of role as a part played 'in society'. Over the latter part of the twentieth century in England, 'socialisation' has become a household word well beyond the earlier middle-class preoccupation with potty training, the intervals at which an infant should be fed, and all the rest of the professionalism of the new maternity. It points to more than the culture of expertise (Schneider and Smith 1973: 47). The 'duties' of motherhood have become transmuted into searching for the culturally acceptable way of ensuring the natural development of the child. Parenthood is not simply to be elicited by the presence of the child: roles must be learnt, the natural bond between them culturally nurtured.[26] Natural development is to be deliberately encouraged, then, or the person will not appear as properly socialised. And that socialisation is evinced not only in the 'control' persons have over their emotions but in a flow of emotions that must be protected from abuse. Healthy emotions are seen to be at the base of well conducted familial relationships.

14   *Advice to a wife, fourteenth edition*
From Chavasse's Advice to a Wife.

In this context, socialisation takes on a new dimension. It does not simply inculcate the regimen of social life into the person; it must also make sure that the individual person is properly reproduced. Such a person fulfils him or herself in personal terms by reference to inner emotional growth. Hence persons are seen as subject to their own individual development.

The term development has a double edge; it can make the person equally the passive object of a process or the active subject of it. The individual person, by our reproductive model, is like the kinship that reproduces him or her, perceived as the outcome of a domesticating process, a natural entity socially constructed. At the same time, society itself is not constructed by any force other than the actions of persons; indeed, in the 1960s and 1970s, social order was assumed to be an artifact of particular interests, the product of ideology. There was a tension between these views, and one that held apart the perspective of each.

The mid-twentieth century leaves us with a double image. On the one hand the person is seen as a construction (produced by society); on the other hand society is seen as constructed (produced by persons). The two sides of the polemic, each the obverse of the other, echoes the double vision of civility that Jane Austen had her characters debate about. But whereas the question in her day was the extent to which social and natural breeding was combined in persons, in this mid-twentieth-century view the question is the extent to which persons either act or are acted upon.

English perceptions of social rank, of middle-class morality, of public duty and of the welfare state have all produced persons as individuals. But the forms vary. However hard we look into the nineteenth century, we shall not find the single traditional English individual, the self-evident and typical 'Victorian', so prominent in latter-day twentieth-century rhetoric. What we find instead are the very different ideas about individuality from which ours have come. And, most recently, in the mid-twentieth century, a highly articulate double. When the individual appears as a product of society, moulded by external conventions, the collectivised person speaks; when the world seems to be full of individuals, a plurality of persons and interest groups, each speaks from the centre of their own network of relationships, and of their own motivations.[27] Indeed, this Jekyll and Hyde appears in Leach's dictum, quoted by Fortes who lets the prescription go unremarked (1969: 288, my emphasis): 'In all viable systems there *must* be an area where the individual is free to make choices so as to manipulate *the system* to his own advantage'.

But those perspectives are to be flattened, the tension dissipated. We shall find that the two faces subsequently merge with each other – there will be no obverse. The individual person who is the microcosm of convention becomes elided with the individual person who makes his or her own choices. In the process, this figure will present a different kind of image, a composite, a montage, of itself. That sleight of hand can only involve an extraordinary cancellation of many of the assumptions which polite society, among other enterprises, generated five or six generations ago.

4

Greenhouse effect

One of the dottier enterprises projected into the 1990s is the attempt to build a tunnel underneath the English Channel to link Britain with the Continent. A fantasy since at least 1856, the date of an early proposal, it seems that our enabling technology[1] is good enough cause to literally go ahead with it. In the meanwhile, ferries ply the seas. Between northwest France and southwest England, a French company links Brittany to Cornwall and Devon. Despite these Celtic affinities, the company's publicity leaflets are concerned to sell 'England' to the French. Making the passage on the Brittany ferry, Mary Bouquet, herself from Devon, was intrigued to find 'Bed and Breakfast' featuring as an English attraction. Devon has long been associated with that kind of tourist accommodation – in the form of the bed and breakfast farmhouse – and I dwell for a moment on her study of the domestic image it presents.

Bed and breakfast is not translatable into French; it appears as *le B et B*. Bouquet (1988; also see 1985) observes that the invitation is at first sight as pragmatic and literal-minded as anyone might imagine the English to be. But there is more to it than this. It makes play, she suggests, with a contrast between 'modern conveniences' and 'home comfort', and opens out a domestic domain for public consumption. Accommodation will be found within the domestic space that a family might otherwise occupy – bedroom, bathroom and downstairs dining room and lounge are put aside for the visitors. Although they can expect evening meal and colour television, meals are set rather than being offered à la carte, and the television will be in the lounge rather than in the rooms. It is understood that what enables the proprietor today to run her business are modern conveniences such as the deep freeze, tumble dryer, microwave oven.

The proprietor is invariably female, the wife in a household who as it were sells housework from her own doorstep. Tourists become visitors; they recognise the resident's hospitality, a reciprocity that elicits a certain style of politeness to deal with the fact that although they are not at home, they are in *someone*'s home. The farmhouse proprietor in turn is expected to be more forthcoming, more intimate than a hotel or even guest-house proprietor. In short, it is the privacy of home life which is laid out for public consumption. Perhaps this is a version of that other form of English self-advertisement: the opening up of stately homes as tourist attractions while the occupants are still in residence. Intense interest is provoked by the more private quarters – not just bedrooms, but the behind-the-scenes kitchens or servants' passages; one feels slightly cheated if one has only been shown the 'public rooms'.

The domestic image of bed and breakfast arrangements, Bouquet argues, is sustained by the fact that while the private is made public there is always a further private domain that is out of bounds. Privacy is also preserved. Hence the conventions of politeness. In stately homes, the private 'private quarters' are visibly cordoned off. In the case of the farmhouse proprietor, I would add that what has also become private is the business that she is running. Her profit, her investments, the improvements of her own house, are all her own affair. In short, her commercial interest – also true of the owner of a large house faced with upkeep – is taken for granted.

Literal metaphors

Homes within homes

Inversions are always neat. If what is for sale is traditional domestic comfort, then the 'real' private domain becomes constituted by modern conveniences – the enabling technology and the financial acumen which makes bed and breakfast into an enterprise. The inner sanctum of the farmhouse includes the taken-for-granted commercial interests that the housekeeper certainly does not share with her guests. They only eat her cooked breakfasts. Bouquet suggests that the images work because the person as such is defined in many respects like a home. Out of reach of the duties imposed by public life, and behind the role, exists a further, more private person, the real interior whose doorstep is not crossed. The English always imagine another recess, a privacy beyond public reach. But I wonder if *that* image itself – the home within the home – does not belong to an epoch that in other respects we have left behind.

It is significant, I think, that while it looks as though behind the doors marked 'Private' the proprietor is leading her own life, in fact the visitor knows that she and her family do not have a parallel 'home life': the hours of the day when they should be sitting down to their own breakfast, they are serving it to others. In other words, the real home is not within.[2] What is there is the domain of commerce and the exploitation of new technology.

Bed and breakfast at a farmhouse is not the special case it might seem. Rather, it advertises an English way of imagining the person that has in recent years become taken for granted in general public discourse. Persons must once more be managers.

In the late twentieth century this is above all a question of financial competence: the person is an individual with means. But although such competence may be taken for granted, it is no secret and indeed is an axiomatic presence in many of our dealings. Thus the English have become habituated to treating others as though they were dominated by financial considerations, as is happening to public institutions such as schools and hospitals. No need to build imposing edifices – the late 1980s assumption is that a concern only keeps going if it is financially sound. No need to advertise anything else. Finance is the enabling technology of the new 'active citizen' who shows his or her individual sense of responsibility through (a deliberate revival of tradition) charity. Moreover, management is required whether the context is public or private. There is no difference in the bookkeeping skills. Indeed, balancing the household books is a homely idiom sometimes used to make explicit the requirements of public accountability.

Yet those differences were once very salient, and in relation to their former salience I make three suggestions. First, the difference between public and private had its analogue in the way objects of knowledge were created. The English imagined that the 'real' nature of something lay within, if only one could see. Thus one looked inside the genteel person and found morality; one looked beyond decoration to structural form; one went into the front room of a house, thinking the real home was behind closed doors. Second, however, that very activity of looking, that externalising of the interior, seemed to create fresh objects. Morality made public became respectability; the form was no longer intrinsic to ornament; the home that you could enter as a paying visitor was not the same home for the family that lived there. And third, once something was brought outside and made an object of knowledge, it stayed there, with other assumptions presumably displacing its former taken-for-granted status. Public works must be planned; form had an order of its own; privacy was forfeited for other advantages. These assumptions in turn would become explicit, as there is a new explicitness to the way in which in the 1980s/1990s the English insist on public enterprises 'paying their way'; fund-raising has become one of the objectives of good management, and not merely a means towards it. In short, in valuing ourselves we both exaggerate what are perceived to be the natural and social bases of life, and search for more evidence that will shed light on what we are really doing in order to be really effective. The result of such constant scrutiny is to bring things to the surface all the time, such that more and more things are known – and in the idiom that caught the mid-1980s, such that there now seem only surfaces. There are no more depths.

It is that which makes the home-within-a-home allegory rather nostalgic. If a sense of surface has become part of a current representational (literacy, aesthetic) repertoire, the boundaries between inside and outside, private and public, appear sometimes inverted, sometimes flattened. The transformations are of interest.

Modern English made meanings for themselves by insisting that meaning is always partial and incomplete – that any one perspective will (merographically) overlap with others. Past tense here indicates what we may imagine of the past; present tense a contemporary interpretation and experience of this 'past'; the future that this was part of a model of expectations and outcomes. I continue to evoke perspectival overlap in the tenses that govern the immediate narrative.

A family farm in Devon consisted of 'various, partially overlapping' groups of interests (Bouquet 1986: 23). The elucidation of numerous different systems or domains, each with their own logical principles, each affording a particular perspective on something, only exemplifies the impossibility of imagining a totality. There will, in this kind of thinking, always be more to know. The perception of knowledge beyond the knower can be reproduced as though it were a change of scale. It may be a question of magnification, as when one perceives individuals in aggregate or holds that a collectivity is larger than the sum of the parts. It can also be effected by a switch in the medium of perception, as in the displacement of a sound image by a visual one, and thus by a change between different orders of measurement. Changes across scales in this latter sense occur at what are perceived to be the 'boundaries' of systems or domains: on the one hand you can look at a family as an intimate circle of relatives, on the other you can look at it in terms of industrial production and the exploitation of labour. Magnification in turn has its own boundary effect; to see 'more' is to see 'differently'.

This indigenous facility for scale change was sustained, among other things, by those homely images of public and private space, exterior and interior, which made every threshold the boundary of a domain. Taking in visitors leads to a 'partitioning of the wife's status and identity within the family' (Bouquet 1986: 35) – the external connection will activate internal differentiation between diverse areas of domestic life. The same is true of kinship relations. Behind the relative is a person; conversely, and I think here of the psychoanalytic assumption that individual disorders arise from familial relations, behind the person is also a relative. Despite their partial connection, the phenomena change scales – neither 'relative' nor 'person' acts as the complete analogy of the other. A hidden domain has its own intrinsic nature or character because of this boundary effect at the (perceived) threshold.

We could put it that interior and exterior were not manipulated as totalising analogies of each other: what appeared on the outside seemed a different order of phenomena from what is within. The sense of differing orders invites one to see more and more, further and further, whether to the most intimate personal experience or to the massive impact of global culture, whether to the tiniest elemental particles or to the hugest expanse of the universe (Haraway 1988). Society is telescopically distinct from its individual members, in the same way as the foetus is microscopically distinct from its mother. In either case, what is seen fills the field of vision, but the field of vision *is never taken as all there is to see*: one can always alter scale and whether on the 'inside' or 'outside' always see more.

It seems that the English saw no reason to put an inside back once it had been taken out.[3] This is the obverse of their interest in making discoveries not only explicit but communicable. Ever since the Enlightenment, the Western systems of knowledge in which the English have participated have rested on the proposition that one should aim for a state of permanent revelation, to demystify and make things more and more apparent in consciously conveying it to others. This seems true whether one talks of human nature, cultural artefacts or inanimate things. But cumulative knowledge of such global proportions rests only with an imagined collectivity, in libraries and archives, on someone's discs and tapes. For the individual person, to switch perspectives involves losing vision as well as gaining it, as we shall see in a moment.

Modern English pragmatism, so-called, thus consists in the fact that knowledge is invariably and merographically defined as useful for or relevant to some *other* purpose beyond itself. That the reality of things lies within them is a counterpart to the idea that knowledge is also conveyed by thus making explicit the external rationale or the principles on which it is based. I have already indicated, however, that these counterparts may themselves be treated as whole other orders of knowledge.

In rendering the nature of things apparent or explicit, the English might attend to the context or environment of the entity concerned or to background assumptions or prejudices, but in either case would be attending thereby to the connections that affected its identity. Thus, the flow of emotions becomes perceived as the content of a relationship. It matters when the human foetus can be regarded as a person, for time turns a cellular mass into a living human being. But of all the locational images on which we draw, that of bringing depths to the surface seems (or seemed) to have (had) a particular power.[4]

Power may well have come from the very equation of interior space with privacy. When the English conceal themselves behind front doors, it seems one of their intrinsic characteristics [Chapter One], and thus there is a characteristically secluded or enclosed nature to the ideal home. Privacy as family privacy is sustained through the combined connotations of exterior surface and interior depths; the change of scale is enacted on the doorstep daily. Private lives may overlap with public ones, but the one cannot stand as an analogue for the other. Farmhouse visitors know this. They are treated to a version or representation of family hospitality, for its outer presentation does not equal its inner character. The same is true of interactions between persons. One person cannot suffice as the measure of another, but reflects only that part which is invested in the relationship in question. Thus from others one ever only gets a partial perspective on oneself. In the same way, one's own external presentation remains out of proportion to one's internal disposition. We forever play roles as 'parts'.

In summary, since what is within and what is without were not isomorphic, to cross the boundary was to enter another world, another system of relationships. Telescope or microscope, aggregate or particle: whatever is within one's field of vision makes other things either part or context, either intrinsic elements within or ecosystem without. Public is different from private, the role from the person, convention from choice, as tradition is different from change and nature from culture.[5] These are not simple antitheses. When domains are not isomorphic or fully analogous to one another, significance will be eclipsed and importance magnified in seemingly disproportionate ways. To focus on one is to lose another.

The English kinship system was inevitably 'part' of such overlapping fields. Yet in comparison with some other of these domains, it has always appeared curiously reduced in its effects. Kinship was seen as simultaneously dealing in (interior) primordial relations and as insignificant in its (exterior) social dimension. From the latter comes the further effect that in communicating other ideas one is not communicating ideas about kinship. If, for the twentieth-century person, kinship relations were visible as a function of biology on the one hand (maternal bonding, sibling rivalry) or social organisation (the home, the nuclear family) on the other, I cannot describe 'the kinship system' without also describing such conceptualisations of society and of nature. Yet it would appear that I am not 'describing' kinship.

Now Charles Darwin located images of connection in kin genealogies in order to apply them to the natural world. Kin relations could be used as a model for natural ones. But perhaps one result of such usage was an unintended displacement of the human relationships. Insofar as he was insisting on an explicit analogy between the two, he was also separating off the organisation of the natural world from that of human kinship. The moral and social nature that had been elicited from kin connections in the writings of Austen subsequently became the generic and hypostatised Nature of Chevasse whose laws imposed themselves on the person, and especially on the physical body, and did not require the mediation of particular relationships (the mother's duty was to the child's development). Relationships in turn came to be externalised as society, an organisational system, a set of principles and forces outside individual persons. This (naturalised) understanding of society in turn rendered kinship only one of the many domains it encompassed. Kin connections did not seem sufficient to carry the entire imagery of social relations. They became internalised as 'family'.

The insufficiency of kinship as a conceptual apparatus was to become a crucial point of anthropological contrast between Western kinship systems and those of many other of the world's cultures as anthropologists were able to describe them (La Fontaine 1985). Certainly, anthropological textbooks on kinship tend to peter out when they come to the industrialised West (Bouquet and de Haan 1987: 256). Kin relations are understood as domestic relations, and domesticity as a rather minor part of social life. The family circle is, so to speak, the real 'home' within the home, and while the complexities of familial psychology and interpersonal development can take on cosmic dimensions for the individual, they appear not to have an external, radiating impact on society at large. Keeping up with relatives can be subsumed under personal choice.

For all that relatives appear given, empirically speaking 'the principle of choice operated with kin as well as friends' (Firth, Hubert and Forge 1969: 114, emphasis removed). The English capacity to shed kin, the idea that the range of relatives who are given also contains those whom, by introducing non-kinship criteria, one can choose to ignore, and who in the course of time and distance will be forgotten, are domestic versions of the reducing effect. For what might once have been taken as a matter of cultivation (personal choice evincing those discriminating criteria which determined one's social connections) has since come to be understood as an inevitable shading off of relatives at distant boundaries. It becomes a triviality that ego is at the centre of decreasing concentric circles.

The idea that it is natural (inevitable) to forget kin at the edges of the kin universe presupposes their prior existence; conversely primordial relations are there simply because they are primordial, even if people do not 'know' about them. They exist at a simple or primitive level (whom you are related to). It follows that other principles will seem extraneous, and appear to belong to other and more complex levels or systems. As Firth, Hubert and Forge's (1969: 97) Londoners talk of themselves, neither 'family' nor 'relatives' represent clear-cut kin units. Similarly, Davidoff and Hall's naturalistic observation that 'in *any* kinship system, some relationships even when acknowledged [will be] played down, others ... privileged' (1987: 320; my emphasis) universalises what seems to give the English universe its limits. An intriguing revelation in this English assumption, then, is the way that relationships are open to acknowledgement and privileging: the content of relationships can be measured as more or less relational and more or less open to choice. It is the choice offered by those other levels or systems which makes society as a whole appear complex.

Radcliffe-Brown (1952: 63) observed that there is no difference between maternal and paternal collaterals in English kin reckoning. Is it the absence of difference that elicits the sense of choice? There is no choice but to choose whether to treat them the same or treat them differently. Choice can then appear as a natural and inevitable outcome of an interplay between degrees of relatedness and the flow of emotions that particular interactions elicit. This accords with the modern English view that relatedness is about being close, and that the kinds of emotions that flow in kinship relations must evince that proximity. One may feel 'warm' or 'cool' towards different degrees of relatives. In fact, Fortes' universal axiom of amity in the definition of kin relations supposes just such a flow of natural emotion at the heart of social life. Kinship can be seen as the core of social institutions, but then Fortes was talking with non-Western systems in mind.

For anthropologists in general, one of the problems theoretically posed by conceptualising Western kinship as an open system, with a network of relations shading off into the distance, becomes how to give it proper magnitude by comparison with those systems of other (non-Western) cultures where categorical kin relations appear as idioms through which society itself is organised and regulated. For the English, by contrast and consistently, *the perspective of society seems to make kinship disappear.*

What we might attribute to the modern or pluralist epoch, then, is not simply an investment in number and quantity, but the idea that one can always produce whole new universes of numbers and quantities by changing the scale of what one looks at, and thus one's perspective on it. Hence one could consider Western kinship from the perspective of non-Western systems where it seemed a significant organisational frame. What was then recovered from the 'interior' of those kinship systems was society – the economic and political interests they organised. The 'amount' of kinship and the 'number' of kinship systems served to point up the cultural distinctiveness of the Western (and English) case. But it was society, not kinship, that was held to increase in complexity over time; complexity in kinship reckoning had no such purchase on the future, for however complicated the systems of non-Western peoples, they appeared to be dealing with primordial relations that Westerners understood as inherently primitive or aboriginal.

As an organising metaphor for social life, 'society' was able to absorb, as it were, any number of orders or domains, for they could all be aggregated under this aggregating concept. On the one hand, then, society acted as a partial domain; on the other hand, it provided a relational metaphor for the idea of domain itself. Other perspectives could be subsumed under its totalising perspective.

Yet the pluralist epoch is in the past. It has been helpful to my account to conceptualise certain aspects of the mid-twentieth-century imagery thus in order to overcome the problem that diversity (variation and change) seemingly posed for anthropological understanding. I suggested that we had to take these ideas as part of the data, rather than an interference with them, in that what we regarded as unique and novel was an outcome of the way we arranged conventional relationships. The English view of extended kinship as belonging to the realm of tradition, for example, was part of the same constellation of ideas which produced the sense that with increasing time society became increasingly complex, and that the world was constantly filling up with more individuals. It was the modern image of the world increasing in social (and cultural) complexity, and in the range of human choice, that in turn kept kinship as a rather homely domain. To switch from looking at society to looking at kinship always seemed to reduce one's scope for *social* explanation. It is, therefore, of some interest that in a postplural world the perception of different perspectives need no longer evoke scale change. The postplural 'individual' is no longer imagined merographically.

Imagining the individual as a person who is supported by an enabling technology, and who thus sustains an independent existence by virtue of financial means, is a concept of transformative dimensions. Technology enables; it is a resource. Although it may take the form of property, it elicits neither the old proprietorial sense of a given identity or possession nor the constraints of social class or position. Rather, anything – relationships, institutions, persons, minerals – may be assimilated to the idea of a resource. These days, resourceful individuals are those who can find resources irrespective of whether they come from within or outside themselves. I say transformative, because when society itself is assimilated to an enabling technology, regarded as a kind of resource, as it can be, it disappears.

If perspective switching always involved a concomitant sense of loss, then the English have always made certain losses evident to themselves. A long-standing one is the notion of family itself, to which I shall return. But recently new absences seem to have been voiced. I wish to document the successive 'vanishing' of three concepts, Society, Individual, Nature. They were crucial to the construction of merographic connections, not just because they provided the substance of domains that clearly overlapped, but because they provided between themselves a conceptual scheme for apprehending connection or relationship as such.

The first is publicly announced, the second is to be found in the writings of cultural critics, the third I infer, and it is the disappearance of the third that brings about the possibility of merographic collapse.

The English and the class effect

Collapse is obviously a metaphor. More appropriately one might take another and talk of cancellation. Relationships may be cancelled.

Diana Sperling's sketch of Mrs Sperling and Wilkinson (Frontispiece) shows what would in the idiom of the day have counted as a familial relationship but not a kinship one. While the couple are members of the same household ('family'), their different and respective standing is displayed in their dress. On a threshold, poised between interior and exterior, the one is bent on improving nature, the other (presumably) to do his mistress's bidding. They are not really in that sense a couple, for they have different perspectives on their tasks. Each becomes, however, an extension of the other – the patroness who gives the servant reason for his actions, and the servant who is in a manner of speaking the enabling technology for her intentions. In this sense, Mrs Sperling is not unlike the bed and breakfast proprietor, though in the latter case the technology is no longer human, and rather than going after it she would probably like to ensure that nature is something her guests will taste in her cooking. Nor are machines quite like servants. However much they observed the proprieties of place, human servants were also notorious for 'talking back', for behaving unpredictably and speaking with a voice of their own. Machines are simply supposed to give back to the operator her own instructions. That relationship is a domestic one, in twentieth-century idiom, but not one of kinship either.

In the persons of Mrs Sperling and Wilkinson and of the farmhouse proprietor with her machines, I have chosen two images without kinship ostensibly 'in' them. Perhaps they will evoke the conventional portrait that I have not made present. The mid-twentieth-century reader would recognise 'kinship' straight away had I reproduced the affecting group scene painted by Zoffany in 1778 that Macfarlane puts inside the covers of *Marriage and Love in England* or even the collection of plastic dolls (male, female, two juveniles and a baby) on the cover of Barrett and McIntosh's *The Anti-social Family*.

For during the years that divided the late eighteenth century from the late twentieth century, kinship became very much equated with the domestic family in English life (La Fontaine 1985; R. Smith 1973). To have portrayed a family group would have instantly conveyed the idea. Indeed, it is a recent complaint (Wilson and Pahl 1988) that many writings on the family have narrowed the focus of kinship even further, literalising family relations as merely conjugal ('marriage') and domestic ('the household'). One effect is to throw into relief the often asymmetrical participation spouses show in the family itself – one or other may be notionally 'absent', preoccupied by concerns elsewhere.

There is allegorical intention to my choice of portrait. The late twentieth-century person as an individual with his or her enabling technology is as much a product of the earlier reproductive model as was the private domestic circle. In fact, the absent family has always been as strong a motif as the actively present one, as we shall see. At the same time, the *relationships* composed by Sperling give one pause for thought. The conventional demarcation of status difference, the interdependence of proprietor and human servant, the significance of the grandly conceived threshold itself and, despite the rain, the matching of natural improvement with self improvement – these have all since been displaced. It is not, of course, this or that particular absence that is significant but the relationship between absences.

Merographic connections make entities disappear all the time. They reappear by the same device, the same connecting perspectives. But cancelling the connections has to be final. That it is entire constellations of absences or displacements that are significant no doubt makes every epoch think it lives on the brink of momentous change or at the edge of the universe, and so it does (its own universe of connections). The English bring such change about through doing what they have always done: rendering values and assumptions explicit to themselves. It has, however, mattered what is selected as those underlying values and who does the selecting.

I have described the literalist procedure by which the English make things known. They search for specifications of reality that will yield knowledge explicit and available for communication. Each dimension, however, leads to further specification, to the further search for the really real, the literal

In its progress down the centuries Salisbury Cathedral seemed a safe pointer to eternity — today it symbolises the costly struggle against the ravages of acid rain. **John Ezard** reports

vember, you will find crowds of men, women and children wandering around, just gazing in amazement. They come from all over the world. Why? Because this is one of the wonders of the world."

No generation before ours has had reason to expect that anything except the last trump could remove it. What our generation has to face is the forecast that — unless we change our way of life — Salisbury and many other churches, great and small, will be mouldering, defaced and unrecognisable within the lifetimes of our children and grandchildren.

Twelve years ago, a blink of an eyelid in its lifespan, the "family" of 800 staff and volunteers which clusters round it and cares for it began to realise that their dear friend was almost terminally ill. For some time the faces of the famous 90 statues of saints on the

west front had looked as if they were being "torn by some agent of evil", as the clerk of works Roy Spring puts it. But the statues are, ultimately, decoration. The worst discovery was that the same enemy agent is attacking three sets of stone decorative bands on the outside of the spire. They help hold up the 4,800-ton combined weight of spire and tower.

These bands have been melted in parts from their original eight inch thickness to two inches. Like the faces of the statues, they look as if someone had hurled vitriol at them; and that is what's happening. The modern industrial world has been throwing dilute sulphuric acid — in the form of acid rain — on top of the effects of frost, wind and all the other traditional corroders of stonework. Frost is slow, and this artefact can stare down hurricanes. But, thanks to acid

rain, the rate of decay has doubled in speed during Roy Spring's 20 years in his job. "The statues are now just a mass of decayed stone," he says. The spire would have fallen in an estimated 20 years.

In 1985 — it takes 10 years to survey every stone of a cathedral and plan a good appeal — a restoration trust was launched for the "horrifying target" of £6.5m, with the local peer Lord Tryon as chairman and his old schoolfriend Prince Charles as president. On the letterhead which is a legion of the great, the good, the influential and the gossip-worthy. The trust's director-general, for instance, is Nicholas Tate from the sugar family.

Unfortunately Salisbury wasn't alone. Suddenly a number of British cathedrals were competing in a scarce market-place with appeals totalling £47m. But Salisbury had

done better than Winchester (£1m) or Hereford (£1m unless the Mappa Mundi sale goes ahead). So far it's got £3m nationally and from the diocese. Salisbury diocese was asked to raise a daunting £1m and divvied up an extraordinary £2m mostly from coffee mornings and w˙ ˙ows' mites. With Tate moving i˙ ˙ the international appeal stage, and the 28-strong cathedral choir due to barnstorm the United States in April, the trust is quietly on course to have the £6.5m by maybe 1992. The original Chilmark quarry has been reopened Thirty five full-time masons have already begun a ten-year task. Even with £75,000 laser machines which cut stone 12 times as fast as a saw, they will still take over a quarter as long to restore mutilated parts of the cathedral as their medieval predecessors did to build it.

This is what the world knows: a

cheering picture of devotion and endeavour. What this picture omits is that the acid rain blitz will continue between now and 1992 and thereafter. We shall have to wait till 1991 for the report of a national monitoring by the Building Research Establishment on the impact of acid rain on ancient fabric. Meanwhile York Minster and Lincoln Cathedral are among the great British churches bothered about it. Further afield, Cologne Cathedral is being ravaged.

But for Salisbury the background picture is the starkest yet described in Britain. Roy Spring says: "The decay is accelerating so rapidly that some of the statues added by the Victorians are now in as bad a state as the medieval ones. When we have finished the appeal we are now in on eight years time, we will have to have another major appeal to deal with stonework which is

15 *Progress, cost and rain, 1989*
From the Weekend *Guardian* dated New Year 1989.
Reproduced by kind permission of John Ezard and *The Guardian Weekend Supplement*.

relationships or connections behind the connections. (To want to make metaphors is regarded as the artificial inclination of poets and artists.) This activity is by no means confined to the English, but it is one they accomplish in a certain style. The point is that one and the same procedure – making the basis of one's current values explicit – both constitutes the nature of present reality as it is perceived and leads to its displacement. Like the sequencing of generations and the downward flow of time, the effect of literalisation seems irreversible.

This literalisation is embedded in a literate culture. My reflections are derived from a limited range of cultural productions and, in the twentieth century, from the educated middle class. In the mid century, the latter lived in a bookish milieu, and I draw again on the London ethnographers. As Firth, Hubert and Forge (1969: 460) remarked, a 'characteristic of our middle class families affecting their patterns of kinship behaviour was the literate intellectual quality of their culture ... [and] a somewhat self-conscious analytical attitude towards their social relationships with their kin'. The anthropological investigation of kinship was part of this reflection on the nature of relationships, and the account I have given of it here has kept largely to readily available material and to sources meant for dissemination. The outcome has been an enquiry into English kinship from a middle-class perspective. Throughout the twentieth century, this has been the class concerned with creating perspectives, and communicating them as knowledge.

My unrepresentative 'we' is intended to indicate the fact of class perspective, and from it I have focused on a prevalent view of English kinship as it informed modern anthropology. Its recognisable components included the idea that kinship was the cultural construction of biological (natural) facts, that one studied society as a set of conventions external to and internalised by the individual, that Western kinship systems were cognatic or bilateral in nature, and that what was peculiar to the English was their individualism. These components encompassed the very relationship between nature and culture that Schneider, for its American counterpart, related to the middle-class underpinnings of anthropology as a project. I have added the invention of English as a national culture. Purportedly a cultural designation that matches a specific population, the idea of Englishness has had its own momentum, and I have tried to give some sense of the nature of that idea as it formed at the turn of the present century. It both contributed to the merographic sense of amalgam in the English character, and presented itself as the whole to which past diverse ancestries contributed.

Certain features may be held to have distinguished 'English' thinking from its American and Continental counterparts. Over the past two centuries, one may point to the particular way in which social class has entered the English construction of knowledge.

The changes described in Chapter Three had parallels elsewhere in Western Europe and North America. What is distinctively English lies in the manner in which social class is used as a source of dialogue and reflective commentary. Thus it is with a sense of triumph that Conservative intellectuals today insist that we now witness a return to a traditional, pre-Socialist individualism. In evoking 'families' and in evoking 'tradition', these politicians are also recalling values that evoke specific social strata – the caring stewardship of the upper classes or the respectability of the middle class as twentieth-century people imagine the nineteenth-century people to have been.

Over the last two hundred years, the English have repeatedly returned to a picture of society divided either 'naturally' and inevitably or else 'socially' and open to reform, and divided either by pre-existing inequalities or by individual merit and attainment. They recreate social heterogeneity thereby.[6] Handler and Segal (1990) suggest that such capacity for commentary developed from, *inter alia*, the eighteenth-century promotion of parties in the political sense, for that brought in its train the idea of a permanent representation of different perspectives as so many different viewpoints. The nineteenth-century concept of social class, we might say, also came to embody the permanent representation of different viewpoints.

Whatever generalisation a nineteenth-century person and his or her twentieth-century successor might wish to make about human nature, social class could enter as a qualifying difference. Over this period, society was characterised by the fact that one could not generalise across class boundaries. Political and academic analyses of class that sought to define a single basis for class formation had to contend with an amalgam of indigenous perceptions. For the classes, composed of diverse criteria, were not equivalent to one another. That is, they were not formed by the same rubrics: what made one upper class (inheritance, estate) was not the same set of circumstances that made one working class (selling labour). Social classes worked like scales; to 'move' between classes was to switch scales of measurement.

While upholding class loyalties and status conventions may have made people think they were clinging to old ways, the perceived differences between social classes throughout the modern epoch speeded up, one might say, reflection on the interaction between the givens of people's circumstances and what they made of life. The picture of the English village with its residential core and mobile periphery encapsulated this relationship. Mobility and immobility, choice and non-choice in relations: the dimensions of English social class meant that one might at once belong and not-belong, claim origins and move, be embedded in a family network and be free of it (Strathern 1981). The possibility of moving 'up' or moving 'down' was, in effect, afforded by the possibility of moving between different domains – there was no simple set of criteria by which the classes were ranked. Individual persons as a consequence were not to be ranked by any single measure.[7]

As Austen's characters knew, different criteria could always be played off against one another, wealth against birth, good management against pride of position, and so on. Class in turn was not the only source of internal commentary and reflection; others lay in the difference between town and country and between the generations. But social class provided an effective medium for the dissemination of ideas, for talking about habits at a remove from one's own milieu. Notions of morality, decency, thrift – key values by which people lived – shifted in meaning between class, and gave everyone a vantage point from which to comment on their neighbours, whether or not they wished to imitate their style.

The possibility of transclass 'dialogue' (or, in its colloquial form, prejudice) has also had the general effect of speeding up a sense of change in English life. Other classes of persons were seen to be doing things at a different rate or in a different quantity (more divorce, more child neglect, more second cars). And other people's styles could also be an affront to one's own. One might refer to 'the family' as a contested concept, and mean that it was a political or ideological concept, historically created.[8] But what also made it contested were the different perspectives that could be brought to bear upon it, and the most significant of these were class based. The middle-class family appeared a quite different phenomenon from the working-class one.

One perspective thereby detracted from another. This was exaggerated in the English tendency to *pull down* what was already in place when what was in place was regarded as elitist or privileged or as incorporating a hegemonic vision imposed on others. But whether to pull down or elevate, the English have had to work through their social class idioms. Thus the mid-nineteenth-century idea of a common culture negotiated middle-class claims to morality and respectability through aristocratic claims to a privileged appreciation of polite society. A common culture was then in the late nineteenth century rediscovered in the rural working class, whose urban counterparts became politically visible in the twentieth century. It is partly because of such a class dimension, one suspects, that the mass institutions of the twentieth century – most notably the totalising idea of the welfare state itself – could subsequently be attacked not only as unwarranted intervention in people's lives but as somehow protecting an undeserving minority of people who 'live off' them. These days the poor find themselves being cast off as a kind of elite.

Middle-class people used to observe that England has no constitution because it has never needed one, whereas Americans had to build up their society.[9] An outcome was that the English felt free to un-do what they had. Democratisation did not entail elevating slaves to the status of freemen but entailed extending the privileges of the ranked or propertied to commoners. This particular possibility of social un-doing, has had a profound effect on the development of ideas. It promotes the radicalism of the philistine (to use one of Arnold's epithets), with her general distaste for elitism and for the planned intentions of others.

In the late twentieth century, however, there has been a further and curious flattening effect. Class no longer divides different privileges. For anything that looks like privilege is nowadays worthy of attack, including the 'privileges' of those on state benefit, and including the prerogatives of the state itself. Present high Conservatism rides exactly because it un-does or pulls down. The policies of this party are highly selective, but not along class lines: it is state intervention in private lives that must be pulled down. By contrast, the power of the transnationals or of established domestic lobbies for commercial interests survives untrammelled, for these bodies are not seen as class based. Super-private, super-individualistic, they seem only larger versions of the private individual. There is, we might say, no perceived change of scale (of different orders or domains) between the individual person and private company, only a magnification or diminution along the same scale of virtues.

I have been surprised at the extent to which this account has had to take notice of the present political dispensation. But that is partly because of the extraordinary force that the policies of the current Government in Britain appear to command. They are putting into effect a cultural revolution of sorts, and one which has had a flattening effect far beyond the dreams of the self-proclaimed levellers. It has not flattened privilege or property differences. On the contrary, material inequalities are as entrenched as ever in the new divide between persons and non-persons: to be an effective person one must have means. ('All lifestyles now require money' is an American comment (Barnett and Magdoff 1986: 416).) What is flattened in the political promotion of this view is a sense of perspective itself.

To put it in extreme terms, there is no permanent representation of different viewpoints any longer, because such viewpoints are no longer locked into class dialogue. Class dialogue has collapsed. This is hardly a return to the England of the eighteenth century any more than it is a return to the nineteenth; nor is it a 'new middle class' which is emerging. Rather, a quite novel constellation of interests has been created by policies such as the encouragement of home ownership among council tenants or turning over state industry to private shareholders. The financial dimension is significant. The new person is the financial manager; and if universal upward mobility makes a nonsense of the old three-step strata, then perhaps we should also find a designation other than middle class. Plasti-class will do for the moment, after its preferred mode of credit display.

The plasti-class seem everywhere, representing diverse and multiple interests, and concealing social division between those with such flexibility and those without. For the nature of the enabling technology – financial flexibility – suggests that perspectives are constituted merely by the choices that resources afford. Those without the means to exercise choice are somehow without a perspective, without a communicable view on events.[10]

Loss should be understood in a strictly relative sense. All the English have lost is what they once had, which was the facility for drawing partial analogies between different domains of social life. Referring to one class from the perspective of another went along with the ability to compare different domains of activity – to talk of individual responsibility towards the general public, or to assume that the welfare of the family meant the welfare of the community. But now, so long as one manages one's affairs, there is no difference between whether one chooses to act in a role or act as this or that personalised individual. So long as it gratifies the consumer, there is no difference between French bread and Viennese pastries. So long as the exercise of choice is possible, the plasti-class expands.

If there is a feeling of helplessness attendant on all this, it is that the most

plas⋅tic (ˈplæstɪk) *n*. **1.** any one of a large number of synthetic usually organic materials that have a polymeric structure and can be moulded when soft and then set, esp. such a material in a finished state containing plasticizer, stabilizer, filler, pigments, etc. Plastics are classified as thermosetting (such as Bakelite) or thermoplastic (such as PVC) and are used in the

-plastic

manufacture of many articles and in coatings, artificial fibres, etc. Compare **resin** (sense 2). ⁓*adj*. **2.** made of plastic. **3.** easily influenced; impressionable: *the plastic minds of children*. **4.** capable of being moulded or formed. **5.** *Fine arts*. **a.** of or relating to moulding or modelling: *the plastic arts*. **b.** produced or apparently produced by moulding: *the plastic draperies of Giotto's figures*. **6.** having the power to form or influence: *the plastic forces of the imagination*. **7.** *Biology*. of or relating to any formative process; able to change, develop, or grow: *plastic tissues*. **8.** of or relating to plastic surgery. **9.** *Slang*. superficially attractive yet unoriginal or artificial: *plastic food*. [C17: from Latin *plasticus* relating to moulding, from Greek *plastikos*, from *plassein* to form] —ˈplas⋅ti⋅cal⋅ly *adv*.

16 *Plastic*
Entry from Collins Dictionary (1st Edition 1979). Computer data file designed: Aylesbury, Computer typeset: Oxford. Manufactured: the United States of America.
Reproduced by kind permission of Collins Publishers from *Collins Dictionary of the English Language*, 2nd edition, 1986.

radical, most conservative government of this century has also collapsed the difference between political Right and Left. ('I don't know whether what I've seen is pure Thatcherism or pure socialism', are the reported words of a member of a Downing Street Policy Unit *apropos* a cooperative management venture in Scotland (*The Guardian*, 6 September 1989).) The collapse is not something, of course, for which it can claim complete credit. For instance, feminists have found that with respect to the new reproductive technologies their interest in defending women's rights is echoed in the anti-abortionists' interests in defending the rights of the unborn. Rather, by hastening the collapse between Right and Left, the Government merely but powerfully embodies it. And we had always imagined that 'totalitarianism' would have been the crushing implementation of one or the other!

The speed with which such changes seem to be occurring is like watching something on fast forward wind. Meanwhile, the Government itself seems to imagine it is midwife to a natural process of social evolution that will also restore traditional values. It can do this because it simply appears to be making the 'nature' of individual motivation explicit, and thereby conceals its own process of selection. As Handler and Segal (1985: 697) remark, however:

'Existing social relations are always presupposed in the interpretive construction of subsequent relations, but they have no inherent inertia, that is, they have no inherent tendency to continue or to determine the future ... social relations are not fixed without the possibility of alternatives.' But if dialogue is flattened, if there appear no alternatives, then what happens to the idea of relationships? Where is the negotiation? There seems no negotiation over how we should define persons. Of all the interpretations of the person that could have been selected, we are presented with an individual subject or agent who knows how to deploy resources or the means at his or her disposal and whose personhood lies in the capacity for choice. We seem to have no choice in the matter.

I refer to flattening by way of alluding to so-called postmodern discourse. Yet the allusion must seem out of place. Of what relevance is it that artists may interpret their images in terms of pastiche and collage, or critics see in films the imitation of dead styles? What does it mean to say, as they do, the 'death of the subject', when choice is all around us and we have more means than ever before at our disposal? The English are still here in their suburbs or their town houses, and who cares what postmodernism means? It is quite true that there have been momentous changes in people's attitudes towards the constitution of the family, and towards such issues as premarital sexual relations (e.g. Jenkins 1990), but the family is appreciated as a lifestyle to a greater extent than ever. In any case, individual persons appear to walk around solidly enough. Above all, the nation has Government reassurance on the matter. The then British Prime Minister publicly pronounced:

> There is no such thing as society. There are individual men and women and there are families. (Margaret Thatcher, 1987)[11]

But while one might be reassured about the individuals and the families, it seems that they can only be made to appear if 'society' disappears.

This was no haphazard remark. The pronouncement has been quoted and requoted, was made the subject of television debate, and has been set as a university examination question for anthropology undergraduates. There has also been some anxious backpedalling, which led the following year (1988) to the energetic promulgation of the concept 'active citizenship'. But the statement is irreversible.

Mrs Thatcher could in fact have used any one of those three terms – individual, family, society – in any one of the three places she deployed them, and the meaning would have been the same. No such thing as the individual, only families and society; or no such thing as families, only society and individuals ... What is breath-taking is that the leader of an elected political party should have chosen the collectivist idiom to discard. What vanishes is the idea of society as *either* a natural *or* an artificial consociation. What also vanishes, then, are the grounds of the class dialogue (the naturalness or artificiality of social divisions) that has dominated political debate and reform for the last two centuries.

Yet in a sense her judgement was unerring. To cancel society is to cancel all three concepts. Not being able to 'see' society is rather like the old literalist problem, one that Western anthropologists projected on to others, of not being able to see paternity. We have literalised our perceptions of human nature to the point that we make social relationships as such very hard to visualise.[12] In fact the English cannot see the individual except by insisting on its rights to display its own individuality: and then all they see is the display. They insist on making families visible by their lifestyle, and then all they see is the lifestyle. What is cancelled, then, is a certain relational facility.

The Prime Minister could, I believe, have 'chosen' any of those terms to discard, in the same way as one may nowadays 'choose' to be a public figure or private person, 'choose' one's lifestyle, and so forth. The meaning would have been the same. We have cancelled the power of analogy: the facility to see that individuals are defined by society, or that families are analogous both to individuals on the one hand and to social communities on the other. We seem to have lost motivation in drawing such parallels. The state must not appear paternalistic, rights must not be trammelled with duties, citizens do not have to be members of a community.[13] The most powerful image one can devise for such a Head of Government is that of household manager, the proprietor selling family-style accommodation.

Disappearing family, disappearing society

Family living can be seen as a lifestyle of sorts. Bed and breakfast offers family-*style* accommodation – the flavour of domesticity. A recent English textbook on the sociology of the family (Goldthorpe 1987) argues that while it flies in the face of variability and change to reify 'the family' as a thing, everyone has had experience of 'family life': accordingly we should be studying such life as events and processes. Interestingly, the author throws in 'society' as a similar entity. To present society as though it were composed of categories and groups is to falsify the reality of human social life (1987: 2): we should study human actions as processes in time. (Everyone has had experience of 'social life'!) A feature of this argument is the assumption that a proper subject for study is what individuals experience. All the variability of family forms are thus flattened out in the assertion that everyone has some sort of family life.

On the surface, such views seem to give the family a new lease. It no longer appears problematic. For like the anthropologist's perspective on Western kinship that makes it always subsumable under other, more significant social factors, the perennial problem of the modern study of the English family has been that it was always on the verge of disappearing. The very variability of individual forms as well as the careers and different life patterns of individuals have seemingly interfered with a clear view of typical families or of a sense of continuity. Valuing family life, however, brings its own twist. When its future turns on individual experience and, as we shall see, on choice, the family is simply made to disappear in a new way. A certain matrix of connections or associations no longer holds it in its former place.

The family in decline was a particularly salient theme in the postwar period, and was among the assumptions that prompted counter-studies to show the historical antecedents of small domestic groups (most notably Laslett and Wall 1972). Jonas Frykman and Orvar Löfgren (1987: 150ff) observe of middle-class Sweden in the mid-twentieth century that the idea of the sorry state of the modern family has in fact been coterminous with the spread of familial lifestyles and of the nuclear family as the basis for the household. Yet a small family can seem somehow 'less' of a family. The idea is that in the past people had more relatives, families were larger, there was more of a community, in the same way that people imagine that village life was once communal. Dramatic changes in people's attitudes towards divorce and single parent families are held to prove the point. As a consequence, the family seems to have become 'fragmented' though, as Jon Bernardes (1988) also notes, the idea of family life enjoys as strong a hold as ever. Martine Segalen (1986: 2) nicely captures the emphasis in her observation that to think of the family in crisis glosses over the real problem: it is society that is in crisis.

Throughout the modern epoch, it seems that the English family has always been vanishing. The same is true of the English village, terminally on the point of disappearing (cf. Strathern 1984), and equally true of the organic community of rural England (Williams 1985). The reasons seem to lie in people's social activities, in their mobility, their capacity to move in, to move out, and thus down or up in social status; consequently it is the naturalness of the pre-existing village or community which is felt to be perpetually weakened. When a suburb of a large Northern city was called a 'village', it was community survival that was at stake. The survival of the Village 'had to be fought for, protected against incessant, hostile forces' (Young 1986: 130). At the same time, nostalgia for community was not necessarily nostalgia for egalitarianism: the vanishing of 'the gentry' ('the old-fashioned English type of family', as one Woodford resident said (Wilmott and Young 1960: 7)) could be cause for regret. Woodford – an Essex village/London suburb – was at the time of the remark coming to seem 'less rural'.

Another contemporary strand to arguments about the family is reproduced in English textbooks (e.g. Elliot 1986): the revival of questions as to whether or not it is a good thing – whether there ought to be families. The most sustained critique comes from feminist enquiry, but is not restricted to it. The individual's natural freedoms, development and emotional life are held to suffer at the expense of family organisation, which may therefore be regarded as an instrument of other (say, capitalist) purposes. At the same time, pro-family movements turn support for the family into an issue of political choice (see Thorne and Yalom 1982 for American observations on the point). Although support may be voiced on the grounds that the family is a natural institution, to have to put forward a political or legal argument for its preservation removes any taken-for-granted position. Family has become natural only for some. Hence the very idea that one might be 'for' or 'against' the family is today fuelled, as Faith Elliot (1986: 202ff) implies, by the conscious promotion of 'alternative' forms of domestic living. Alternatives to the family invariably appear as alternatives to domestic living arrangements. The family thus acquires definition as a matter of living style.

We have here a new virtue. Style in turn acquires definition as a quintessential exercise of choice, and what is new in this late twentieth-century rendition of an old question is precisely the place given to choice. An individual cannot choose into which family to be born, but evidently he or she may well choose whether to opt for a family-style lifestyle or not. The family as a natural consociation vanishes in the promotion of family-living as an experience. Experience is held to affect the opportunities individuals have available to them.

Consider the following:

> [T]he right-wing argument for the 'right to choose' in education ... means that parents should be able to choose what sort of state school system there is and whether to send their children to private school ... [T]his 'right to choose' is often presented as opposition to outside interference: in fact it means parental control over children instead of social control ... [The question is how to offer] everyone the best possible opportunities.
>
> The issue of child-neglect and the role of the social worker raises perhaps more thorny questions. Even when it is suspected that young children are being battered by their parents, local authority social services departments are reluctant to remove the child from the home. The logic of our collectivist position might seem to be that ... children should more often be taken into the care of the local authority. Yet social work also represents an intrusion into people's lives – and especially working-class lives ... Here again, then, we meet the problem of the rebarbative character of the existing class forms of collectivity. Yet here again we would argue that we must not retreat into the individualism of 'the family', but must fight for better kinds of collectivism. So we should recognize that at present we should often want to defend a parent's right to keep her child. But at the same time we should be working to improve the quality of children's homes to open them up so that teenagers unhappy at home might actually *choose* to go to them. (Barrett and McIntosh 1982: 157–8, original emphasis)

The authors point to the elision in many contemporary arguments on the issue between 'choice' and 'rights'. The 'right to choose' is problematic; but at the same time the *ability* to choose appears as the mode through which 'rights' are exercised. The subjects who exercise those rights are individuals. Relationships, such as the relationship between parents and children, cannot have such claims and the family disappears from view as the natural locus for a collectivist position. In its place is the desirability of improving the quality of home life.

We have here a complete about-turn from Eleanor Rathbone's 1924 plea for the provision of a Family Allowance on the grounds that 'the well-being of the family concerns the community as a whole'. She added that 'there seems something strange in the assumption so commonly made, that the question of the maintenance of families concerns only individual parents and can be safely left to them; or that, at most, society need only take cognizance of the matter by, as it were, mixing a little philanthropy with its business and influencing employers to pay wages which will enable their male employees to indulge in the praiseworthy leisure-time occupation of keeping families' (1927: ix–x). The about-turn lies in the symbolisation of personal welfare. Rathbone was concerned with the miserable living conditions of the working class and the inadequacy of state provisions for the lower paid and unemployed. But she was also concerned to give 'the family a fuller recognition and a more assured and honourable status' (1927: 304) against those of her day who put forward contrary arguments on the grounds of individuals' rights to determine their private lives. She took the whole unit because the individuals distinguished by such rights often excluded the women and children of the family. We might argue that *because* of the provisions of the eventual Welfare State in the intervening years, that is no longer the issue it was: the family having been protected, 'individualised' in Barrett and McIntosh's phrasing, the new collective can only be formed through undoing or decomposing its members.[14]

Such collectivist arguments from the Left seem to have this in common with the individualistic arguments of the New Right: to exercise choice is a good thing in itself. Barrett and McIntosh (1982: 134) offer two general aims for political strategy on the family:

> (1) we should work for immediate changes that will increase the possibilities of *choice* [their emphasis] so that alternatives to the existing favoured *patterns of family life* [my emphasis] become realistically available and desirable; (2) [w]e should work towards collectivism and away from individualism in the areas at present allocated to the sphere of private family life, especially income maintenance, the work of making meals, cleaning and housekeeping, and the work of caring for *people such as children* [my emphasis], the old and the sick or disabled.

Children are here individuals at a stage of personal development, not offspring or relatives.

Distinguishing their argument from that of liberal individualism does not disturb the assumption that choice as such is a good thing. It makes very evident the individual person as a subject and an agent of her or his own destiny. All that seemingly differs between Left and Right in this is the means by which such destinies may be realised:

> socialism is bound to give a positive value to collective rather than individual concerns in questions of reproduction. What socialists must do is not deny the existence of individual rights, for these will surely exist and even flourish in socialist society, but challenge the private content attributed to such rights in bourgeois thought. (1982: 136, emphasis removed)

Now in the manner in which we make explicit just how the individual person is constituted by the choices he or she makes, I think we might find ourselves facing a new absence.

The family as a set of kin relationships disappears in the idea that the quality of home life has an independent measure. But what about the person as an individual whose opportunities, decisions and opinions are so significant? If the process of making assumptions visible indeed changes perception, then the chances are that 'the individual' will become eclipsed by the enhancement of 'choice'. Or perhaps individuality will be juxtaposed *as* a choice.

The result could be an apperception of person which has the individual vanish. The individual would not vanish in the old way – seen to be absorbed by its social construction or by the metastructure of society – but would vanish quite simply *from the exercise of its individuality*. The repository of choices: what we shall see if we look will be the choices, the experiences that evince 'individualism'. Individual-style living! Prescriptive individual*ism* displaces the individuality of the person. We are already there of course, and have arrived at a view of postmodern imagery. For that is exactly how certain postmodern reflections in aesthetics, art and literature have redefined the individual subject of the previous epoch.

I take up the words of one American exponent of the condition conceived by some to apply generally to the Western world. His question is why modernism is a thing of the past, and why postmodernism should have displaced it. The new component, he says (Jameson 1985: 114), is generally called 'the death of the subject', or more conventionally 'the end of individualism as such'.

What has disappeared is the modern premise of the individual with its unique vision and private identity – the great modernisms, he observes, were predicated on the invention of a personal private style. He relates two just-so stories.

> [O]nce upon a time, in the classic age of competitive capitalism, in the heyday of the nuclear family and the emergence of the bourgeoisie as the hegemonic social class, there was such a thing as individualism, as individual subjects. But today, in the age of corporate capitalism, of the so-called organization man, of bureaucracies in business as well as in the state, of demographic explosion – today, that older bourgeois individual subject no longer exists ... There is a second more radical position, what one might call the poststructuralist position. It adds: not only is the bourgeois individual subject a thing of the past, it is also a myth; it *never* really existed in the first place; there have never been autonomous subjects of that type. Rather, this construct is merely a philosophical and cultural mystification which sought to persuade people that they 'had' individual subjects and possessed this unique personal identity. (Jameson 1985: 115, original emphasis)

Yet such a proclamation (the death of the subject) of itself, is no more nor less interesting than other deaths – the father absent from the family, the family absent from the community, the community absent from the country-side, and so on. It is only interesting in conjuction with what is also cancelled. In Jameson's speculation, this includes linguistic norms which vanish in the value put on idiosyncrasy, on private codes and mannerisms,[15] which in turn vanish in pastiche, in the imitation of unique style. Where collage invalidates the very notion of style in its mix of genres and materials, pastiche is the emulation of past styles and other moods. Innovation is no longer possible. We can speak of the 'failure of the new' (1985: 116). Diversity and heterogeneity, in this view, no longer reproduce new forms: all forms have already been invented, and there is no novelty to be generated from recombinations.

Let me use my English argument, then, to comment on why the hyper-individualism of the late twentieth century is simultaneously the death of the individual. The simple reason is that the Individual has lost its elicitory power to make Society appear. For that depended on its further (merographic) connection with a third concept, Nature. The individual once appeared – like the kinship that produced it – as a connecting hinge between these two domains, between society on the one hand and nature on the other. But styles that are after other styles do not need to be after nature at all.[16]

It is the potential cancellation of that connection with nature which has, I think, led us to see the world as myriad surfaces, to lose a sense of perspectival depth, and which thus makes the threshold imagery of scale-change work with less conviction, which has undone a pluralist and merographic perception of relationships. Perhaps in turn we think there is 'less nature' in the world because we have lost the relational facility for making a partial analogy between nature and society work as the context for the way we think about individuals. To cancel the merographic person is in effect to cancel the natural individual as a microcosm of the socialising process.

Now the modern(ist) concept of nature encapsulated within itself a significant relation: between what is intrinsic to an entity (its individuality) and that entity's context or environment. The individual vanishes not just from a surfeit of individuality. It vanishes when it no longer seems relevant to talk about its environment and thus – as Mrs Thatcher discovered – about 'its relationship' to society. The point is worth pursuing.

The processes by which the concepts discussed in the previous chapter were professionalised or 'naturalised' had a dual outcome. On the one hand, I referred to the way in which such concepts created their own context: thus society was to be understood as a type of (social) organisation, or persons were to be understood as agents exercising (personal) choice, individuals as unique entities, and so on. Instead of imagining society as a contract among persons or persons as God's creatures, each reference point became self-defining. In thus creating its own context, a concept such as society created its own domain of explanation, which then required 'relating' to others. The domain – society made proof, for instance, in Durkheim's realm of 'social fact' – became typified by the kinds of facts appropriate (that is, natural) to it.[17] On the other hand, there was the literal sense in which nature served to model such facticity. The natural world was apprehended as full of facts, and facts appeared a natural feature of the world. Their social counterparts were made proof, for instance, in the new quantifications under way in the mid-nineteenth century. From the 1830s onwards, as Corrigan and Sayer remark (1985: 124–5), central government departments emerged as fact-collecting institutions, a proliferation of Royal Commissions mounted enquiries into this or that state of affairs, inspectorates spread like a contagion, and above all statistics were gathered. Facts relating to social conditions could be collected, as natural items might be assembled.

I do not wish to stress too much the new statistics of the nineteenth century, but note that they may have laid the grounds for an analogy between social connections and the abstract (causal) connections that could be revealed between social phenomena.[18] Society as a summation of relations could be grasped not just as sets of relations between persons but as relations between abstract but nonetheless effectual entities such as 'living conditions', 'family size', 'level of education' – that is, between characteristics at a remove from the populations to which they pertained. The possibility of seeing such links as 'relations' was exemplified in the mid-twentieth-century interest in 'the relationship' between individual and society.

It is, if one thinks about it, and *pace* Radcliffe-Brown (Chapter Three), a most peculiar notion. The concrete person who had (social) relations with other persons could, when thought of abstractly as an individual, also be seen to be in some kind of relationship with society, another abstract entity but of a quite different order of reality.

The model of kinship as the social construction of natural facts is the outcome, then, of various shifts not just in the meanings of society and of structure but of the facticity of nature and the naturalness of facts. I have suggested that 'nature' itself provided a model for the very domaining (or professionalising) of concepts themselves. It in turn was naturalised in the image of the life of organisms and became understood as biology. Yet there was always more to the matching between kinship and nature than the perception of biological affinity between mammalian forms of nurture or the mechanics of sexual reproduction. Kinship in the modern, pluralist epoch preserved the idea of variable genetic heritage and the fruitful production of new, vigorous individuals. This dual connection between individuality and diversity on the one hand and natural and social forms on the other has since altered. If we are in the position of imagining for ourselves the multiplication of neither individuality nor diversity, perhaps we should also be imagining forms of relationships that are neither 'social' nor 'natural' in character.

No such thing as society: does this mean that the context for action is internalised? Is intrinsic worth the same as an external environment of constraints and reference points? Can we imagine overlap without domains?

Referring to other orders or domains of life once conveyed convention as a question of morality. The individual should listen to society. Has such regulation become superfluous?

The present dispensation convinces because it appears to be merely revealing the character of or making explicit a figure already in place: the person who in his or her dealings with others exercises individuality. Individuality signals choice; it would also seem that it is up to the individual whether or not to adhere to convention. Choice becomes conventional, and conventions are for the choosing. It then becomes redundant to externalise other domains, or even think of social relationships as an object of or context for people's communication with one another. This explains why the active citizen can be relied upon to behave responsibly in her or himself; why the New Right can talk in the same breath of the duties of the citizen and the freedom of the individual without any intervening image of a community.

People forget, and still refer to society,[19] but society is orderly (I quote from a televised discussion among self-defined Right Wing thinkers in 1988, *Right Talk*, ITV Channel 4) simply by virtue of individuals following their own habits – not by following 'society' and certainly not by looking to the Government. Such talk is accompanied by looked-for reassurance that the new individualism, far from contributing to a break down of law and order, relocates it as personal motivation. Those who would backpedal and think it too dangerous to abandon society just yet (the same programme revealed) instead say that what is really targeted is the state and its associated evil, the idea of a national culture. As a speaker on *Right Talk* said: nationalism is a modern heresy – there is no single (no such thing as?) 'national community'.

I have probably extracted too clear a devolution from confused and mixed metaphors. But I write from the hindsight of how, through exactly such imaginings as these, that figure of the individual person vanishes. In the late twentieth century it is possible to think that morality is a question of choice. Prescriptive individualism: choice requires no external regulation. As a consequence, the individual is judged by no measure outside itself. It is not to be related to either nature or society (*vice* national culture). It is not analogous to anything.

Now if morality becomes perceived as a question of individualistic choice, then nature appears as what a person consumes. From the perspective of the symbols of the modern epoch, this double transformation far dwarfs the particular policies that speed it up – truly making God's ants[20] of us all.

No 'nature', hardly any 'law': two pivots on which Schneider's account of American kinship so persuasively rested cease to persuade. Insofar as the same was true of English kinship at the time, it is clear that whatever cultural account I might have wanted to produce, it could no longer take the same form. It is not just dichotomies that will, in many cases thankfully, go. We have potentially abolished the particular relationships on which our symbolic capacity for relational imagery was grounded.

Reproducing preference

The morality of choice

On the face of it, however, the Active Citizen of late twentieth-century propaganda seems to embody rather than negate everything one might wish to say about a sense of responsibility towards others. It also appears to be the epitome of individualism. Actually it was a slip of the pen to say 'responsibility towards others'. As Lord Young has declared,[21] the important thing is that individuals in developing their own skills take responsibility *for themselves*. There are clear resonances here with ways in which the typically English have been depicted in the past.

I refer to Dixon's musings on 'The English genius', which includes a discourse on the stock type, 'the English gentleman'. Consider the concept of duty, which a century before Mrs Taylor had located as a question of moral decorum between persons, and between persons and their God. Duty in Dixon's panegyric may be attached as a defining outward characteristic but has become detached from relationships. The English gentleman does his duty without knowing quite what it is. The important thing is that he does it.

> [I]nto this one word, duty, the English have distilled [a] whole body of ethics . . . 'To do one's duty' suggests nothing exalted, magnificent, spectacular . . . [The words] adjust themselves to the simplest intelligence and to the circumstances of every hour, it may be to no more than the performance of some daily drudgery; and yet again on occasion may lift their standard to the heights of Spartan heroism. There is a notable plainness about the word 'duty'. It stands merely for what is proper, appropriate, becoming, to be expected of one . . .
>
> I am far from saying that the men who were guided by this conception understood either its origin, or the nature of the obligation they felt. Without inquiry they responded to its call. In some way incomprehensible to them it gave, when obeyed, a happy sense of freedom, of release from further responsibility. The rest was not their affair. What is English here is the sense of conduct as the test of a man. Not what he thinks or feels . . . Let others judge by the state of their emotions or of their minds, by their personal inclinations or disinclinations. What do they matter? Brushing all these aside as irrelevant, the Englishman judges simply by the act, his own or another's. (1938: 78–80, *passim*)

Duty is no longer a fashionable word. But this 1930s evocation of individual motivation anticipates a most interesting feature of the active citizen: that he or she is her own source of right acting. Importance is placed on convention, yet it is not specific conventions that are the object of the exercise but a specific orientation of the person. As Dixon might have said, provided the person has the right motive ('duty') it will follow that whatever the sense of duty is attached to will be the right thing; one may perform one's duty without knowing what its ends are. The individual in (him)self personifies convention ('the sense of conduct'). To attend to the individual is thus a highly moralistic stance.

For the late twentieth century, however, the promotion of such a figure seems at the same time a complete turn around from the socialist–welfare oriented propaganda that influenced public life when Dixon was writing. That propaganda helped shape the collectivist idioms in which 'society' was then conceived, and anthropology's discovery of society as a source of morality endorsed the significance being given to public institutions and the idea of a common good. Contemporary propaganda appears to change these precepts out of all recognition. Yet what some might interpret as political reactionism, or as a swing of a pendulum, can also be regarded as a devolution of or a process of literalisation in the development of ideas. The concept of moral society produced, so to speak, the concept of the moral individual. However, while this conceptualisation of society has reproduced itself in the idea that the individual contains convention within, it has not reproduced itself as 'society'.

I sketch one of the paths such devolution may have taken. To regard society as having a life of its own and to regard human institutions as having ends of their own, as I suggested was a personifying proclivity of early and mid-twentieth-century anthropology, presented abstractions modelled on persons. Persons in turn were imagined in culturally specific ways. As a consequence, society was 'personified' in the English sense, evoking persons as individuals and as subjects or agents, in short as autonomous organisms. So, if the form that the person took were that of the individual subject, the form that society took was that of a collective organisation of separate elements which communicated with one another to compose an individual system. The same might be true for particular components, the groups or institutions that 'made up' society. Yet I have also suggested that insofar as the analogy (between society and individual) was partial, each concept also participated in or extended into the other. A relationship between institutions and persons was replicated within the person, who showed its effect (as a microcosm of the socialising or domesticating process), as indeed society in turn was held to show the imprint of human ingenuity. Considerable effort was put into making such connections explicit. In particular, the relationship between individual and society was interpreted as bearing on *motivation* in human action. This in turn privileged the image of the individual person as an agent with a purpose in life. Here is the figure who will turn into the late twentieth-century person for whom convention is a choice.

The substance of some of these notions was described towards the end of the last chapter. Here I present a set of propositions illustrative of the modern epoch, and then add late twentieth-century outcomes for them. The outcomes have no logical status. That is, they are not inevitable precipitates of the propositions; rather, they are excavated, with hindsight, from these propositions in the light of certain contemporary values. The illustrations come from anthropological and other social science writing. All the propositions are ones I have embraced myself at earlier times.

(1) Society was an agent. The relationship between human institutions and persons could be imagined as one between subject: object.

Either society or person might render the other object to its subject. Social science took for granted that its task was to uncover determinism or direction in this relationship, and thus the causes of behaviour or action. This was conceived as an explicit aim of investigation. One recent overview of 'the relationship between the individual and society', points out that the problem turns on the political ability of persons to pursue their own interests as against interference from others (Sharrock 1987: 131). Interference could come from society itself: in interactionist terms, discussion about the relationship between society and the individual appeared like a discussion of the relative effects of two persons on one another (cf. Barnett and Silverman 1979).

> Society is *both* a subjective and an objective reality. Society is built up out of the actions of its individual members... Spontaneously constructed patterns of relationships, however, become stabilized and relatively immutable, and so something which began as a 'subjective' creation, the product of the aims and actions of individuals, develops into something 'objective', into a fixed arrangement which presents itself as a given and constraining environment for subsequent action... We must recognize that we have the power of 'agency', that we can act and achieve things, but must also appreciate that we act within and upon structures, and that, in addition, those structures themselves shape us [and] affect the kinds of things that we want. (Sharrock 1987: 153–4, original emphasis)

Thus the answer to the question of whether or not society was made up of individuals or of collective phenomena or even of structures (Sharrock 1987: 146) was given in the aesthetics of personification. Yet because of a democratising sense of plurality, it was also imagined that the collectivity was of a different order from the individual, more powerful because of its magnitude, an impersonal person. In short, when determinist and voluntarist positions were set against each other, the debate appeared to be over which exercised the agency: whether individuals produced structures or were produced by them. What was made visible was agency, and the dichotomies boiled down to the question of where to situate the agent. In that it had a distinctive natural form of its own (its structure and organisation), society appeared to have its own reasons for existing, which is what social scientists investigated. Concomitantly, individuals were perceived as having their own reasons for existing, and for existing 'naturally' as subjects who would prefer to be able to act as subjects rather than as the objects of another's subjectivity. Any demonstration of an object-like status indicated a relationship of domination.

The outcome: individuals in their natural state act as subjects.

(2) Society had needs. A justification for human institutions acting according to their own goals was the maintenance of their own life. Institutions needed persons in the same way as persons needed institutions; as well as having certain needs that must be met in order to sustain themselves, then, institutions were also regarded as meeting human needs.

Although social scientists repeatedly claimed to have outgrown functional-ism, the notion persisted in their explanations of institutions such as 'the family'. The family was based in a need to 'regulate' sexual and parental relationships (e.g. Elliot 1986: 1). This echoes Ronald Fletcher's (1962: 19) rendition.

> The human family is centred round these same biological propensities and needs: mating, the begetting of children, the rearing of children ... It can therefore be said to be a 'natural' grouping in so far as it is rooted in fundamental instincts, emotions, and needs serving important biological functions; and a 'socially necessary' grouping in the sense that it exists in all societies for regulating sexual and parental behaviour in order to achieve those relationships and qualities of character which are considered to be desirable.

The regulation of relationships found an external justification in the idea that however variable the social form, there was a natural necessity for regulation itself. 'The natural propensities involved require regulation, both with regard to their relationships with each other, and with reference to the wider stability and order of human relationships, and the allocation of claims and duties, in the community' (1962: 20). Family organisation was regarded as a correlative of collective organisation and social order. Similarly, Macfarlane argued that marriage (1987: 139) was a solution to the need to regulate sexual intercourse, even as convention was a general solution to what to do with human emotions. 'Love' was not so much constituted in kin relationships, but was something that flowed between persons prior to relationships being made. Especially in relation to its romantic form, he was thus able to postulate love as an 'ideology of individualism': emotions arose spontaneously within the individual, or, if triggered by other persons, nevertheless fulfilled the need for self-expression. So an emotional bond between persons could be seen as a result of their respective individualities.

The outcome: the individual has pre-existing capacities for emotional self-expression which are simply channelled or regulated by convention.

(3) Society was self-regulatory. Society was composed of conventions, and imposed them on individuals, but individuals also willingly entered into relations with others in the same way as they subordinated themselves to the overriding necessity for social order.

Rules were made by persons, and persons made by rules; convention was seen as intrinsic to an orderly and organised life, and to a human one. The issue as anthropologists tried to explicate it was the extent to which people appreciated or recognised the necessity for convention. Thus Fortes (1969: 44) pointed to Radcliffe-Brown's interest in the mechanisms of social organisation – the 'principles' by which institutions are preserved – in terms of how people make them known to themselves through their models. Fortes' axiom of amity depended on a 'consensus in accepting the value of mutual support in maintaining a "code of good conduct" for the realization of each person's "legitimate interests" ... in the last resort, even by acts of violence regarded as legitimate' (1969: 110). Non-amity implied non-relationship. In many systems, this reach of amity was coterminous with the recognition of close kin relations (cf. 1969: 123) insofar as these had both an affective and a moral dimension. Personal interest and social legitimation were thus fused. Convention could be taken as a good for its own sake; it was understood to be the cultural counterpart of natural law, embodying the order necessary for sustaining a complex (and civilised) life. It was externalised as 'social order' or the 'norms' of good conduct to which people subscribed.

The outcome: the individual who perceived the importance of convention (respecting amity, doing one's duty) for its own sake.

(4) Society became an object of collective sentiment.

The point was rehearsed at the end of the last chapter. I note Michel Verdon's (1980: 136) observations on kinship groups. By linking the problem of a group's internal cohesion to boundary and regulatory mechanisms,

> the proponents of the jural model rested their notion of group on a behavioural foundation. If internal solidarity is problematic, it follows that the focus will have to be shifted from problems of structure to considerations of behaviour and normative mental representations (such as values, beliefs, norms, etc.). Indeed, there seems to be only one way of solving the question of internal cohesion, namely, by describing and explaining how a set of mental representations has a psychological effect on individual feelings or sentiments, thereby drawing individuals together. Despite their claim of divorcing social anthropology from psychology, the structural-functionalists were only rooting it more deeply in the study of behaviour.

Examples are to be found in former writings of my own (e.g. Strathern 1972).

The outcome: an individual with motivations that could be oriented in different directions.

(5) Society was a property holder. It treasured and valued its conventions and sought to pass them on; socialisation was likened to transmission, and values and conventions to the property of society, its estate.

The period when society was discovered in the conventions that the individual person followed, the roles he or she played, was also the period of socialisation theories. In British social anthropology property seemed important, for there was an elision between two conjoint ideas of inheritance: society was transmitted from one generation to the next much as real estate was. This was evinced in the early work of Jack Goody among others. Not only did he connect property and role in the idea of 'office' (1962: 276), but he placed emphasis on the socialising agent. There has to be someone who could pass on information to the next generation. The induction of ideas was done via a 'tutor' who was thus a mediating person, one who teaches and transmits (1962: 274). This bookish English image of the person passing on his skills, like father to son, simultaneously reified the values and items transmitted and personified society (society is like a father who hands over assets to his heir). It also assumed that property is uniquely possessed, that what one person has another cannot. Goody gave the example of a person who divides his plot among his children and thereby loses part of the land himself (1962: 274), contrasting possession with the non-exclusive transmission of information. Yet such a distinction could only work in a culture where on the one hand transmission of information was not regarded as loss and where on the other possession of property was always at another's expense. This fitted the English understanding of society as made both of persons in communication with one another and sharing their meanings, and of individuals divided against one another by their material interests.[22]

The outcome: the individual as the expectant heir (of society), and thus an entity with inherent rights against others.

(6) Society allotted roles to its members. Social roles were, so to speak, part of the property of society, the distillation of its traditions and heritage. In playing their parts, individuals as role-bearers thus brought conventions to life: they 'did' convention.

The analogy between the person as a microcosm of convention and convention personified as having a life of its own was thereby externalised in the mediating image of persons as role-playing individuals. This constituted one of social science's direct contributions to popular ideas about kinship. Anthropology became the study of how other people 'do' their conventions (and had endless trouble in describing peoples who do not do convention). A person did convention by acting out being a good mother or a good nurse. In Chavasse's time, the choice was between good and bad role playing; the conventions were not in question. But convention came to be perceived as expressive and thus also a question of cultural style. What one did informed others about one's class, gender, ethnic origins or whatever; behaviour reflected category, role.

The outcome: whether or not individuals observe convention at all becomes itself a style of life, as though roles were there for the choosing.

And the outcome of that is that convention is internalised as personal style. Over and again we find in this constellation of ideas the notion that it is the individual person or role-player or member of society who takes it on him or herself to show convention at work. The individual is thus revealed as a socialised entity. Society is thus revealed in its success as a socialising agent, and its effects are literalised in its impact on internal motivation. But the consequence is that the individual person comes to contain within him or herself the knowledge for right acting, and thus becomes his or her own source of morality. If society itself vanishes from this drama, then, it will have done so quite simply *from the exercise of its socialising faculty*.

With such possibilities in place – individuals personifying convention, giving it life and reason by their acts – one can begin to see how Mrs Thatcher could make the remark she did.

> There is no such thing as society. There are individual men and women and there are families.

Although her critics seize on the atomistic and self-interested attributes of prescriptive individualism, the then Prime Minister herself and the Conservative intellectuals who still debate the matter no doubt take the pronouncement as one of profound moral significance. The reference to family evokes the notion of a circle of persons enjoying life in their own homes, where decency is axiomatic, in the same way I think that she intends us to take the individual. An active citizen will shoulder the responsibilities that the lazy leave to the state; there will be a new era of respect and orderly behaviour based on individual responsibility as there will be prosperity based on individual enterprise. The one proposition is the enabling condition of the other. Our proprietor will combine her financial management of herself with public decency and charitable dealings towards others. So where, then, does morality now come from? How can it be 'seen'?

It appears to come from within. But that interior has itself no structure. No public/private difference is required. Individual and the family are taken for granted in this pronouncement as natural and self-evident units, that is, evincing a unity manifest in themselves. There seems a potential analogy here between them. However, and emphatically, the family is not being modelled upon society or vice versa; since society is eliminated in this formulation, its organisation and systemic, relational character cannot be invoked.[23] Instead, that people will know what is right is taken for granted, rather like the stereotyped English gentleman who knows his duty even if he cannot say what it is until the moment is upon him.

The pronouncement is an outcome of the image of the socialised individual, and indeed does not make the moral sense that Mrs Thatcher wishes to convey without that prior image. But there is a new qualification, for the individual is now abstracted from the socialising agent, society. 'Socialisation' is apparently dispensed with as a structured process of relational interaction: it is simply there in the home.

On the surface, this seems to recapitulate those early nineteenth-century assumptions about civil order and natural law that characterised polite society. But there is a difference: the intervening epoch externalised the concepts of law and order, arriving at the idea of society as a set of collective and objective controls over the individual. I have suggested that it is against that specific collectivist vision that the individual is now reinstated. In the moral decisions she or he makes, what is revealed is not rank or good breeding, or respectability or social worth, namely a place in society as the outcome of connections with others or as the outcome of following the examples others give. What is revealed is the fact that the individual is arbiter, choice-maker, naturally knowing what to do.[24] He or she merely needs to become *conscious* of the fact.

In a way, Mrs Thatcher has pushed the image of the socialised person, microcosm of the domesticating process, into another frame: the individual (or the family) is all there is of society. But see what has happened. It does not appear as a 'society' composed of relationships, as an organisation, but a composite or collage of human nature and processed convention, a kind of auto-socialised body.[25] Perhaps that possibility draws on the ease with which the English have in the past personified convention: the 'forces' or 'principles'

THE TIMES HIGHER EDUCATION SUPPLEMENT   25.11.88

Andrew Vincent on what it means to be an active citizen

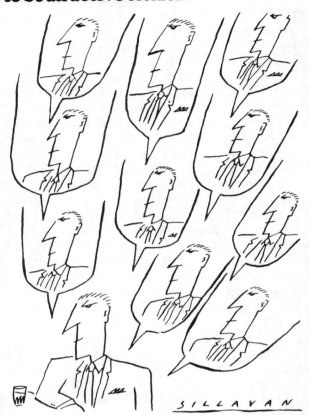

The call for active citizenship has a pleasant ring to it. No doubt for some it gels with the rhetoric on Victorian values. The clever advertiser could make some headway with the idea. However, the debate raises some queries.

The notion of active citizenship implies that there is something called passive citizenship. Active citizenship denotes a "doing" in the community (neighbourhood watch, looking after your own old or handicapped family), without relying on the state. Passive citizenship implies a kind of moral lassitude; if one pays swingeing taxes then the state should do the "active bits" for you. This involves high taxation, delegated concern and denial of personal responsibility. The irresponsible 1960s (and dependency culture) rears its ghastly mythical head again.

Intentionally or not, this formulation is a clever turning of the tables. The conventional images of citizenship in politics are: (1) that the more activist idea, demanding involvement and participation, is to be found in doctrines such as Jacobinism or Leninism, and, as any Karl Popper, Friedrich Hayek or J. L. Talmon will tell you, this can lead to totalitarianism; (2) negative or passive citizenship, a conventional liberal bourgeois view, implies, conversely, the right to protection of one's person, property and liberty. Active citizenship, favoured by Jacobins, demanded positive duty, *les vrais actionnaires de la grande enterprise sociale*. It involved a positive conception of an objective common good – *a volonté génerale* – which is the ground to our true positive freedom. Passive citizenship ties in with a more negative understanding of freedom. However, now the active participating citizen is seen to be the necessary concomitant of a successful liberal market society.

In the passive sense of citizenship, the argument is usually based upon a distinction between the public and private realms. Individuals choose their private senses of the good life, as long as they do not infringe a like freedom for others. Value (specifically moral value) is largely an individual matter. Many liberals have admittedly wanted some kind of broad regulative moral consensus in society. Not, however, generated by government. Value is a matter of individual choice. It is not impossible for a consensus on certain values to evolve in a classical liberal society, but it could not be a communally generated moral goal. If the government were to define the moral goals or individuals, something significant would have been undermined in liberal thought, the private/public dichotomy.

Another element of the varied classical liberal vision is the free economy. Individuals must be able at liberty to pursue their own interests and have

Looking after number one

munal moral goals; (6) human nature is seen to be social, developmental and growing in ethical awareness; (7) the state is part of an enterprise to make humans more virtuous. This is not an exhaustive list, however, it indicates the general ethos within which one important sense of active citizenship

ism. The weakness is that a citizen might be persuaded a neighbourhood watch scheme would better defend personal property. Yet would citizens identify personal interest in working long hours on a school governing board, where they had no child or relative, or looking after a senile

17   *What it means to be an active citizen, 1988*
Reproduced by kind permission of *The Times Higher Education Supplement*.

for morality, good conduct and the rest can be apostrophised as existing of themselves, so that people can respond to these forces without the intervention of (contrived, collectivist) human institutions. Morality is set free from such institutions. Indeed, they are in Right Wing thinking a block on its proper exercise by the individual – hence the minimalist role that is seen for government. People, we are told by the Government, do not need government to tell them what to do. Since ideas and values are seen to exert an influence by themselves, they do not have to be mediated by others, but can be taken for granted as embedded in the minds of right thinking individuals. All that individuals have to do is manage their lives properly. Government intervention is in this view properly reduced to making the resources individually earned individually available, principally by reducing taxes.

The prescriptiveness of this move cancels the idea of a correlation between inner and outer law: it instead becomes incumbent to do everything that will clear the path for individuals to exercise their individuality.

Bypassed in the new prescription, then, is any idea that people are part of an organisation, or that people make society, and thus what people do when they act is to enhance sociability. Indeed, the whole question of ideology and thus of the 'authorship' of society – in whose interest social conventions are manufactured – that characterised political thinking in the 1960s and 1970s is laid to one side in a sweeping gesture of plasti-class anonymity.[26] What displaces the plurality of other persons who might be held to 'make society' is the single individual with means. 'Society' thereby becomes unimaginable.

Writing in the 1830s, Arnold's father summoned the image of society in order to offer a biting condemnation of laissez-faire. He wished to make evident the effects of individual acts. Thus he could say that laissez-faire is

> one of the falsest maxims which ever pandered to human selfishness under the name of political wisdom ... We stand by and let this most unequal race take its own course, forgetting that the very name of society implies that it shall not be a mere race, but that its object is to provide for the common good of all. (Cited in Williams 1961: 123)

His critique would cut no ice with 1980s propaganda. Society becomes unimaginable as an associational dimension of people's affairs if they can entertain no analogies for relationships of commonality. And in any case, when one has no choice but to be defined as a customer in respect of social services, there is nothing laissez-faire about prescriptive consumerism.

It becomes impossible to invoke selfishness with the same axiomatic condemnation. Attention to one's own interests is now a virtue. Moreover, since morality is within, then it must necessarily take the form that in turn typifies the individual: the capacity to exercise choice. Here appears that flattening to which I alluded at the end of Chapter Three. The individual person who is the microcosm of (what was once external) convention is also the individual person who makes his or her own (what was once internal) choices. The individual does not just follow convention or have it imposed but 'does' convention, that is, shows his or her capacity for morality, and thus makes explicit the fact that moral behaviour is contingent on the capacity for choice. But what the choice should be between, the norms and canons of behaviour, no longer need lie in institutions outside the individual. The person is his or her own reference point, a position that requires no negotiation or bargaining with others, least of all with a collective will.

The question might then be posed: how do we know that choice is being exercised? How can we 'see' choice being made?

One answer is simple. Exercise of choice is shown in the style that the individual affects, not just in dress or food but in almost anything that a person does. We might epitomise the contrast with ideas in circulation at the turn of the eighteenth and nineteenth centuries by saying that if 'then' individual behaviour revealed the natural basis of morality, 'now' moral behaviour is a question of individual style. This involves a further cancellation: style and taste are exercised in public, but for their own sake, without polite society as an arbiter. Aesthetic canons are on sale – magazines show one how to choose kitchens and office furniture – but good taste does not reveal social standing or natural breeding and cannot reveal one's proper station in life. Indeed, 'style' is an appropriately more democratic version of 'taste', good or otherwise. And one that only reveals an exercise of itself. Late twentieth-century people talk consciously of lifestyles, and style is done because individuals do (live) style.

Despite the incipient analogy, there seems little difference here between individuals and families. When in her study of the family Elliot (1986: 1) put alternatives alongside 'traditional family ideologies', she called them 'alternative lifestyle ideologies'. The former assert that the family is basically the same everywhere; the latter assert the variability of sexual and parental relationships, and she suggests we should talk about fami*lies* rather than the family.

There has been an explosion of information about diverse lifestyles available to the English over the last twenty years, not only through travel abroad, in ethnographic film and the like, but through widespread attention to local and ethnic differences at home. If they have a common significance, it is for home life. English television serials deal with the niceties of difference: they are not only period pieces but are subtly classed, regionally placed and above all domestically nuanced. No one would dream of showing a typical English family: we are shown the insides of styles whose essence is variety. What was once largely an area of status-consciousness has been heightened by what one would call a general cultural or ethnic consciousness about the specificities of life. It is through such lifestyle that choices are evidently made. But that explicitness has had in turn its own effects.

Since individuals (or families) 'do' lifestyle, the style can then be attached to the individual rather than the kind of life that is imagined. In an arena of self-conscious displacements one should not perhaps put too much emphasis on this or that shift, but the following comment on perceived advertising and marketing futures seems apt. The reference is to a major furniture retail and design business that dominated middle-class taste in the 1960s and 1970s. Aimed at professionals who were flat-dwellers or recent house-buyers, its distinctiveness was that it did not just sell individual products but 'entire ensembles of things for the home', based on 'modernism married to natural, unadorned materials' such as timber, earthenware and rush matter.

> The eclipse of [   ], in common with the resounding crash of [former fashion chain], signals a profound shift in retail and consumer culture, away from the two-decade-old strategy of 'lifestyle' marketing... Tomorrow's more mature customer, educated by two decades of consumerism, will choose products from many sources in a much more individual manner. The growth of 'car boot sales' and antique shops (the consumer equivalent of re-cycling) are just manifestations of a desire to escape the tyranny of manufactured lifestyle, to rediscover distinctive products outside the commercial arena. (Carl Gardner, *New Statesman and Society*, 9 March 1990)

One way of literalising choice-making is to define it as the capacity to purchase commodities. But as Daniel Miller argues (1987; see Gullestad in press), commodities may in turn be re-appropriated in the service of distinctive and individual family identity.

Choices appear exercised when they are exercised in certain well-defined 'choice-making zones'. For many, family-style living may only be a real *option* when choosing where to have one's holiday. As we have seen, however, the idea of a family lifestyle is invariably imagined as domestic style – the kind of household one runs. The appurtenances of domestic-style living have been self-consciously thrust on individual decision makers as a question of market choice – to the point of their being able to choose between different 'designs'. I draw on Miller's 1986–7 study[27] of kitchen furnishings on a London Council estate where we witness, so to speak, the delayed plasti-class effect of middle-class preferences. While in one respect people appear to monitor their furnishing according to external evaluations of social worth, it is revealing about other aspects of the choice-market. I make two points.

The first is the massive scale of the industry which has created choice-making zones as against the relative paucity of 'styles' available. Middle-class owner-occupiers spend large sums on fitted kitchens, in an industry worth about 1.5 billion pounds. Miller observes that most commercial kitchens are based on essentially identical melamine-faced chipboard carcasses; function differences are minor. Substantive difference rests in the style and materials of the doors and in the name of the company. Here trade journal advertisements make it evident that a major stylistic dimension lies in the evocation of time. He lists three principal options:

> (a) Solid wood doors evoking an olde-worlde nostalgia style associated with carved insets, leaded glass, items of copper and brass, preserves, dried plants, old masters

18 *Tailor-made at ready-made prices.*
From *Signature* January 1989.
Reproduced by kind permission of Neville Johnson Offices Ltd and Reed Publishing Services
Ltd for Signature magazine.

and pewter; (b) A laminate fronted modernist form associated with geometric designs, bright colours, spotlights, non kitchen equipment, stainless steel, fruit and cut flowers; (c) A mixture of laminate and wood associated with a mixing of nostalgic and modern items and more often associated with practical functions such as cooking.

Underlying the temporal symbolism were two modes of organisation. On the one hand was heterogeneity and bricolage with for example china from a number of different sets, such that the objects were not united as visual style but implied memorabilia related to the householder's own past. The opposite organisational principle was one of homogeneity, in which all items related stylistically to all others, and it was the visual cohesion which determined the meaning and acceptability of particular forms ...

[I]n advertisements the young are shown with modernist forms and the elderly with the nostalgia style. Historically however the earliest fitted kitchens in the 1950's were universally modernist, the mixed pine and laminate developed in the 1960's and the nostalgia style based on oak did not take off until the 1970's. For the present generation, therefore, it is modernism that is historical, nostalgia that is relatively new. (1988: 358–9)

The images portrayed in the commercial brochures associated fitted kitchens and their carved or beaded doors with 'middle-class' life-styles. The (white) residents on the estate were in fact highly conscious of their tenant status. The two households with such kitchens were amongst the few who provided unsolicited and quite vehement statements about being 'ordinary working-class folk'. However, although the idiom is that of class, the issue seems the nature of home ownership. There is nothing in Miller's account to indicate that were tenants to move into a different style of accommodation, other aspects of their working-class status would inhibit them from obtaining such furnishings.

Miller points to the gulf between what people 'felt they were supposed to like' and 'what they actually identified with', and to the gap between advertiser and consumer. It is almost as though to incorporate a commercial design into the home were itself an act of pastiche, an evocation of other contexts (minimally the 'home magazine' itself). That also had its own value. Despite the possibilities for semantic conversion (Werbner 1990: 143) from purchased commodities to expressions of personal identity, it seems that some people at least wanted the commodity form to remain apparent.

My second observation thus concerns the mode of action through which choice is conceptualised.

[S]everal informants [on the estate] claimed that what they really wanted was a 'fitted kitchen'. This suggested that although they already had a fitted array of floor and wall units, as in advertisements for fitted kitchens, for them a 'real' fitted kitchen was one purchased, not allocated. Certain tenants when asked to select preferred styles from examples, noted that they would have chosen the nostalgia mode but for the fact that they were in a council estate – that is, the ideals they associated themselves with were rendered pretentious by their circumstances. (1988: 365)

In other words, decisions thought to be appropriate to one's lifestyle are set against an abstract sense of what one could choose if choice were the only factor. Actual decisions come to be perceived as the outcome of constraints (here tenant status), of not being able to exercise choice, there being no tenant-style decor among the choices. What the Council provided they had to put up; the meagre alternatives offered in the advertisements on the other hand were interpreted as offering scope for preference. Visible choice is thus exercised between certain well-defined styles that are purchasable as styles. Indeed, choice can appear most visible when it is inscribed in a purchase: 'for the individual consumer, spending is a duty – perhaps the most important of duties' (Bauman 1988: 808).

When choice is consumer choice, the motivation is neither private nor public. And insofar as the range of styles appears to be taken for granted, the advertised 'culture' is not presented as a set of criteria open to critical scrutiny: these modes of design are simply present in the world, available from the manufacturers, and people's concerns are with the preferences they feel able to exercise. The difference between choice and no-choice conceals the extent to which, insofar as the styles come from a limited range of acceptable commercial alternatives, one might also perceive choice itself as, in fact, lack of choice.

What is there, then, to preserve difference between the styles, to sustain the facility to choose 'between' them? It can only be through the active participation of the consumer in the perpetuation of individual designs. Miller describes how, in the two instances of commercially purchased kitchens, people strove to preserve decor integrity (1988: 363).

> The [first] new fitted kitchen was white with 'classic' internal rectangular beading and a white worktop. This was set against the blue-grey found in the new flooring and curtains and picked up by a variety of objects such as a set of three cylindrical containers, a cassette radio and a grey tray with an internal white rectangle and some blue and white china pieces. Virtually nothing remained from the previous kitchen, even the array of houseplants was replaced by one in a dominant grey ceramic plant pot ...
>
> The overall look, evoking the pictures in advertising brochures, was also found in the [second] ... although this kitchen had been built four years previously. It incorporated a split level oven and extractor fan, neon strip lighting, a wallpaper of fake 'terracotta' tiles and a floor of 'fake' stone. Apart from a double spice rack, some matching china and a utensil rack there was a marked lack of additional objects.

Whereas the majority of tenants personalised their kitchens in their own ways, the advertised kitchens that these two households were preserving remained visible as a multi-dimensional unity. Whether as 'homogeneous' or 'hetero-geneous', decor itself makes a unity out of the different flower pots, work surfaces, cupboards and the activities they indicate. Perhaps it is the further requirement for the active participation of the consumer in sustaining the uniqueness of design that has led to the plasti-class counter perception: it is (really) the individual who is stylistically reassembled through consumerism.

What one might have perceived as diverse grounds for negotiated behaviour and moral judgement may also be elided in the composite but not otherwise structured image of the person. Like homes, like persons: the new individual is also a multi-dimensional unity.

In a polemic against the traditional notion of the family, Bernardes offers a new theorisation of 'family life', though he is concerned with social conditions rather than designer objects. He introduces the concept of multidimensional developmental pathways based on the unity of human social existence.

> That is the way in which a given life-space structure upon a given life-course and perhaps shared upon a given pathway is the centre (not necessarily outcome) of a huge range of different interacting factors – personal background, history, age, gender, class and so on. This is to conceptualise individual human social existence as a *multidimensional unity*. I am a sociologist, and a lecturer, and a male, and at a certain age, and a father, and of a certain class etc. (1988: 65, original emphasis)

We must commit ourselves, he says, to the unity of everyday and actual experience: people's lives should not be seen as disparate segments of health, education and so forth.[28] It is a stirring call, except that the notion of a definitive unique and single life-course as embodied in the individual has no dimension. Internal plurality apparently requires no organisation. The do him justice, Bernardes does hypothesise an external organisation in the form of a the local 'democracy' that will discharge public functions. But in his account this is an internally undifferentiated body, and he gives no indication of how one democracy might differ from another.

Here is decomposed that merographic image of the individual person as a *part* of diverse systems or domains beyond him or her. The individual has become an internal constellation of plural elements. Instead of composing 'a life' merographically conceived as belonging to many different external systems (health, education and so forth), life is reconceived as decor, as a whole with diversity and multiplicity contained within. Yet if in this plasti-class rendering diversity and multiplicity have no external analogue, what preserves the difference between being a lecturer, a male, a sociologist? We do not really get an answer. There are only the multidimensional developmental pathways of collectivities of other individuals. 'Such collectivities may constitute a "unity of interacting personalities" or a "temporal form", which may regard themselves as "a family" (1988: 56).[29] People may share pathways, and even interrelate. The choice to do so is presumably theirs.

Bernardes states his theoretical position as encompassing the unity and indivisibility of what are often seen as dualities: Macro/Micro, Reality/Ideology, Agency/Structure.

> Thus the activities of individuals within temporal forms, some of which are 'families', *are* social structure. In making sense of our lives – in negotiating identity and stability in the life-space structures of our daily existence (probably but not

necessarily as a member of a temporal form) – in doing this we are society. Society is not 'out there', but rather 'in here' in our minds and given perceptible form in our mutual and shared activities. (1988: 63, original emphasis)

But in here and out there are already collapsed in this formula. The one side of his equation does not encompass or determine or give rise to the other – there is no switch in scale to make one move from reality to ideology or from agency to structure. His 'inside' might as well be 'outside' anyway. These hypostatised elements are seen as adjacent, coeval dimensions within the frame of a single form (the individual subject). Overlap without domains. 'Unity' works as no more nor less than an aesthetic device. Let me contrast this with the position of David Morgan.

In his critique of analyses of the family, Morgan observes:

[O]ne of the key issues of sociological theory is the establishment of relationships between various levels of analysis, specifically the relationships between the personal and/or interpersonal at one level and the social/structural at the other. (1985: 275)

He comments on the forms that 'the relationship' may take (the one determines the other; the one arises out of the other; or they are mutually reinforcing, or appear as two sides of the same coin). As far as the institution of the family is concerned, he emphasises the difference that perspective makes. In observing the way many writers have placed the family as somehow 'between the macro and the micro, the societal and the individual, the institutional and the personal and between the public and the private' (1985: 282), he states that for himself

I prefer the alternative formulation of the 'place' of the family in social space, not simply as lying between ... but as being both ... at the same time. In short, the family is both societal and individual, both institutional and personal, both public and private. (1985: 283)

The contrast[30] with Bernardes is that Morgan locates his different elements as different theoretical, and indeed political and ethical, external perspectives on the family, corresponding to different enquiries we might wish to make and thus to different referential domains. That (theoretical) externalisation constitutes the distinction between merography and pastiche or collage.

Were it just the case that society is vanishing, the thought might prompt the further thought that someone should conserve it. Our government spokesman on the state of the world instead suggests that it never existed. The death of the collective! In its place is pastiche: the authentic individual from a traditional past. And collage: men, women and families, a mix of genres and materials.

A government that does not identify with 'society' not only out-radicalises the radicals, but consumes its mandate to govern. To bypass the idea of social legitimation, to interpret the electoral mandate as no more than the outcome of individual acts of choice, like so many multidimensional pathways, contributes to a kind of greenhouse effect. All that requires is maintaining our present levels of consumption. And all that requires is continuing to assimilate our own precepts – in this case for public figures to make explicit already held values concerning the propriety of individual choice. The self-gratification of the individual as consumer is then bounced back to the consumer in the form of publicly sanctioned individualism ('privatisation'). The exercise of in-dividual choice becomes the only visible form of public behaviour. Like photographing the foetus, the result is to extract the person from its embedding in social relationships.

The consumption of nature

Fantasies that the world might run itself without human intervention have no doubt a long history. One twentieth-century version lies in the idea that the artefacts human beings create are capable of sustaining themselves. Perhaps this is a kind of delayed counterpart to the vision of society as having a life of its own – so too may technology or, as one recent televised dialogue had it, Culture.

This was a programme on life forms, including the 'artificial life' that can replicate itself within computer programs.[31] The thought of life based on other than DNA as a mode of self-replication led to the observation that, in some possible future, 'culture' may be able to reproduce itself without the presence of human beings. Culture was rather anachronistically imagined as a robot-driven universe of factories sustaining communication between them-selves. Two observations are of interest for us. First, this culture that was given a life of its own was imagined literally in terms of replication. It thus borrowed from a model of genetic mechanism: life is defined as the autonomous capacity to replicate forms. Second, it also borrowed from modes of human interaction: what is transmitted is information which provides models or templates for future forms. Although they do not yet, it was said, computer viruses could in principle replicate with variation. But absent from either of the above analogies was any idea that diversity and individuality were intrinsic to reproduction. These are qualities by which the English have in the past characterised the future of animal and especially human populations. Diversity entailed the fertile reproduction of vigorous hybrids, individuality the uniqueness of organisms. Such qualities were regarded as having adaptive potential, suited to the idea of populations sustaining life within an environment that was the context for their life.

To think of reproduction as replication seems at first simply a matter of locating the reproductive process further back in time, in the communication devices by which the transmission of the appropriate messages is effected. However, the image of self-replicators such as computer viruses is breath-taking in its own way. No environment appears necessary when what is at issue is the replication of communication devices themselves. It is as though genes did not need to be embodied: what is reproduced is simply the informational capacity itself. Models with a life of their own!

18 COMMENT

The cost and the quality of justice

IGNORE the squeals from the legal profession. The three green papers on legal services published by the Lord Chancellor yesterday were not designed for the profession, but for its clients. Their purpose is to increase competition, improve choice and raise the competence of lawyers. These objectives can only be achieved by removing the restrictive practices and shameless privileges of the most cosseted profession in the land. Hence the wails from all sides.

For nine years the lawyers have been protected by their Old Boys from the chill principles applied elsewhere: competition, efficiency and economic cost. But not any more. Belatedly, concern for consumer interests has been given priority over professional interests. Belatedly, the legal Big Bang has begun, provided the proposals in the green papers are implemented. They represent the biggest restructuring of legal services this century.

The best test of the green papers is to apply three consumer tests.

Will they increase access?
Will they reduce charges?
Will they improve performance?

The key proposals, although presented as the Government's provisional views, are believed to reflect a firm intention to end restrictive practices in the professions and encourage free market competition.

compared to what has gone before, this is a truly radical package. Lord Mackay of Clashfern is a revelation. He deserves wholehearted support from all those who seek to consume the essential commodity called justice.

19 *Natural justice, 1989*
Extracts from *The Guardian*, January 26th 1989.
Reproduced by kind permission of The Guardian News Service Ltd.

It would be something of a future anachronism to call such replications culture. Meanwhile, one human model for the concept of culture is, so to speak, already there.

To think of individuals as motivated by choice and choice as evinced in style is already to render individuals redundant. The modernist sense of style as unique expression is displaced in pastiche and collage. Styles appear to imitate other styles, replicating them by an inner momentum that is contained in the very notion that style itself is an imitative act. Not the imitation of nature or of more noble ages, as it might have been seen a century before, but imitation of versions of itself. Representation without reference is in fact 'a description of the way film or tape functions as a "language", receiving exact copies of sights and sounds ... [lifted] from their contexts' (Ulmer 1985: 92).[32] But if it were the context that once elicited the adaptive uniqueness of individual forms, and thus the individuality of modernist styles, style now becomes self-consuming. The individual disappears from a surfeit of individuality, in the same way as society has disappeared from its too effective techniques of socialisation. It would seem that Culture emerges as the new totalising concept that can gather all human enterprise to itself, including its own capacity for regeneration.

Yet hopeful as the possibilities for its future reproduction might seem, there is a small problem. This imaginary Culture may be able to reproduce itself without either Individuals interfering with its plans for replication or Society determining its goals. But without Nature, it will indeed only have itself to consume. Without nature, there is no context for its existence.

In mid-twentieth-century thinking, nature provided a model for a process of consumption that was also one of (re)production. The conversion of raw materials into energy, inanimate into animate life, was imagined as an ecological relationship between individual organism and its context or environment. The three concepts could be played off against each other. The 'individual' modelled ways for thinking about diversity and the uniqueness of forms, 'society' ways of thinking about relations and connections, while 'nature' combined both of these as an at once single and manifold phenomenon. Nature *was* reproduction. Like the composite image of the relationship between individual and society, nature accounted simultaneously for the diversity of individual organisms and for the relational or systemic ('adaptive') nature of their interactions. But what does one do with the idea of cultural replication? Of self-consumption? If the question seems claustrophobic, this is greenhouse heat. Nature does not represent or model this new reproductive process: on the contrary, it is the substantive entity that is being eaten up without being regenerated. In some present visions of nature, consumption has become the very antithesis of reproduction.

I earlier noted that there have always been English protests against the spoiling of nature. They were certainly vocal in the Sperlings' time. Nature 'was being destroyed by the new, and growing, industrial society' (Urry 1987: 214). Nature was being destroyed, but by a society that was thriving, in the

same way as the assertion of individual choice was made against the
background of assumptions about the conventions of social rank. And when
industrial society was criticised for squalor and greed, it could be shown up
as unnatural – neither attending to the necessities for a natural life nor natural
in its own terms, that is, recognising the human relationships on which it was
founded. Such analogies have since lost their plausibility.

Nature is no single concept and I have tried not to treat it as one; it has
always meant many things, and in changing constellation. In modern
parlance, it covered at least five different areas (after Urry 1987: 214). They
comprise the essential quality or character of something; the underlying force
that directs and controls events in the world; the entirety of animate and
inanimate objects in the universe; the physical as opposed to the human
environment; and finally the countryside, rural as opposed to urban, the realm
on which industrialisation was seen to encroach. These elements were
connected in the merographic mode. Each thus inhabited and created specific
contexts, so that to invoke one was to recall or eclipse other contexts or
domains. While each element thus appeared as a part of a wider range of
meanings, the combination meant that it was also legitimate in English to talk
about nature *as though* it were one thing. This habit of thought gave a further
sense that there was an identifiable entity under attack from diverse sources.
The English could bundle these elements together in the same way as they
bundled together diverse perspectives on society or the individual. Conceived
as discrete entities, any of these (and other) salient entities could also be
brought into partial analogy with one another.

Analogy implies perceived difference as well as similarity (cf. Fernandez
1971). Among the analogies by which nature and society were compared was
their respective internal organisation or structure. Insofar as the analogies
were never complete, neither domain was wholly modelled on the other (cf.
Jackson 1987) – and indeed either could be thought about through models
drawn from parts of each. Thus idioms of reproduction and biological
function could be used to describe the maintenance of social institutions;
idioms of engineering or architectural form to describe nature's design. Each
could also be imagined as participating in the other, evinced in composite
entities such as 'the individual' who appears as both a natural and a social
product. The elements of such a merographic figure were kept distinct by the
domains from which they were derived, in the same way as the composite
figure itself constituted a further distinct individual.

That sense of distinctiveness rested on the evocation of environment.
Environmental forces had an effect on the individual organism, to which the
organism responded, and environments were perpetually modified by such
responses. This modern model indicated possibilities for interaction and two-
way feedback. It is a little different to imagine that we are consuming
environment itself.[33]

Just such an image, however, is contained in the idea of appropriating nature to personal ends, of literally ingesting it. What is taken to be part of one's body becomes coeval with the destruction of wild habitats. Moreover, there seems no difference in the way the individual or in the way society is seen to consume nature. The dilemma of consumption is regarded as a dilemma that affects all life. As protest movements and alternative lifestyles proclaim, personal and social responsibility are fused. Indeed, the kind of society one lives in seems much less an issue than the kind of culture: the aggregate lifestyle of its individual members resolves into how much how many households consume. But there is a new quantity effect here that is very different from the old sense of culture as a community of shared meanings. (Lamenting the passing of hegemonic middle-class texts, of the place national newspapers once held as a common denominator of cultural experience, a *Guardian* writer (18 April 1990) comments: 'Mrs Thatcher set out to abolish society. She may well have abolished culture as well'.) The new culture, if one may call it that, is contained instead in a new common denominator, technology.

The late twentieth-century English consume nature in two modes about which they talk. The first concerns the using up of resources, and it is to feed technology, including the technology that sustains present home comforts, that resources are being used up. General awareness of world depletion of natural resources is sometimes dated to the oil crisis of the early 1970s; yet if people think that new technology will always overcome shortages in this or that material, such as oil, that speeds up rather than slows down their sense of a diminishing natural world. Similarly the effluents of technological production are seen to speed up the disappearance of natural habitats and wild life. While one might date growing public apprehension to about the same time, in England the greenhouse effect changed from being an outlandish metaphor to a literal apprehension in 1989.[34]

The second comes from depicting continuity between human and other species in a mode which tries to sustain a natural continuum: food is marketed – in supermarket chains as well as Health Food stores – as 'natural'. Quite literally we are invited to free ourselves from artificial additives. The technology that appears as gratuitous additions can also supply the means for purification. As a result, even natural products (such as coffee) can be further purified, made allegedly more healthy (decaffeinated). Various natural options are available in other spheres, of which childbirth has received considerable critical attention. With the elision between nature and biology, bodily functions have long been regarded as the special province of nature; what is new is the scale on which a natural style to certain aspects of living is presented as consumer choice. Indeed, the duty of the consumer to purchase is reinforced in the idea marketed in 1989–90 that one is helping the environment by buying particular products. A preference for X against product Y is thus re-presented as a consumer preference for sustaining nature.

One of the great discoveries of the social constructionist era in social science was that the manner in which the body is thought about has social or cultural origins, whether one refers to gesture, habits, the expression of emotions or to sexuality. What receives new (cultural) attention is the body as a digestive tract and its physical requirements for resources, for protection from pollution. We do not just simply attempt to 'improve' the pleasures of the body (in the phrasing of Dreyfus and Rabinow 1982: 257). The cultural construction of biology has been overtaken by the (cultural) necessity to sustain biology itself.

My remarks are not meant to detract from a present sense of crisis, but to point to the conceptual collapse of the differences between nature and culture when Nature cannot survive without Cultural intervention. It is hard to imagine that there will not be consequences for the way we imagine intimate human relationships. These include possibilities as well as actualities, the kinds of things it is conceivable to think about in the late twentieth century. It is not that human relationships or social life or the natural world or whatever have disappeared, but that we have potentially cancelled the basis on which certain relations of similarity and difference were taken for granted. Consider once more the image of person as consumer.

Attention to the body and to bodily functions is not simply a manufacturer's conspiracy to make customers consume more products. It is a consummate literalisation of modern(ist) concepts of human nature. I refer to those concepts that assume that knowledge about human life is to be gained from inspection – that if one looks (inside) one will find the real thing, that one can always bring to the surface the reasons for behaviour, that motivations are explicable. It is to such literalisation that manufacturers contribute in putting themselves into the hands of 'the new intensive forms of market research ... designed to offer a social map of desire which can be used to determine where exactly which products should be "pitched" and "niched"' (Hebdige 1989: 53). Persistent literalisation of knowledge practices alters the perception of the terrain. Self-consciousness is both means and ends.

I have argued that the English have always made assumptions explicit to themselves; making apparent their conventions is also to make apparent the contexts for their values. The danger is that something no longer taken for granted will disappear, as Zygmunt Bauman (1990: 435) observes of communities that 'fall apart the moment they know of themselves as communities. They vanish ... once we say "how nice it is to be in a community"'. But the nesting box effect of insides within insides, homes within homes, formerly controlled this movement as one between different perspectives.

I have also argued, then, that one powerful if homely set of imaginative devices has been in the interplay between public and private domains. Thus what was within could become the object of overt attention, even as convention could turn into individual role-playing. As we have seen, movement between the perspectives of public and private domains, like potential movement between social classes and thus between different orders of phenomena, acted as a source of reflexive English debate on the nature of social life. It also sustained the difference between the individual and his or her social/cultural/natural environments. An abstract relationship between a value and its conventional context was made concrete in the image of an organism in its habitat or a person at home.

When the person is defined by what she or he takes inside, the difference between exterior and interior is merged. The generic consumer image is that of ingestion. And consumables are neither simply part of one's public presentation to the outside world nor do they simply reflect one's inner moral or social worth. Outside does not mediate inside, or vice versa, because the individual's gesture towards the outside world – the choices to be made – are simply choices about what she or he is going to take inside. Nor can these movements sustain the merographic sense of reality, such that one finds 'more real' dimensions to an object the 'further' one looks. To look inside the consumer is to see the items the consumer has ingested from outside itself; to look outside is to see producers apparently moulding their products to the consumer's desires. Choice of style turns out to be choice of style, serial substitutions that create images of change by altering surfaces (Barnett and Magdoff 1986, quoting Baudrillard). Surfaces only 'reveal' other surfaces. It then appears contrived and melodramatic to point out that choices have political consequences, that it matters what style people adopt, or that the figure of the consumer conceals power relations. And that is because the consumer image *does not contain any depictions of a relationship within itself.*

It is as though we had all been photographed: as though the individual person were a walking foetus/floating spaceman. In Petchesky's words, the human organism is imagined as a self-contained unit, free floating apart from its life-line which is attached to something not in the picture and (bar discharging waste) taking-in not giving-out. The foetus – the spaceman – is also our individual as consumer. Given the enabling technology (a life-support system), the consumer imagines the person as a package, an enterprise with nothing to do but manage his or her own affairs. The ultrasound image of the foetus and its enabling technology ceases to be merographic when the domains of 'person' and 'technology' are no longer discrete contexts for the multidimensional whole.

The Warnock Report (1985) on human fertilisation and embryology gave vent to numerous concerns about the social consequences that might follow advances in the new reproductive technologies. One question was how to protect transactions in human gametes from market forces. As critics have commented, it is thought proper for the technicians to be paid for their services but not the donors of gametes, and especially not those who act as surrogate mothers. The Report was concerned to discourage commercial exploitation of surrogacy (1985: 46); it thus recommended that it should become a criminal offence to set up agencies to facilitate the recruitment cf women for surrogate pregnancies. At the same time, it recognised that private agreements will take place, and acknowledged the argument that individual women have the 'right' to enter such an agreement just as, it sweepingly claims, 'they have the right to use their own bodies in other ways' (1985: 45). Together with that right to private agreement went the assumption that the decision to choose surrogacy will be made either in the context of a marriage by a couple who want children, so that it is their private affair, or else that the carrying mother will enter into a private contract affecting only the management of her own body. Consequently it looks as though there is no commerce involved. Exploitation only begins when financial interests come in. That persons should be allowed to exercise choice in the matter for their own ends goes without question.

The recommendation depended on a prior cultural premise: that people reproduce *themselves*. Reproduction can thus be construed as a private matter. And that people have a natural desire to do so is reason for the desire to be protected. A concomitant assumption of the Report seemed to be that, of all that they transmit, people naturally desire to pass on their genes and should if they can, especially as this has consequences for legal inheritance and succession. (Glover *et al.* [1989: 67] suggest that a surrogate mother may find her task easier when 'the egg is not hers, [since] it reduces the feeling of giving away her own child'). The kind of rights and obligations that attends the actual 'donation' of gametes is another matter. Donation is seen as a specification alienation, and the donating person cannot assume parental rights over the eggs or semen once they have been given (Warnock 1985: 54). Yet because of the intimate nature of the transaction involved, the donor still remains a 'parent' of a kind: indeed, it is recognised that children may want to know who the 'genetic' parent is. Egg donor is referred to as 'genetic mother' (1985: 37): however, she is a mother without rights in and therefore presumably without obligations toward the child.

This is not just the English belatedly recognising a split between biological and social mother, as anthropologists might have framed it, for the split is not simply about relationships. This is also language, an expressive capacity for imagery, stretched to some kind of limit. A similar flattening occurs between the terms nature and culture. When nature becomes a question of cultural style and culture the exercise of natural choice, the one ceases to be 'inside' or 'part of' – contextualised by – the other. The language will not work. Let me spell out what I mean by these phrases.

Pfeffer related current concerns to a new, and what she regarded as insidious, assumption. Why is it, she asked, that in the late twentieth century, personhood is equated with the capacity to reproduce? She pointed to various discrediting images of infertile men and women. Accused of selfishness or of spiritual irresponsibility, they may also be regarded as 'the sort of people' who would equate children with stair carpets, microwave ovens and other items available for purchase (1987: 97). At the same time what makes their behaviour in seeking assistance explicable is the popular notion that to be infertile is to be desperate and that one is driven to desperate means.

We can answer Pfeffer's query in one way.[35] Personhood is equated with the capacity to reproduce insofar as language and imagery presents the act as one of choice. Persons who otherwise did not have the choice now do have the choice to reproduce themselves, for they now possess access to the enabling technology. But the 'choice' to reproduce is like 'choice' for style; to not so desire is somehow to be less of a person. The assumption is that, given a chance, one will take it, part of the wider nexus of prescriptions that presents failure to exercise one's capacity for choice as failure of motivation. The fact that one should reproduce oneself with as close an approximation to natural process as possible is a point I return to in a moment. As we shall see, if one cannot reproduce one's genes, one can reproduce (be parent to) choice itself.

Chapter Two referred to the observations of Stanworth and others on the way medical doctors appeal to the natural desire, natural right even, of people having children 'of their own'. At the same time, there is increasing criticism of the whole language of artificial reproduction – either because it ignores the continuity of natural processes, of nurture and parental bonding beyond conception and birth, or on the contrary because it ignores the fact that all parenthood is socially constructed. Exactly. What is in crisis here is the symbolic order, the conceptualisation of the relationship between nature and culture such that one can talk about the one through the other. Nature as a ground for the meaning of cultural practices can no longer be taken for granted if Nature itself is regarded as having to be protected and promoted.

After nature: modification of the natural world has become consumption of it, in exactly the same way as modification of the world's cultures (through colonialisation) has become consumption of them by the international tourist. The old double model for the production of culture – society improves nature, society reflects nature – no longer works. The individual consumes cultural and natural products alike, but in consuming them him or herself reproduces only him or herself. So consuming the world is turning it to already anticipated ends: the pleasures of the closed circuit (Haraway 1985: 88–9), the body as the place of private satisfaction that completes its own desires.

Perhaps a new ground for individual action will be this very capacity to combine desire with the appropriate enabling technology. If this is a change, then the change has occurred as a result of people becoming self-conscious about values already held. When the traditional yearning for parenthood can be satisfied by 'artificial' arrangements, it is the yearning that seems 'natural'. Stanworth is right, I think, to comment that accelerating rates of divorce and remarriage hardly signify the breakdown of the family or marriage as institutions; on the contrary, people are perpetually re-composing family style lives. But how should we visualise *kinship*? For what is signified, she says, is markedly greater uncertainty in the 1980s about relationships themselves, 'about the ties that bind individual parents to individual children' (1987: 19).

Chapter One noted the shift over the last thirty years in English views about artificial insemination. Far from being regarded as an attack on the family and promoting family disintegration, DI may now be held to enhance family life

(Smart 1987: 106–7). The difference between the hapless 'illegitimate child' of the 1950s and the DI child of the 1980s is that the DI child is likely to be openly wanted by both husband and wife. They have simply resorted to artificial means to implement their wish. That the husband, for instance, wants the legal status of father is an overriding plea for recognising legal paternity (1987: 108). Paradoxically, if the couple complete their natural desires by having children, these desires seem to have been fuelled by the increasing assimilation of social roles to biological ones. As far as paternity is concerned, the old assumption that within a marriage the husband was the father to his wife's children was based on the further assumption of his genetic parenthood; but now people talk of the reverse. It is widely accepted that the child born outside marriage should be socially recognised. The new question has become the status *of the parents* who reproduce outside marriage. The Warnock Report debates the right of the child to know its 'genetic father'; the Glover Report similarly speaks of 'biological parents', of 'the right to know' and of the claim of 'the biological father'.

This very desire for a *real* match between biological and social parenthood seems in the case of fathers the obvious outcome of kinship thinking, of the modelling of social on biological ties. But see what has changed: what is 'biological' is no longer subsumed under the parent–child relationship itself, the flow of blood that was supposed to connect parent and child through the act of procreation. It is literally the donation of genes. Blood could be imaged as some kind of metaphor for a bond; like the act of procreation it worked as a trope for a relationship between individuals, a symbol of a communicative event. Genes are the bits of information themselves.

Biological process is literalised as genetic donation, a technical act open to artificial assistance. The resultant emphasis on 'donation' fits older models of paternity more closely than those of maternity (Stolcke 1986), but I remain with the general case.

If parenthood is fragmented into particular components, as the going language has it, decomposed, deconstructed (Stanworth refers to the deconstruction of motherhood; Glover *et al.* to the fragmentation of both motherhood and fatherhood), then what makes a parent (cf. Smart 1987: 114–15)? All the various contradictions in the material with which these Reports had to deal, with increased value being placed on genetic parenthood on the one hand and increased possibilities of supplementary aid on the other, resolve into a single answer: the parent must be the one who desires to be a parent.

A woman who gives birth from a donated egg can be seen as the mother of the child because she wished to have the child; if a man consents to his wife having DI then the Warnock Report recommended that the child be regarded as his legitimate offspring (1985: 23–4). In this view, the parents will be those who planned and wished for a child to be born to them. It completes their desires. Yet there is still an equivocation for they do not supersede the 'genetic father' or 'genetic mother'. As far as possible, then, such desires should also be completed naturally, so that an approximation to genetic parenthood will be the natural choice of all intending parents. That needs no justification.

Natural choice can even appear to inhere in the pre-natal material itself. Thus the anti-abortionist movement anticipates the child's (natural) choice to live. Janet Gallagher (1987: 148, my emphasis) quotes from the 1979 *Michigan Law Review*:

> One 'foetal rights' advocate writes that legal provisions for foetal protection can be justified . . . by the expectation that they will provide people with 'the gratification at the thought that *their wishes were significant even before they were born*. They can thereby escape whatever insecurity may be aroused by the notion that at one time in their prenatal existences they were deemed wholly undeserving of legal respect'.

Yet when choice has to be exercised on another's behalf, it comes up against the other's exercise of choice. Thus the new reproductive technologies also 'interfere' with women's bodies. 'Reclaiming our bodies and bodily integrity means renting [tearing] the entire fabric of sexual subordination', for under attack is bodily integrity because 'our bodies are *parts of* ourselves' (Raymond 1987: 62, original emphasis). It is not society or social relationships that are in jeopardy, or even in this case the mother–child bond or the right to be a parent to a child. But, then, as one contemporary writer on English kinship has observed, relationships may conflict with rights. 'Women must have the right not to care, and dependent people must have the right not to rely on their relatives' (Finch 1987, quoted by Hicks 1988: 252).[36]

Women's reproductive rights are in turn defined as rights to dispose of bodies.[37] As a result, paternal interest may be read as an intervention.

> Some are wary of this increased role for men in parenting . . . One anxiety is that if men do get involved they will in fact take over, leaving women with *no* sphere of influence: 'He creeps in like another mother, between the mother and the child'. (Rowland 1987: 70, quoting Elizabeth Badinter, original emphasis)

Choice by oneself on behalf of others is evident in certain areas such as genetic counselling,[38] and over abortion decisions that have the child's future in mind, as it is also embedded in the desirability for protective legislation. Within the framework of 'assisting nature', however, whether choice is pro- or anti-technology, the capacity to choose is above all validated by reference to the individual and her or his fulfilment or development. The involvement of others can be regarded not as intensifying relationships but as intrusive, as in the case of the male parent just quoted.[39]

It is the exercise of choice, then, that will enhance human capability; where earlier visionaries experimented with social forms (Utopias, Erewhons, 1984s and so on), we re-live our recent modernist past in the hope of being able to go on exploring further, seeing more, extending our capacities, and above all in enriching personal experience. But in one area, such possibilities are almost uniformly met with dismay, the area that concerns the reproduction of the consumer him or herself, the reproduction of the maker of choices.

Recall that remarkable projection: that alongside the development of reproductive technologies have consistently gone popular fears for the consequences of genetic engineering, eugenics and the rest of it. These are epitomised in science-fiction fantasies about creatures who are half human–half machine, or human–animal transplants, 'parts' of different worlds that stick on to one another. These figures are often presented as terrifying and unnatural, or where the combination is poetic or the result aesthetically pleasing – as in Anne McCaffrey's *The Ship Who Sang* – with pathos for the incompleteness of the sentient being.

Such negative reactions represent choice at a kind of limit. The individual consumer's capacity to choose this from nature, that from culture, has turned into the person itself. A composite of bits from different sources, literally a conglomerate, a collage of physical materials. Not metaphorical parts, but tissue and plastic. But for how long will amalgams of human and non-human parts seem grotesque? Dental amalgam is one thing, and chemical stop-gaps to decay acceptable medicine. These new images introduce the further idea that a fusion of materials is also a fusion of identities. Persons who pride themselves on individualism, as the English do, are right to be suspicious: for the fantasy supposes a creature who is no longer an individual. It might be repaired but how should it reproduce?

Yet as Cecil Helman points out, we are already familiar with transplants (organs between bodies) and implants (non-organic substances introduced as substitute organs). He speaks of the blurring of the boundaries between nature and art, and of a social consequence. The new industrial body

symbolizes a new type of society, and new types of social relationships. The creation of implants or prosthetic organs, for example, requires an elaborate social organization of production, distribution, marketing, maintenance, and repair of the artefacts. The individual's body is now part-industrial. His implants link him permanently to the world of industry and science. He is also the ultimate *consumer*, incorporating the products of industry into his very body, and a living, walking advertisement for their efficacy. He is not only a unit of production in the workforce of that society, but also a unit of consumption in every sense. The new parts of his body are mass-produced, impersonal, replaceable... Having an implant also links the individual to a huge team of experts: surgeons, radiologists, anaesthetists, nurses, physiotherapists, hospital technicians, as well as the designers, producers, suppliers and repairers of the prosthesis. While the implanted body may have more of these 'social' links to other people, the links are really those of consumer to producer. (1988: 15, original emphasis, note omitted)

The reappropriation of the consumer's identity by the makers of commodities!

In passing, Helman comments on the practice of allograft – the transplant of tissue from one body to another. 'The closer the kin relationships between

· · · as a prelude to the privatization of higher education. In a leaked policy paper Mr Robert Jackson, junior minister for higher education, ruminated on "an alternative paradigm". Instead of the state providing higher education its role should be confined to "enabling individuals to purchase services from providers". With their own money, at least in part, not the taxpayers', of course.

As to what sort of structural changes there will be, I believe that we may be approaching a fundamental choice between two different patterns of evolution. One route towards mass higher education could be through an increasingly state funded and therefore state-organized "system" of higher education. There is a real possibility that this will be the course followed on the Continent. If this is the path we follow, the difficulty which the institutions of higher education will face is that the expansion of provision by the State – with taxpayers' money – will be expected to take place without substantially increasing the burden of public expenditure and taxation, and in the absence of mechanisms for engaging private funding. The other route would see the movement towards mass higher education accompanied by greater institutional differentiation and diversification in a market-led and multi-funded setting. But much depends upon the willingness of the institutions, of the heads of department, of the teachers, to go out and market what they have to offer, rather than to wait for applications to roll in.

In the first scenario, the structures of mass higher education will tend to be increasingly rationalized, under pressure to stretch public funding as far as it will go. The effect will be to offer a limited variety of institutional structures and missions, providing a range of broadly similar experiences to all, and producing a range of similar outcomes for all. In the second scenario, the structures of mass higher education will be much more diversified, as they are in the United States. The traditional modes of provision will still, of course, be cultivated: but there will be a much greater emphasis on a variety of approaches better able to meet the needs of different types.

Why do I prefer that we in Britain should take the second of these two routes, that of expansion through diversification and differentiation?

continued: see plate 1

20 *Baker's two paths, 1989*
From *The Times Higher Education Supplement*, 13 January 1989 and 30 December 1988. Reproduced by kind permission.

recipient and donor ... the less likely the graft is to be "rejected"' (1988: 15). How, then, are we invited to think kin relationships?

Perhaps what is being consumed in this process is that relational facility, the idea of a symbol itself. We cannot in any simple way talk of the new body as 'symbolising' a new society if we cannot externalise or differentiate the one from the other.[40] Helman argues that there is a reciprocal relationship between images of the personal and the political body (1988: 16):

> The parallel for replaceable body parts is, therefore, replaceable people, par-
> ticularly in the workforce. However, this new society – like the new body – is a
> collage of different elements: some living and contemporary, some artificial and
> industrial, and some ancient and traditional.

Yet society and body are equally collage. On what are 'reciprocal relation-ships' and 'parallels' between them modelled? Where is the analogy for analogy?

The English have made explicit to themselves the partial nature of the various social systems that once met – and Bernardes would like us to think still meet – in the person of the multifaceted, many-role playing individual. But their insistent cultural search for literalising that multiplicity, for showing up how fragmented people's lives are, how partial their descriptions, how hesitant their grasp on the scope of life, along with their celebration of the plurality and diversity of form, and of individuality itself, have made the individual vanish. Instead of becoming *more* individuated, we become more parts of one another – ethnically (French bread/English marmalade) and personally (evoking the idiosyncracies of other ages, other epochs and, following the Chicago Bears, other cultures). The English consume culture, as they do nature, in the information they are constantly consuming about ourselves. They wish to be conscious of their experiences. Not parts of other domains but parts accreting with other parts.[41] This makes everyone into versions of one another's particularism.

In the modern epoch, the individual person was equal to neither nature nor culture but could be imagined as participating in the realms of each. What the English used to think of as their kinship system was the keeper of that partial analogy. But persons can now be imagined as simply composed of elements of other persons – whether in terms of organ transplants, or the borrowing of cultural forms or the imitation of other individual lifestyles, or even the transmission of genetic particles. We move from the unique amalgam of elements drawn from different domains to a literal assemblage of parts perceived as substitutable or replaceable for one another. The relationship between these components cannot be conceptualised in other than terms of self-management. So let us return to our foetus/spaceman, or our farmhouse proprietor for that matter.[42]

A photograph of a foetus with its umbilical cord cannot model a social relationship if social relationships are not the model for it. In terms of natural substance, the baby is all human tissue. But the protest against medical 'intervention' is about intervention in the relationship between child and parent. Technological enablement becomes reproduced in cultural dream-work (the phrase is from Zoe Sofia, quoted by Petchesky) as rendering the mother herself like a machine. In that sense, the baby is properly regarded as part machine. The organism connected to a life-support system evokes the family photographs in the front room of the farmhouse, above a flickering fire where visitors sit, with the quiet hum of white goods singing away to themselves behind doors misleadingly marked private.

A perceived relationship between inner and outer worlds, part of the way modern English have understood knowledge, worked as an analogy for the change of scale by which social science in the earlier part of this century construed society as containing a plurality of individual members, and construed the individual as having internalised social norms. Does a postplural world imply that we can no longer change scale? Changing scale was visualised as an exemplification of perspective – society seen as more than the sum of individuals; an individual seen as more than the social conventions it observed. Is abandoning that relational facility, then, abandoning the facility for calibrating difference and similarity through partial analogy?

And might literalising as such lose its power? One of the popular academic debates of the 1980s assumes that the referencing facility of words can no longer be taken for granted – words do not have 'meanings' either inside or outside themselves. They do not provide contexts for one another. Words simply summon other words.[43]

It is very obvious, I suppose, that if one imagines away society as a collective plurality, then one imagines away the individual elements of which it is composed. Less obvious perhaps are the potential consequences of the present ecological necessity – namely that we make explicit the participation of nature and culture in each other. Literalisation's last stand? Insofar as the individual has long been regarded as the site at which nature and culture fought it out, to remove the battle is also to remove the battle ground. I use the military metaphor as a reminder that loss is not always a matter of regret. It is certainly a matter of interest. At least such a potential absence should be of interest to anthropologists, for that particular conception of the individual has not only been at the centre of the English education and welfare systems in previous decades, but also at the centre of what, for a time, anthropologists called kinship.

Greeting card: late twentieth century
Reproduced by kind permission from Camden Graphics Ltd and Fine Art Photographic
Library Ltd.

Recapitulation: nostalgia from a postplural world

Thirty-five years ago, at the end of his study of types of civility, which takes him to many countries but ignores America, Nicolson predicts the future:

> I do not foresee that the social habits of this island will ever be imitated from those of the French, the Germans, the Australians, the Dutch, the Trobrianders, or the Portuguese. I imagine that it will be the American model which will in the end impose itself on the English-speaking world. (1955: 284)[1]

But he professes not really being able to understand their type of civility. His clinching reason brings us back to enclosed gardens and fenced properties. Trying to look at the English through American eyes, he writes:

> There is again the curious indifference to, or disregard of, what to us [the English] is one of the most precious of all human possessions, namely personal privacy. To them, with their proud belief in equality, with their rather ignorant affection for the pioneer spirit, privacy denotes something exclusive, patronising, 'un-folksey', and therefore meriting suspicion. Thus they leave their curtains undrawn at dusk, have no hedges separating their front gardens, and will converse amicably with strangers about private things. How can a European dare to discuss the manners of a people who seem to ignore, or to be unconscious of, what to him is civilisation's most valued heritage? (1955: 18)

The ignorance, so-called, informed an oppositional culture. An American exhortation published in 1927 deliberately promoted the idea of 'foundation planting' – plants pushed up against the house rather than, as was taken to be the style of the Old Country, forming a hedge on the street line. 'The American way called for uniformity of landscape design: no fences or hedges, only foundation planting and lawns. Anything else was vaguely unpatriotic and morally suspect' (Ottesen 1987: 21). The reason was that the home was the greatest institution in America, and should be open to the street.[2] In the 1980s, it is the lawn that now seems the problematic import; it is taken to be an English influence that interferes with American nostalgia for the land as it once was. Nowadays, 'sophisticated gardeners learn to appreciate what is unique in the American landscape', to restore beauty in natural bogs and to stylise meadows (1987: 27, 29).

186

For England in the late 1980s, US-style popular design (stars and stripes, block letters, American football on television and icecream in the super-markets) have made a new and explicit entry into the advertised aesthetic repertoire. We are officially told – and I refer now to Higher Education – that our provision for state benefit should learn from the American model of financial competence. So it seems that I have been describing the outcome Nicolson predicted: what happened when the dichotomy between public and private disappears. Indeed, I have flowed between English and American examples insofar as I think we share certain cultural forms in common. But the situation is not quite as simple as the idea of adopting – or resisting – a model would suggest. As far as that public/private dichotomy is concerned, it might appear flattened but it has not 'broken down' any more than the family has. Nor have the English simply imitated the apparent American disregard for it. Rather, we might say, it has worked itself out in people's imagination in a particular way.

The epoch of bourgeois revolution, that one might date to 1780–1820, led in Williams's view to terms such as class and culture being used in their modern sense, and in Roy Wagner's (1986) view made God a function of nature. It anticipated the period in England when a division between public and private worlds was realised in the middle-class, kinship-based image of the home away from the workplace. The home in this sense was not some timeless attribute of the English, however precious a human possession some English have claimed for it. Here was a particular devolution of ideas, an interpretation of human nature literalised in domestic architecture and the conduct of family life with as much particularity as the countryside was steadily enclosed through deliberate, individual acts of parliament (2,341 private enclosure bills between 1780–1810). Those enclosed fields that so strike the visitor were made step by step as a practical necessity which the new agricultural technology had presented as the only choice a landowner bent on improvement could take.

Like their formulation of social class, the reappropriated distinction between public and private became one of the modes through which the English reflected on the relationship between individual and society and between nature and culture. Certainly the distinction was the hinge of Nicolson's interpretation of types of civility: what floored him was that he could not use it as a framework for the American case. Yet to present it as 'traditional' is as profound a mis-reading of English tradition as is the embrace of American individualism in current political rhetoric. American postage stamps celebrate constitutional figureheads; one recent frank came with the declaration, Freedom under Law. Our English commoner, by contrast, can throw out the notion of constitutional society as a source of law precisely because of the way the language she uses is able to recapitulate a changing relationship between public and private priorities. That language makes a vernacular appeal to individualism a self-sufficient, intensely moralistic and nostalgic gesture.[3]

But we also participate in the promotion of one another's cultural forms. The American essay on foetal photography was published in a volume put out by an English press; this book originated in my talking about English kinship in America, hoping that I would simultaneously convey a sense of distinctiveness and speak to common concerns. That capacity to participate is promoted by the way the English have thought about kinship over the last 200 years. It led in the pluralism of the modern epoch to the indigenous perceptions I have labelled as merographic, where meanings seem always to be partial, where there is always more beyond the field of vision than one sees, and where elements that are part of one system are also in another dimension conceived as parts of others. The mid-twentieth-century view of kinship as a set or network of relations between individual persons is a beautiful example. A system itself is thus regarded as an aggregation of elements – natural insofar as it displays their internal relations, artificial insofar as it never encompasses their entire definition.

The vantage point of the postplural world disaggregates. Its own characteristic lies in the notion that wholes have dissolved into parts in such a way that they can only be reassembled as so many parts. Yet the very idea seems sinister (Spallone and Steinberg 1987: 10, original emphasis):

> The 'new' reproductive technologies are thus not really 'new'. They are based on the same old ideology of abusing, disrespecting, and exploiting women as objects that can be manipulated according to the needs of the group in power. What *is* new is the emphasis today on *parts* of women's bodies being used in both unprecedented ways and to an unprecedented degree. Will the body that is allowed (or forced) to reproduce in the future be White, middle-class, heterosexual, able-bodied?

Nostalgia here is for difference, for variation, for diversity, for the multiplicity of human cultures and bodily forms. When what is reproduced are not bodies but choices themselves, the spectre of choice is conventionalised desire.

> In 1984, we heard the suggestion from an Australian IVF clinic director that people may want to use donor eggs and donor sperm with IVF rather than their own because they do not like their own or their partner's characteristics – for example, intelligence, personality, or appearance. (1987: 5)

Technology enables people to substitute for a random outcome their own all too predictable wishes.

The nostalgia for multiplicity is also the nostalgia for whole forms, where elements are intrinsic and parts non-detachable, for the integrated home and unique landscapes. At its extreme we might say that it is *nostalgia for the idea of the individual*. I include here persons as individuals.

Vanishing forms was always a perspectival analogue to receding horizons. Thus for as long as the individual person was an emergent form, it was 'community' – including communal family life – that was ever receding. British anthropologists for their part never had much doubt about the chimeric nature of such a construct. Their object was the study of social relationships on the ground and the cultural values (including notions of community) that attended to such relationships. It was the collective ('social') dimension of life that they took as their subject matter. So if there is a particular loss that lies in wait for anthropology, it will not be for the idea of societies and cultures themselves, for their holism is apprehended as an artificial (constructed) tool of analysis. It will be *nostalgia for a relational view* of the world.

Or rather, this is the point at which I locate my own sense of being after an event. Drawing Melanesia into this account (Chapter Two) was not meant to evoke the kind of community life for which Westerners conventionally yearn and never existed. The intention was to make explicit certain understandings developed within the discipline of social anthropology that address the manner in which human beings create society for themselves. In the words of one Melanesianist, (modern) anthropology 'has at its core a commitment to making the social component of human life visible' (J. Weiner 1988: 5). To convey a Melanesian world through idioms of relationship, to describe persons as composed of relations, imparts a sense of sociality that makes the systemic and individualist tenor of English-language-based perceptions equally apparent.

That tenor was contained by the general Western perception that relations were to be appreciated after the fact, for they comprised a distinctive order of being, *sui generis* one might say. Thus the relationship between different parts of social life was held to inhere in principles of structure or organisation that was not equivalent to social life but 'underlay' it or were 'superimposed'. Social life itself could be shown to have 'a relationship' (expressive, constitutive) to those principles even as an individual person, in that peculiar colloquial English on which I have dwelt, could be said to have 'a relationship' with society.

A relational view of the world encompassed the connections people made at all levels. That ideas should not be considered in isolation but in relation to one another was the starting point of this book. This tenet has been modern anthropology's professional contribution to social science. 'Social anthropology is about relationships' (J. Weiner 1988: 5). As in the manner in which society was professionalised or naturalised as an object of study that provided its own frame of reference, so too with culture and symbolic constructions. In putting things into context, anthropologists assumed that there would be sets of relations internal to the domain in question whose elucidation would reveal its own structural form. The present cultural analysis has been just such a relational exercise. It also bears its own relationship to other works.

Much of my account can be read as an English exemplification of Wagner's *The Invention of Culture*. He not only demonstrates just how modern Western culture invented 'society as man's relation to nature' (1975: 132),[4] but analyses the symbolic mechanisms by which this most unstable of cultures has perpetually destabilised itself. While there is no culture that is not itself constantly reinvented in people's views of the world, Westerners took on as their own cultural project the ever-receding goal of inventing convention both for and against ('after') a plurality given in nature – after individuality and diversity. Thus they came 'to embody, and to live in a world of natural diversity, united by [their] own efforts to master and understand it' (1975: 130). The project entailed the counterprocess of conventionalising inventions, of their constantly making evident to themselves the principles upon which they constructed society and culture itself. Westerns sought to draw out the relations between things, to make the connections that underlay their understandings obvious.[5] Indeed, they made these the literal reference points for their own individual acts.

The precise dates in my account, and the unfolding of ideas as though they succeeded one another in time, has been a specificity or literalisation as awkward as my ascriptions to 'the English'. Though his archetypical Westerner is American, Wagner's sequel, *Symbols that Stand for Themselves* (1986), attends to developments in Continental European and English thought that provide a substantive schema for the various epochs to which I refer.

Wagner's epochs are, literally, tropic constructions. They are turning points in the devolution of what he calls the Western core symbol, for which his own starting place is Latin Christendom in the eleventh century. The core symbol consists in the changing relationships between divinity, humanity and sacrament on the one hand and between nature, society and symbol on the other. These internal relations are themselves in relationship with each other, and the entire figure consists in a 'turn' of perspective. The first set of relations, which he calls the Medieval cycle, contains within its configuration the second, Modern cycle, which may be read as an everted or displaced Medievalism. This is meant in the sense that the whole is a figurative construction (trope) containing relations that may (in a literalising mode) be drawn from it, as the author does. For the perspectival turn consisted in 'man taking responsibility for the conventional [relational] rather than trying to compel it as "mystery"' (1986: 112–13).

Each cycle constitutes several epochs, themselves turning points of prior perceptions. Epochs can be of immense or of no duration, but what is germane to the present account is the way in which Wagner imagines them as so many historical periods. An epoch is experienced as a 'now' that gathers perceptions of the past into itself.[6] An epoch will thus always be what I have called post-eventual, that is, on the brink of collapse, for what it gathers together in its own apprehension of the world is all those antecedent ideas – as I have done here – that bring one to the present moment but not beyond. For one who perceives the world relationally, it is always the eleventh hour, the implosion of the evolutionary clock, the moment of terminal realisation.[7] Thus the entropy in my account, the falling cadence to the chapters' ends, are given by this epochal gathering that also constitutes a 'then'. The End of Nature is really After Nature: a point of apprehension, in this case of the constructional roles that particular concept has played in our perceptions.

The Modern cycle made nature a ground for knowledge. I began rather arbitrarily at a mid point, and rather arbitrarily with a writer who dealt with the ambiguity of improving on a nature that includes the essential person. In place of the eighteenth-century understanding of society as an artificial construct, like reason, for Jane Austen's era rational society had been internalised. If reason were a human function, then civility lay within persons and was to be exhibited by them. Nature was thus embellished by the exercise of talent, a point that in the decades that followed became the literal improvement of talent itself.

That early period also introduced ideas about the plurality of human artifice, a numerical democracy that was to be made evident in succeeding decades. Here I have gathered together the hundred years or so between 1860–1960 as a single 'epoch'. We may think of it as modern(ist) or pluralist in character. It is divided in turn by two points that constitute epochs in themselves.

The 1860s presented a turning point in what Wagner calls modern conceptualisations of society with its tropes of quantity and spatiality. This was the time of Arnold and Ruskin, of the deliberate production of social institutions, of morality externalised, of education moulding good habits. This was also Morgan's era of 'nature as evolution' and 'culture as man's production of himself' (Wagner 1986: 119). The question was how far and to what degree improvement was possible. It led to enthusiasm for productive activity, to complex organisations of all kinds, to factory reform, the duty of management, the institutionalisation of hospitals, schools, prisons and, for anthropology, to ideas about cultural evolution. We could call it the production-centred or institutional epoch of pluralism. If anthropology was being institutionalised as an academic subject, civilisation or culture was being institutionalised at large. Yet, in retrospect, from the perspective of the succeeding epoch, it seemed it were the individual that had been in-stitutionalised. It was persons that turned out to be the result of education. The unique person now had to be freed from such constraints in the same way as, from the anthropologists' point of view, each unique culture had to be apprehended from its own point of view.

From the early twentieth century, 1910 or thereabouts, society was presented as a collective enterprise and as a representation. Structures evoked sentiment and social forms incorporated the value individuals gave to them. Indeed, culture became the counterpart to people's self-conscious apprehen-sion of uniqueness and diversity. Social life, like the natural world, appeared intrinsically plural – full of individuals, species and diverse ethnic groups and thus, for anthropologist, of cultural relativity. This was the person-centred epoch of pluralism. It is the one to which my three facts of modern English kinship belong.

In this latter phase of modernity, then, diversity became a guarantee of natural vigour but people's consciousness of collectivity and institutionalisation also produced the idea of the person as the subject of or microcosm of the domesticating process. This was the socialised individual, the consumer of values whose individuality was in danger of being suffocated for a collective good. In thereby discovering the social construction (the representation) of the individual, mid-century anthropologists began undoing that collectivist idiom. The aggregate appeared instead as a heterogeneity. A fresh sense of pluralism came both from the discovery of internal critiques of social systems (the rediscovery of political economy, for instance, as marxism and feminism) and from the revelation that the individual as an object of social construction also resisted complete construction. But if one sees pluralism as the final epoch within the larger Modern cycle, one would then imply that it was the transformation of the entire Modern cycle that is contained in the present epoch I have called postplural.

This is to exceed the possibilities of relational exposition. – The restaurant at the end of the universe. – Let me return to the moment before, to the 1980s, as though the postplural world were simply devolved from a plural one. At that moment, '[s]ociety, the ideal and the goal of the Enlightenment, is internalized and taken for granted' (1986: 121). The move appears to repeat the internalisations of 200 years ago. But in being freshly internalised, society now vanishes as an object of people's dealings with one another. For the late twentieth-century mandate is not longer of reason but of consciousness, and the society internalised is not rational society but the elicitor of emotion and preference. The choice is not how to behave but what to consume.[8]

Wagner writes 'This is the age of consumerism, the technological ... production of the individual through the special properties of machines, drugs, and ultimately the computer. It is also the era of the synthesis of human needs and meanings through the media' (1986: 120). It is the moment at which his exposition stops. Intriguing as it might be to speculate beyond this point, a trope, he asserts, is elicited not determined and certainly not predictable.

In certain parts of our imaginings, at least, the individual has already become something else; it has ceased, so to speak, to be reproduced. I have dwelt on the particular fantasies of reproductive engineering that not just the English but also others with access to Western technology have thought up for the future. They persistently include that of cloning, of being able to produce *individuality without diversity*, endless replicas of unique forms. Yet it is merely to extrapolate from present medical practice to imagine the joining of human and animal parts, of producing beasts that are neither one nor the other, that is, *diversity without individuality*. The old assumption, the more individuals are produced the more diversity, will not work. I have suggested that these dreams/nightmares are already visualised in an area currently given highest moral value: the capacity to exercise choice.

As Jencks and Keswick (1987: 54, my emphasis) unwittingly assert: 'the options *force* us to reassert a freedom of choice'. Without such prescriptive variation one could not create a market for customers to exercise their preferences. In the view of the chairman of a public funding body in Higher Education, the role for the (British) state is 'just to make sure the system works, just like it regulates a free market'; funding should 'encourage diversity ... If they [the services to be funded] all look the same: 'we'll say we've got enough of those'" (*The Times Higher Education Supplement*, 14 October 1988; phrasing transposed). Individuality without diversity: the customer is pressured into the exercise of choice, an emphatic promotion of preference, as a mandate impressed on all consumers alike. Diversity without individuality: the riot of consumer preference collapses all other possibilities, all choice becomes consumer choice, not just rearranging the same variants but converting social relations into market forces. Individuality does not produce individuality.

This, we might say, is the demise of the reproductive model of the modern epoch which was, if the reader recalls, a model not just of the procreation of persons but for conceptualising the future. The individuality at issue was the special individuality of parts elicited by merographic connection. Parts have ceased to be merographically connected.

The merographic capacity to put the individual into different domains or contexts, as now a social construction and now a natural and biologically given entity, depended on one consummate perspective: that these were all (plural) ways of knowing the world. For the world was composed of numerous relations between entities of which symbolic sequences themselves (constructions, representations) were a part. Relations were in the nature of things, this being at once a symbolic and a social statement. However, relations were not all relations of comparable (analogous) order and while concepts such as Individual, Society and Nature could always be connected with one another, each term carried its own substantive or tropic effect. They were not simple substitutes,[9] and their interactions led to varied outcomes.

We have seen the way in which concepts participated in one another. Let me separate out differences in their effect. 1. When people personified ('individualised') society or nature, they were conscious of creating a metaphoric construction. The point of resemblance was understood 'symbolically' and as no more than resemblance. The resemblance thus remained in the domain of symbols, as a cultural artifice or figure of speech. 2. The idea that the individual person was socialised, however, drew not on resemblance – the individual was not really thought to be 'like' society – but on a perception of process. Society *was* the human construction of the world, and persons were moulded by it. Nature might also be perceived as a human construction, either in the sense of humankind's impact on the environment or in the sense that the very idea was a category of thought. But nature was not 'socialised' the way a person was. When we talked of the social construction of natural facts we meant a construction that remained in the domain of social life and artifice, even though it attended to or incorporated aspects of the natural world such as biological processes. 3. Finally, then, nature itself composed an autonomous domain, for that is how nature came to be defined. Its twentieth-century assimilation to the concept of environment was no accident. It created its own context, and did so because it worked as a kind of grounding conceptualisation for knowledge, for understanding the intrinsic character ('nature') of anything. To speak of the person as a natural individual was to point to what was taken for granted about the autonomy of organism, and here the person was seen as a 'part' of nature.

Now because human constructions already had their own autonomy, anthropologists also regarded the representation of social institutions as 'naturally' belonging to the domain of symbolic construction (thus one could compare, for example, different representations of family forms as symbolic constructs). But that was because for them society was the entity that was naturalised in its own self-regulative and context-providing aspects. A context was generated from properties seen to be inherent in the object itself, as in the perception that social science was the study of social facts, and therefore to be named by itself (social, pertaining to society).

The perspectives that these three concepts gave upon one another were not reciprocal: none was a complete substitute for the others, and where analogies were perceived, they worked only to a partial extent. Hence the concepts had different controlling effects. 1. Persons evinced an essential consciousness which properly resided within them as individuals, and was only 'metaphorically' or 'symbolically' extended to non-human entities. 2. Society was the exemplification or sign of human enterprise, so that social life was coterminous with the activities of human beings. 3. Nature, at once intrinsic characteristic and external environment, constituted both the given facts of the world and the world as the context for facts, thereby providing a ground to the life of persons and results of social enterprise. Although it could be made into a metaphor or seen to be the object of human activity, it also had the status of a prior fact, a condition for existence. Nature was thus a condition for knowledge. It crucially controlled, we might say, a relational view between whatever was taken as internal (nature) and as external (nature).

Making these concepts explicit extended the concept of consciousness, and thereby brought about a further range of effects. 1. To be conscious of the agency of persons was simply to recognise the nature of persons for what they were (individual agents). An already explicitly recognised element of human life was given its due. 2. To be conscious about the social construction of the world, however, made an implicit realisation explicit. As soon as it was said it became self-evident, by virtue of the fact that society was coterminous with human enterprise, and that included the way human beings 'construct' their worlds. Society became joined to symbolic practice. Yet its new visibility also meant that what had been taken for granted no longer was. Both these positions were, in fact, well rehearsed in anthropological debate in the 1960s and 1970s, and devolved from what I have called the mid-twentieth-century view. 3. But to bring to consciousness the context or grounding for one's sense of the world could not be confined to recognising what was already explicit, nor to making the implicit explicit, though we might have thought we were doing both of those things. Its effect has been to make context or ground itself disappear.

The Modern cycle, to recall Wagner's terminology and as we might remind ourselves, was ushered in with a new conceptualisation of the ground for knowledge.[10] The discovery of social enterprise, the point at which human kind took responsibility for the conventional or for law, was also the point at which nature had become that ground.

Of course, Nature does not 'really' disappear. On the contrary, late twentieth-century culture renders it more and more evident. What has disappeared, so to speak, and for which we seem to have nostalgia, are persons as individuals and society as a relational view of persons. Easy to kill off the individual as the originator of private worlds and original symbols when one can substitute cosmopolitans as consumers of world society. Easy to dismiss society as a symbolic fabrication when it seems to ignore the mainsprings of individual motivation and enterprise. But postmodern aesthetics and Thatcherism alike most interestingly pull out from under our feet the grounding or reason for these constructs, and thus an anterior assumption about the conditions on which we so freely play. They take from each its former context in the other. The sense is that context itself has gone.

A perception of the uniqueness and intrinsic nature of forms created a context for the modern or pluralist concept of the individual. A concept of society created a context for perceiving that social relations formed an (external) environment to people's dealing with one another. Unique form and relational knowledge: Nature grounded both these contexts. It held the twentieth-century notions of individual and society in relation to each other as though one could apprehend inherent facts and self-regulating systems simultaneously. It was also the context for the idea of symbol as humankind's consciousness of its own place (context) in the world and of symbolic constructions as the environment (context) for its own understanding.

If nature has not disappeared, then, *its grounding function* has. It no longer provides a model or analogy for the very idea of context. With the destabilising of relation, context and grounding, it is no surprise that the present crisis (epoch) appears an ecological one. We are challenged to imagine neither intrinsic forms nor self-regulating systems.

To recapitulate: the English of the educated middle class have merely practised what they had always practised. It seemed a matter of pragmatics. They valued their values, and in doing so slid from making more explicit what was already explicit to searching for the assumptions or principles behind their actions and thus making the implicit explicit. The mother's role in caring for the development of the child was seen to include the vital relationship between mother and child itself. That relationship then ceased to be taken for granted and became the object of attention and elaboration. If one may choose to see a relationship either as socially constructed or as a natural state of affairs (socially) assisted, one is in fact choosing what to consider natural.

To introduce consciousness about one's own practice is, in the late twentieth-century idiom, to introduce the possibility of choice. This is not the choice about which Jane Austen or Mrs Taylor wrote, nor quite Bell's exhortation that we should choose our forms of self-expression, though it has devolved from all of these. Chapter Four suggested that choice has since become naturalised by the aesthetics and constraints of consumer culture. To have choice about the grounding of one's motivation in this way is to simultaneously render trivial any relationship between external context and internal character. Plasti-class does not even sound like a class. Let me amplify through a further recapitulation.

Clumsy as the expression might have been, I have needed to name the particular kinds of past connections I have called merographic. They produced overlapping domains that in the end made a relative matter out of the concept of context itself. They rendered Nature context-dependent.

In the manner in which the English have in the past valued their values, they literalised a particular kind of relationship, namely that between an entity (a person, value or principle) and its necessity or rationale, that is, its context. In the example I have given, the child's healthy development provided a context for the mother's interpretation of her role. We may think of it as a reference point for her motivation, though it was not the only one.

What was literalised, then, was the relationship between a value (role, duty) and its rationale (healthy development), so that the whole formed a referential or conventional domain. The relationship was not between persons but between entities of non-comparable order. Hence the constant effort to make evident the individual's 'relationship' with society. Spelling out the connection made it evident that at the same time the individual is not completely comparable to society, and therefore this was not a wholly self-referential domain. Indeed, it was the constant perception of the fact that entities could always be re-described from further perspectives that revealed merographic connections between domains. One could displace one context by another, and thus alter one's perspective in that part of one domain now seemingly part of another. A principal example has been the very figure of the individual person, who could be assimilated now to a context thought of as nature, now to a context thought of as culture or as society or for that matter as psychological selfhood. From the perspective of the individual, we can see that any of these entities, nature among them, could be a ground to this figure.

There was, in turn, a constant tendency to render the analogy between these contexts partial, to turn them merographically into parts of each other and make one the momentarily encompassing context for others.

Contexts seemed real (they provide the rationale for the properties of things), where analogies once made conscious seemed artificial or incidental, 'metaphorical'. Indeed, contexts were real insofar as they provided a perspective, even though they could always be displaced. In short, contexts have been 'natural' to the twentieth-century viewing of the world. We were organisers of the spectacle but it was in human nature to so create the contexts (perspectives) for understanding, and thus humankind created for itself its grounding for (self) knowledge. This was modernity.[11]

But the spectacle was still, in the mid-twentieth century, at a remove. It was persons who suffered crises of consciousness about what anyone could 'really' know. Nature might appear in this or that guise, or as an illusion, but the existential problem of consciousness and representation seemed contained within the human frame and its capacity for symbolism. The new crisis (epoch) is not so contained. A crisis perceived as ecological contains all.

We are still After Nature: still act with nature in mind. But I have suggested that the concept that grounded our views of individual consciousness and symbolic activity on the one hand and a relational view of human enterprise and society on the other has been transformed. And because it is ground that is transformed, an equally devastating effect is of triviality. Insofar as the plasti-class person of the late twentieth century also perceives him or herself as a consumer of it, nature seems turned into a mere artefact of consumer choice. Its image may be borrowed here and there, slapped on to products as a new dimension, a kind of marketed contextualisation that reinvents human responsibility as a matter of discriminating between products – even where the greater responsibility might be not to buy at all. But nature as a superadded dimension to human products makes the point nicely.[12] The idea of autonomous form seems old-fashioned.

There is a final effect for this, that lies in knowing that knowledge will (so to speak) cease to search for its own grounding, for its contexts will no longer be significant.[13] There will be no need to extrapolate a new 'grounding' for the future.

As a consequence, it would seem that we are as free as we like to go on talking about 'nature' and the importance of 'natural' products and will no doubt do so until, as the English say, the cows come home. The bovine idiom is at once unfortunate and wholly apposite. In the year (1990) that British cattle reveal they have been infected by a slow-growing virus (bovine spongiform encephalopathy), with its disastrous effect not just on herds but on people's fears for human health, it is also revealed that these herbivores have been fed animal offal. Such plant-eating animals were always, of course, intended as animal meat for our own table; now they turn cannibal on their cousins (the offending offal is thought to come from sheep).[14] Domestic cows no longer belong to the domain of herbivores: as we have always known, they are simply produced to be consumed.

This 'as we have always known' is the fatal traditionalism of the English. It bears one more rehearsal.

To exercise choice over whether cattle should be herbivores or (like human beings) omnivores seems to be quite natural for human beings (who are always 'improving' on themselves, economising in Thatcherite idiom),[15] even if it is unnatural for nature. In any case, opposition on the grounds of unnaturalness seems equally traditional – we have always known that human artifice worked 'against' nature. After all, Ruskin, among other commentators on the industrial revolution a hundred and more years ago, thought it prevented human fulfilment, deformed the capacity to labour, and perverted peoples' consciousness away from the self-evident reality of the world. Along with this idea grew up the twentieth-century notion that different social arrangements not only deformed the natural person but also deformed themselves: the idea of society as composed of internal contradictions and interests pitted against one another meant that the need for social cohesion that was so important to early twentieth-century anthropology gave way to a later perception that some forms of social arrangements were less adaptive than others. Society could thus be seen as deformative of human relationships. But of course these very notions of imperfect lives or maladaptive functions rested on those images of individual form and relational knowledge intrinsic to the notion of nature itself.

There seems to be no real basis (no ground) on which to regard feeding sheep to cattle as shocking when multimedia is the name of the game and computer viruses might be alive.[16] To date, however, BSE is found in neither European nor North American cattle. In this manifestation it is a strictly British disease.

It is impossible not to make the modern English seem either less important or more important than they really were. However, some place should be given to their reproductive model. Kinship was regarded as an area of primordial identity and inevitable relations. It was at once part of the natural world that regenerated social life and provided a representation of this relationship between them. Anthropologists, in turn, apprehended kinship as a symbolic construction that took after the natural facts on which society imagined itself based, a microcosm of the relationship between nature, society and symbol. One cannot say what will become, though possibly the elements of technology, motivation and design are being rearranged in the idea of what it would take to decode the human genome.[17] Natural selection is reinvented as auto-enabling choice. Perhaps replicators that need no base in biological substance merely imagine for us a cultural future that will need no base in ideas about human reproduction.

Notes

Prologue: making explicit

1 Fox (1967: 24) states it bluntly: 'Kinship and marriage are about the basic facts of life. They are about "birth, and copulation, and death".'

2 An original impetus lay in the politics of feminist anthropology (cf. Strathern 1980). Since then I have been provoked by Donna Haraway's question about what constitutes Nature for late twentieth-century people.

3 After Thompson (1978 [1965]: 3).

4 'Coordinates' after Werbner (1989: 14).

5 My interest is primarily in the perception of complexity. It does not require a theory of production, although Sahlins's (1976: 215) comment on consumer markets nicely literalises forms as objects made: 'every conceivable distinction of society is put to the service of another declension of objects'.

6 The contrast is a contrivance, a claim to a particular mode of interpretation, and is obviously contestable. Jencks (Jencks and Keswick 1987) takes issue, for instance, with the influential interpretations of Foster (e.g. 1985) and his colleagues (Owens, Lyotard, Jameson) in arguing that 'postmodernism' is often confused with late modernism. Late modernism is the tradition of the new, whereas in his eyes postmodernism is a recapture of the vernacular that evokes the tradition of the old. But I find his own emphasis on 'superabundant choice' and 'widespread pluralism' (1987: 54) anachronistic. Superabundant choice subverts widespread pluralism, subsuming pluralism under the single gesture of choice – not 'everything goes' but 'everything participates'. Needless to say, these legislations over terms, periods and so forth can be seen either as late modern exercises or as the postmodern traces of a vernacular tradition that in the new context must appear faintly absurd. The sources of the confusion are simple: postmodernism makes evident the pluralism of the preceding epoch, and thus seems to make 'more' of it. But it does not itself reproduce pluralism; for it makes pluralism appear *as a single, all-embracing phenomenon*. Both this point and the quaint personifications of convention implied in these debates (epochs as agents) recur in the arguments that follow.

1 Individuality and diversity

1 A term used of the policies of and promoted by the Conservative Party in power throughout the 1980s (see Keat 1990; Heelas and Morris 1991). Their heavy investment in the need to advertise, the late twentieth-century's locum for action research, has contributed to this self-revelation. Unfortunately, the enterprise

culture is not entirely their product; it is as much constitutive of a cultural revolution as of the political will of an electorate.

2 On the assumed affinity between pets and persons, also see Wolfram (1987: 16). She further suggests that the implied relationship between similarity and difference is analogous to that between blood and affinal kin.

3 I deliberately mix kin terms and names here because I am describing a 'mixed' system. Thus, Firth, Hubert and Forge (1969: 451): 'In any formal context relatives must be properly pinpointed as individuals, with category label carefully qualified to bring out the personal aspect.' To anticipate the argument that follows, such mixing is an example of merographic overlap.

4 He contrasts the use of first names by 'the gay Devonshire House circle, and the sentimental intimacy of Charles James Fox and his friends, [from] ... the tightness in such matters observed and expected by the characters in Jane Austen's novels! Even when happily married, the Woodhouse daughters continued to call their father "Sir". Emma denounced as "vulgar familiarity" Mrs. Elton's reference to Mr. Knightley as "Knightley"; she herself, we may assume, continued to refer to him as "Mr. Knightley" even when they had been husband and wife for many years' (Nicolson 1955: 272). A more sober commentary on Austen's terminology is offered by Isaac Schapera (1977).

5 Of course, the personal name may recall a specific relative or be drawn from a stock of 'family names', or even follow rotation or succession rules. When the personal name is a family name, it becomes a kind of generic. But in so far as it is known by its stock of names that knowledge also individuates the family concerned. As Lévi-Strauss (1966: 188) observes, the one term can 'play the part either of a class indicator or of an individual determinant'. 'John' distinguishes which Smith, and 'Smith' which John. I return to this in the next chapter.

6 Cf. Schneider (1984: 181). Trautmann (1987: 180) takes it as axiomatic that every 'anthropological investigation of kinship sets out from ... the idea that kinship is somehow more important to the working of simple societies than of complex ones, and that in the course of their development complex societies have substituted something else for kinship'. From status to contract; from relationship to individual!

7 Eliciting people's relatives as 'persons' related to one was seen by Nisei (second generation Japanese–Americans) to be an 'American' procedure involving individuals and choice, and not elicitory of their own practices or definitions (Yanagisako 1978: 20).

8 The reference is to Schneider here. I should make it clear that my theoretical interest in the cultural practice of quantification is just that. My colleague David Rheubottom (e.g. 1988) has convinced me that the patterns thrown up by historical demography are as intriguing as one might uncover by other means.

9 In a report submitted to the 1987 Macdonald Enquiry on racial violence in Manchester schools, Elinor Kelly notes that 'English' was by far the hardest term for the researchers to define constructively. It appeared a residual category after all other groups had been eliminated (a set of language, community and religious designations such as Irish, Gujarati, Hindu, Chinese, etc.). I am grateful to Elinor Kelly for permission to cite this work.

10 'New blood' is the antithesis of in-breeding: compare Strathern 1982: 85.

11 According to Rivière (1985: 2), artificial insemination by the husband was first recorded in 1776. I note that the former acronym for artificial insemination by donor (AID) has been replaced by DI (donor insemination).

12 '[The Committee] concluded that whilst it could not condone the practice of artificial insemination using donor semen because clearly it was immoral, it could not prevent it from taking place between consenting adults. Thus the wives of infertile men who were inseminated with donor semen became stigmatized because ... *they were indulging in an unnatural act* in order to conceive a bastard within the institution of marriage' (Pfeffer 1987: 95, my emphasis).

13 See the discussion in Wolfram (1987: 210f). Pfeffer (1987: 97) adds that the 'mercenary image of the infertile, their alleged commodification of parenting, is reinforced by the ways in which the cash nexus has infiltrated the alleviation of infertility. Not only are there now commercial agencies arranging surrogacy [but] ... cuts in funding in the NHS have led many District Health Authorities to cut back on [free] services for the treatment of infertility which they see as an expensive luxury'.

14 In the interwar years, the counterpart fear of homogenisation anticipated an over-exercise of bureaucratic or state control. Machinery, an image of control, was imagined as getting larger and larger, human beings becoming dwarfed as mere cogs in a wheel. A generation on we have dwarfed many of our machines but, by using individual choice to create the outer dimensions of our world, have found a new source for anxiety about homogenisation.

15 A number of the contributors to this last volume set out to allay fears about what might or might not be technologically/medically possible. Ferguson, for instance, points to the way in which the term cloning has been misused in the popular press; while it is possible to take embryonic cells and transplant them across species, and while transgenic animals can now be patented as new life forms, arguments (against experimentation) based on population control through cloning are 'pure fiction' (1990: 23). The reassurance both points to the widespread nature of the fears and is no reassurance about what the barriers of possibility will look like in the future. I should underline the fact that it is the *form* the fears take (the images they engage) that is my interest.

16 This is a particular example of what Sahlins (1985: vii) would argue is a more general case. Not only is history culturally ordered but culture is historically ordered, 'since to a greater or lesser extent ... meanings are revalued as they are practically enacted'. The more things are the same, the more they change.

17 Corrigan and Sayer (1985: 17) remark *of* state forms in England that they display a singular capacity 'to accommodate substantial changes whilst appearing to preserve an unbroken evolutionary line with the past'.

2   Analogies for a plural culture

1 The first 'surrogate' baby in England was born in early 1985, through the assistance of an American agency, and stimulated Powell's private bill [see Chapter One] (Wolfram 1987: 209, 217, n. 13).

2 I subsequently use the phrase 'enabling technology' as a cultural gloss for the perception that technology ought by definition be enabling of the wishes and intentions of persons. In this view, those who see it as disabling 'fail' to appreciate its potential. Thus the view that reproductive technologies are themselves failed technologies has to run counter to the general futuristic assumption that technologies do not 'fail' – they only pass through primitive experimental stages from which they improve. The *Fourth Report of the Voluntary Licensing Authority for Human in vitro Fertilisation and Embryology* (1989) records the following crude rates for all treatment centres per treatment cycle over the period 1985–7:

pregnancy rates 11.2, 9.9, 12.5%; live birth rates 8.6, 8.6, 10.1%. There was a considerable difference in the rates of large and small centres.

'Enabling technology' is used by the European Community's academic programme (New Framework Programme for Science and Technology 1990–4) to demarcate one of three areas of contemporary research interest (Enabling technologies/Management of natural resources/Management of intellectual resources). Under its rubric fall information and communication technologies, industrial and materials technologies. Here technology may thus be 'enabling' of technology.

One might note the increase of 'enabling' legislation, once thought to be constitutionally improper, in the political programme of Thatcherism (McKibbin, *London Review of Books*, 24 May 1990).

3 The words here are adapted from the comments of one of the Press's readers. 'Children who are not bonded to their mothers (not so much is heard about the fate of mothers not bonded to their children), grow up, *à la* John Bowlby, into affectionless and socially disruptive adults' (Oakley 1987: 53). Goldthorpe (1987: 49) reports a comment that when Bowlby's thesis was promulgated, no-one needed convincing of the importance of maternal care, only of the best means to implement it (how to put into practice what one values).

4 I am grateful to Charles Lewis (pers. comm., Reading University) for this reminder. Fathers – and other attendants – may in fact be in a much better position to see the screen at the time than the mother who is on her back. It invites their participatory 'experience'; on the deliberate and explicit promotion of father–infant bonding, see Lewis (1986: 59 and Ch. 7). My own observation refers not to these practices as such but to some of the accompanying cultural interpretations of them.

5 An image of an individual child evokes a relational response on the part of other individuals related to it (that is, the parents), but is not itself an image of that relationship. (The English require a relationship to be visible 'between' persons; a single person cannot represent a relationship. Later in this chapter I consider a Melanesian construction which supposes just this.)

6 'Maternal bonding' is reported to be an outcome of the mother's feelings in the presence of an image of the child; but it is a relationship without interaction, and the mother appears simply as passive spectator. This, I have suggested, contributes to the dissonance Petchesky reports between the evidence of women's strong emotional responses and the voyeuristic scenario as it appears to the outsider of the woman 'passively staring at her objectified foetus' (1987: 71).

7 I refer to the identity of the father rather than his fathering role. On the invisibility of that, see Lewis (1986: Ch. 1). The relationship of paternal invisibility to the absence of biological connection (through childbirth, breast-feeding) is reiterated by G. Smith (1987: 75): 'Unlike a woman, I am not *physically* tied to any one child once conception occurs' (original emphasis).

8 I have since come across Sarah Franklin's observations on what she calls the new genetic essentialism. She notes that the fascination of genetic determinism has roots in beliefs not only about procreation but about human origins. She adds that a 'common-sense ideology of genetic determinism has long been a guarantor of difference and of individuality in Western culture' (1988: 96).

9 I also draw on this analysis in another publication (Strathern 1991). While I extend my interpretations in other directions than Munn's, they derive from her theoretical elucidation of the nature of body, external form and the effects of social interactions.

10 By cultural definition, that is. Contrast the critique in Hobsbawm and Ranger (1983); when it is given a contemporary place, tradition is of course either 'preserved' or 'revived', living by being construed as heritage (Bauman 1990: 435). I hardly need add that it is not only the Melanesian case that underlines the specificity of the English view: Apffel-Marglin (n.d.) reminds one of the Vedic assumption that continuation is not a given of nature but is incessantly constructed by ritual activity. An example of the English assumption I have in mind is offered by the philosopher Simons (1987: 353) who quotes the following remark (from Harré) as *self evident*: 'Enduring is in no need of explanation. We are not required to explain the fact that something remains the same; only if there is a change is explanation called for.' The first sentence is in italics in the original.

11 In inseminating his wife, the husband makes her breastmilk from his semen (Godelier 1986: 52).

12 I extrapolate from Godelier's analysis of Baruya imagery. Indirect justification for this extrapolation is given in an interpretation of a related society, Sambia (see Strathern 1988: Ch. 8 and Ch. 9, after Herdt 1981, 1987).

13 Hence the emphasis given to arguments about the *potential* of an embryo to become an individual (person) (e.g. Harris 1990).

14 On Massim mortuary rituals, see Damon and Wagner (1989); on the importance of having to erase individual memory, see Battaglia (1990).

15 The Molima of the Massim do not embark on full mourning until the signal is given on a conch shell by one of the attendants that the deceased's soul has departed to the land of the dead. This is some hours after 'death', when preparations for the funeral begin, during which close kin must weep only softly and other mourners should desist (Chowning 1989: 103). If mourners weep too soon, their tears may flood the road to the land of the dead, and they (so to speak) prevent him or her fully dying.

16 Hockey and James argue that since medical advances have made the survival of children more certain than in the past, 'children can now more surely symbolise the future than at any other time. For elderly people, however, medical advances ... have simply meant that *more* people live to an old age ... The age at which death occurs has not changed significantly' (n.d., original emphasis). They suggest that the infantilisation of the elderly is a response to this dilemma: the thought of death is avoided, especially by the carers, through drawing parallels with children. On the adoption of motherhood as the role model for the (female) carer, see also Ungerson (1983, 1987).

   While what happens at the beginning of life is thus brought in as a metaphor for the end, there are also obvious asymmetries. One is of particular interest for my present argument about the downward flow of English time, obligation and identity. At the beginning of life, children do not just need carers, they also need (it is held) carers in the specific kin relationship of parent and above all a mother; as was noted earlier in the chapter, the mother provides emotional as well as physical support. While the child is encouraged to grow up in both senses, and finally away from its dependence on his parents, specific kin thus provide a crucial environment at the start of life. At the end of life, however, the elderly and infirm are held to need carers to provide physical and emotional comforts, but there is not the same felt need for the carers to be kin nor the assumption that damage will be done if they are not attended by their children. This leads one to reflect that the earlier parenting of the child constitutes acts which do not just belong to the relationship between parent and child but belong also to the development of the (to-be-independent) individual. This lays the ground for the fact that any expectation that a child will care for its parents can be compromised by the independence of the child, and the often reciprocated desire for independence on the part of the elderly relative (Finch 1989: 38–9).

17 A critique J. Goody (1983) himself offers in relation to terms such as 'clan' and 'lineage', objecting to how they are sometimes used for European materials. Earlier, however, and as far as mortuary practices are concerned, Goody (1962) embedded his description of the Lodagaa from West Africa in a running comparison with early European practices; the Lodagaa disposition of property seems similar to Western modes of inheritance in that inheritance itself comes to have its own rationality (holders must ultimately divest themselves of property to their heirs). But what appears to be taken apart at death is a very different kind of social person from the English holder of property. Goody makes it clear that Lodagaa mortuary ceremonies are ultimately concerned with the reallocation of the deceased's rights and duties among members of the community (1962: 274). In effect, they disperse the social person – in the case of a man his offices, roles, rights in others, activities represented in the handing over of his tools, and his potential for transactions represented in other assets. It seems to me that the English person is not seen as constituted by kin relationships in such a way that death means a reallocation of rights and duties. On the contrary, those rights and duties terminate. They were part of his/her individual presence; if connections endure, it is in memory of the deceased or because absence creates a need such as care of dependants or a debt to be settled. Above all, English rules of inheritance are axiomatic, and only by an extension of his or her 'will' does the deceased affect the subsequent disposition of property – and then as a matter of wish or choice, not as a matter of having to de-assemble and reassemble his or her 'roles' (relationships).

18 Consequently, 'descent abolishes the relevance of the difference [discontinuity] between the dead and the living. This is essential to the notion of a descent group, in that the existence of such an enduring entity depends on a succession of *substitutive* generations' (Bloch 1987: 327, my emphasis). Carsten (n.d.) has demonstrated the retrospective creation of consanguinity between grandparents on the birth of grandchildren for the Malaysian Langkawi.

19 A point he qualifies by adding the 'inheritance' of surnames as 'patrilineal' (*sic*). The terminology of cognation is disputed among anthropologists (e.g. Barnard and Good 1984: 71). For a critique of Fox's usage, see Wolfram (1987: 189–90).

20 Persons may in their lifetime maintain gardens on both father's and mother's land, but rights to hamlet land pass at death through women only. Those related to the deceased through female ties become the 'workers' at burial.

21 Mereology is an established department of philosophical enquiry; my thanks to Gillian Beer who first introduced me to the term. To set it apart, I anglicise my neologism 'merographic' by analogy with the biological term meroblast. *Meros*, Greek, 'part' or 'share'. *Graphic*, since the issue is the way ideas write or describe one another; the very act of description makes what is being described a part of something else, e.g. the description.

The neologism is intended as a substantive cultural (Western) exemplification of the interplay between literal and figurative constructions (see Wagner 1977b; and below, Recapitulation, note 5). Anthropologists have conventionally treated such constructions through theories of metaphor and symbolic process.

But the neologism does not necessarily imply invention. I have not, for instance, paid proper attention to the Derridean notion of 'supplementation', though no doubt it prefigures much of what I have to say here. Culler (1979: 168) points out an originating reference in Rousseau's observation that education supplements nature: the 'concept of nature [becomes] both something complete in itself, to which education is an addition, and something incomplete, or insufficient, which must be supplemented by education for it to be truly itself... The logic of supplementarity thus makes nature the prior term, a plenitude which was there at the start, but reveals an inherent lack of absence within it and makes education something external and extra but also an essential condition of that which it supplements.'

22 A mereological part, by contrast, is commonly taken as a part made up of what makes up the whole (e.g. branch of a tree). As for merography, it might seem that any range of phenomena can be diagrammed as so many intersecting circles (by definition, of meaning etc), like the Venn diagrams Edmund Leach made familiar to anthropologists. So it might, as long as this does not obscure the cultural bias. This rests in the (Western) apperception that persons work to bring into *relationship* with one another whole different *orders* of phenomena, as different ways of knowing the world and as different perspectives on it.

23 See the discussion in Barnett and Silverman (1979: 41, 63, etc.) which follows a similar reasoning *apropos* the dual conceptualisation of an individual person being dominated by other individuals or else by external forces.

24 'Our propensity to "biologize" human life-history may in part be due to a rather fundamental tendency in Western thought to locate the mainsprings of social behaviour in the inherent nature of autonomous individuals' (Ingold 1986: 160).

25 My observation has to be offered naively, but such a naturalistic assumption seems to lie (for instance) behind Simon's distinction between proper overlapping and other forms of overlap between individual entities. Proper overlapping, where individuals overlap without being parts of each other is, he suggests, an uneasy concept perhaps because it is 'connected with its abnormality for human beings' (1987: 12). In his view, most human beings are disjoint from one another; the mother–foetus case where, he avers, individuals overlap without one being part of the other, is a routine exception!

26 Or else are left as some indeterminate referential 'field'. Firth, Hubert and Forge strikingly refer to kinship as a field of relations, an area divided into 'lots' in the idiom of one informant. 'The ideology of kinship in its moral aspect is not a series of one-to-one relationships, each with its separate moral content, but a constellation in which the moral responsibility of each party is regarded as relative to that of others in the field' (1969: 113, emphasis removed). Cf. Cheal (1988: 168), who insists that 'the social order of mass society consists of a plurality of interrelated, and *irreducible*, systems of social organisation' (original emphasis).

27 Goody's (1983: Appendices I, III) critique of the conventional classification of Western European kinship systems makes the point that kin terms have for centuries stressed the distinct (unitary) nature of the nuclear or conjugal family. The conjugal family is itself only 'bilateral' by virtue of an extension of reference beyond it ('the range of kin traced through fathers and mothers', 1983: 223).

28 Johnson (1989: 94) suggests that numerous techniques are in fact used in American kinship to define a person as a relative. The part that choice ('friendship') plays in the perception of relationships is significant – Johnson's point being that this cannot be relegated to the person-centred system. The issue would have to be argued, however, in terms not of normative 'flexibility' but of categorical incompleteness.

29 And the shading off noted above thus has a special character to it that one cannot

assume is necessarily similar to the 'continuum of relatedness' (Carsten 1990: 272) from close to distant kin routinely reported of bilateral systems elsewhere in the world.

30 What Schneider calls the universe of relatives in American kinship 'is constructed of elements from two major cultural orders, the order of nature and the order of law' (1968: 27, emphasis omitted). [From another perspective] 'it is the order of law, that is, culture which resolves contradictions between man and nature, which are contradictions within nature itself' (1968: 109). Gellner ((1963) 1987: 182, emphasis omitted) writes: '[A]n area in which society and nature overlap conspicuously, or seem to, is kinship'.

31 This does not of course distinguish 'kinship' from any other social domain. Taking Gellner's point that kinship as anthropologists understand it consists in the relationship between (socially possible) biological relations and the social systems built up after these, one might look for a Melanesian analogue in terms of procreative practice. We would recognise 'kinship' relations by their reference to a reproductive model of social life.

32 My thanks to Janet Carsten for drawing attention to the Geertzs' early discussion of teknonymy in Bali. Their interest is in the manner in which teknonymy erases the memory of preceding genealogical ties. Consider also that in the parent being named after the child, the parent is thus 'produced' by the child. Hence the Geertzs' observation for Bali that it is not who one's ancestor is that is stressed but whom one is ancestor to (1964: 105). I add that Lévi-Strauss's (1966: 195) interpretation of the phenomenon of the couvade is not that the father plays the part of the mother but that he plays the part of the child.

3   The progress of polite society

1 These details come from the commentary by Mingay which accompanies the publication of Diana Sperling's drawings (1981). The book came into my possession as a gift, and I am grateful to Nigel Rapport for the pleasure it has given.

2 Charles Darwin needed a trope for the organisation of natural relations ('kinship'); each term had to define the other. The analogy itself was already in place in the literature, poetry and philosophising of the eighteenth century. But the work it was then made to do differs. When two generations earlier Erasmus Darwin refers to the natural world as 'the whole is one family of one parent', he is drawing attention to a Creator who has 'stamped a certain similitude on the features of nature' (quoted in McNeil 1986: 171). Conversely, the Creator is understood as Nature itself. Here is Joseph Priestley writing in 1777 (A Course of Lectures in Oratory and Criticism) as cited by McNeil (1986: 198–19, emphasis removed; my emphasis substituted). His disquisition is on the use of personification as a device to make the non-human world intelligible to the human.

> As the sentiments and actions of our fellow-creatures are more interesting to us than anything belonging to inanimate nature ... a much greater variety of sensations and ideas must have been excited by them and consequently adhere to them by the principles of association. Hence it is of prodigious advantage in treating of inanimate things ... to introduce frequent allusions to human actions and sentiments, *where any resemblance will make it natural*. This converts everything we treat of into thinking and acting beings. We see life, sense, intelligence everywhere.

3 The definition of 'family' as a 'course of descent, a genealogy' did not appear in Johnson's dictionary till the 1758 edition. An explicit recognition of the family as a

'community of descent' is linked to the increasing 'rhetoric of genealogy and rank to label newly acquired social positions as traditional and natural' in the late eighteenth century (Handler and Segal 1990: 32).

4 Schapera (1977: 17) observes the manner in which certain affines could be considered 'connections' even if they did not have to be treated as 'relatives'. However, the latter term is here Schapera's, and the contrast is to some extent given by his use of it as an analytical category.

5 From one's own perspective, however, it was also desirable to marry a superior – respecting nature while improving on it. The authors observe that Austen's characters do not so much assign one another to discrete ranks as discourse endlessly upon its effects, thereby evaluating one another in terms of a dual distinction between the low, vulgar, servile and the civil, genteel, elegant.

6 '[S]ocial mobility ... must be understood as an internal, dialectical feature of the hierarchical system' (Handler and Segal 1990: 52). They add (n. 6) 'This suggests that the rise of the bourgeoisie [was not a new historical element of social life, but] an immanent feature of the aristocratic order'.

7 I am not talking of living conditions; to paraphrase Ray Pahl's aphorism about villages, the phenomenon in question could be called 'cottages in the mind'.

8 Along with its separation from work came a gendering of 'the home'. Talking of writers of the mid-nineteenth century, Davidoff and Hall (1987: 181) say:

> Mrs. Ellis ... does not ... write about a whole society peopled by both men and women. Her advice books and novels assume a world in which the domestic sphere is occupied by women, children and servants, with men as the absent presence, there to direct and command but physically occupied elsewhere for most of their time. Similarly, Harriet Martineau assumes a world divided between political economy and domestic economy ... It was recognized that men would be preoccupied with business, and domesticity had become the 'woman's sphere' rather than, as it is for Cowper, a way of living for both men and women.

9 Speaking of change, Maine (1870: 168) says: 'Everywhere a new morality has displaced the canons of conduct and the reasons of acquiescence which were in unison with the ancient usages, because in fact they were born of them.' Such a relative view of society is not, of course, locally English. Trautmann (1987: 187) also cites a paragraph from Fustel de Coulange's *Le cité antique*, published in 1864. 'If the laws of human association are no longer the same as in antiquity, it is because there has been a change in man. There is, in fact, a part of our being which is modified from age to age; this is our intelligence. It is always in movement; almost always progressing; and on this account, our institutions and our laws are subject to change.' He adds that, like Maine, de Coulange writes to undo the French Revolution.

10 And of childhood. See David Morgan's (1985: 163f) contextualisation of sociological interest in this field.

11 For instance, Martin's (1987: Ch. 2) analysis of the American counterpart to these ideas.

12 The evocation of sensibility in this respect has a long history. McNeil (1986: 197) cites the poet James Thomson for whom it is the contemplation of nature which will evoke and thus constitute the capacity for contemplation itself. 'Thomson's *Seasons* (first completed version 1730) represented a new direction for nature poetry. Its main concern and presumption was that each individual's relationship with nature was vital. For Thomson, nature was the primary focus of human life and of poetry: 'I know no subject more elevating, more amusing, more ready to

evoke the poetical enthusiasm, the poetical reflection and the moral sentiment, than the works of Nature."' Mark Akenside contended in 1744 'that Newton's description of the rainbow actually intensified the human experience of this part of nature' (McNeil 1986: 168). Nature developed people's sensibilities.

13 For instance, in *Grundrisse*, published in 1858. Society is conceptualised as the capacity for and precipitate of social relations, a condition that some latter-day anthropologists recognise in the term 'sociality'. It indicates association and interaction between persons, and a source of value for their labours, without the twentieth-century connotations of morphology or structure ('organisation').

14 Williams also states (1961: 148, his emphasis): 'This position was necessarily a fundamental challenge to the nineteenth-century system of production, and to the "laws of political economy" which supported it ... In asserting [a wholly different social judgement] Ruskin was also, necessarily, asserting the idea of a social *order*. At the root of all his thinking is his idea of "function" – the fulfilment of each man's part in the general design.'

15 The phrase refers here in the first place to vital beauty (quoted in Williams 1961: 145).

16 And was partly achieved through a recovery of the laws of political economy that Ruskin had rejected, with a reinterpretation of productive life as social formation.

17 Organicism was not simply a metaphor borrowed from physiology: it had long served to describe human institutions and the wholeness of human life. It was now, so to speak, renaturalised in order to convey the inevitability of an internally regulated system.

18 Fortes attributes to both Morgan and Maine what he finds lacking in Tylor (the idea of a social system). Yet I suspect that Morgan at least uses 'system' in the sense of tabulated or otherwise arranged taxa rather than in the structural–functional sense of a set of principles which interact upon one another, for this needed the intervening image of 'structural form'. We may note that Morgan found system in nature. Morgan's 'system of nature' is presented by Trautmann thus (1987: 137, original emphasis removed, my emphasis substituted): 'The links of kindred are never broken, but the streams of descent perpetually diverge from one another ... "*This self-existing system*, which may be called the numerical, is theoretically the system of nature; and, as such, is taught to all the families of mankind by natural suggestion. It specializes each relationship, and indicates, with more or less distinctness, a generalization into classes of all such persons as stand in the same degree of nearness to the central Ego."'

19 From *Elementary Forms of Religious Life*, 1912. The remarks are quoted with approval by Corrigan and Sayer (1985: 9), who give the concept of moral authority new life in their account of English state formation as cultural revolution. Cf. Bell (1914: 288): '[b]ecause no two ages express their sense of form in precisely the same way all attempts to recreate the forms of another age must sacrifice emotional expression to imitative address'.

20 In laying out 'the structure of the Andamanese society' (1964: 22), Radcliffe-Brown turned first to local and family groups. He later distinguished 'social structure' (manifest relations) from their supposedly abstract 'structural form', as he also distinguished individual from person.

21 And, personified, may 'do' things (see Metcalfe [1987: 78] *apropos* the personification of classificatory categories). 'If any society establishes a system of corporations on the basis of kinship – clans, joint-families, incorporated lineages – it must necessarily adopt a system of unilineal reckoning of succession' wrote Radcliffe-Brown in 1935 (1952: 46). Structure has needs: 'the existence of unilineal

... succession ... can be traced to ... certain fundamental social necessities', such as the need for a precise formulation of rights over persons or the need for the continuity of social structure itself (1952: 47).

22 An example of a structural principle is the manner in which persons trace their relationships to one another through an apical ancestor ('descent'). He gave as a simple instance 'the cognatic principle' (1950: 13).

23 This was another solution to Darwin's problem of personification, insofar as the awkward analogies between nature and society were resolved in the idea that the individual was a hinge to both. The awkwardness had antecedents in the explicit questions people asked about the analogy itself. I quote from Jordanova (1986: 39, original emphasis): 'eighteenth- and nineteenth-century writers also questioned the unity, coherence and goodness of nature. Increasingly, nature appeared full of contradictions, tensions and ambiguities ... By the 1780s, the idea that the natural world contained unambiguous ethical prescriptions was coming to seem naive, at least in some circles. Nature was simultaneously taken as a theatre of human affairs, in a deliberate and celebratory anthropomorphism, and as containing dramas which repel or disgust the human spectator. The parallelism between human social life and the natural world could also take a more abstract form ... Ideas like division of labour, progress and hierarchy appeared to have equal explanatory power in both realms. This raises the question of metaphor – was it that society and nature were *like* each other, that is, linked through a metaphorical language, or was it rather that they were different aspects of the *same* thing for which only one language was needed. social phenomena being merely more complex organic ones?'

24 From one point of view it looks as though this turn of the century moment simply repeats another. The following comes from a review of MacIntyre's *Which Justice? Which Rationality?* (Duckworth):

> It was the late 17th century according to MacIntyre that saw a transformation of the view of the task of moral philosophy. The idea that there could and would be a diversity of views about the good took hold and political theory began to centre on the practical issue of how people with these diverse conceptions might live together. It is in this context that 'the individual' emerges as a fundamental social category – individuals as prior to and apart from their membership in any particular social and political order. The question for political philosophy was set then and continues to be: why should this isolated individual conform to any particular social order? Why should the individual obey the state? For *this* question, neither the ancient answer – that the individual already has an assigned social role within the *polis* – nor the medieval answer – that the order of things is laid down by God – was available as a solution. The question remains, then: 'how can someone moved only by self-interest be motivated to obey the principles of justice?' (Brenda Almond, *The Times Higher Educational Supplement*, 14 October 88, original emphasis).

Yet the question does not really remain in that form. While the 'new' twentieth-century plurality of viewpoints (ethnicisation) seems to have precipitated a similar refashioning of the individual, the assumptions are not the same. The central issue is not that of 'obedience' (to a state which could be personified in its king or legislative assembly) but of 'the relationship' between the individual person on the one hand and society on the other, when society is refashioned as an organisation and system whose authority extends to the very moulding of cultural values and personal attitudes themselves.

25 An example no doubt at the back of Fortes' mind when he generalises about the way the differentiation of persons in the domestic domain feeds into the structure

of the unilineal descent group, this being more (he says) than just a matter of physical recruitment (1958: 6).

26 From the moment of its birth, in this view, a baby embarks on a struggle: between being moulded by all the forces of convention that will turn it into a schoolchild, adult, engineer or whatever, and realising itself as an individual, with its own personality, tastes and skill and successes in life. The one is played off against the other, so that the best institutions are those which 'allow' the individual to 'express' him or herself. Hence we make very little of the fact that the (biological) capacity to be a parent is already within the child: rather, we distinguish different processes. The child must both naturally mature and culturally learn what parenting is – and thus do parents evince convention [Chapter One].

27 For a recent Anglo/American formulation, see Paul (1987: 80):

> One of the enduring differences of opinion among anthropologists . . . concerns the degree to which society is understood to be an entity in itself, with some power to determine the behaviour of its constituent members, as opposed to a position according to which society is nothing other than the product of the summed behaviour of a number of individuals . . . [From] Holy and Stuchlik (1983: 2): 'If society . . . is an objective reality to whose demands people respond in specific ways, then it is an autonomous agency and individual people are its agents, and the only acceptable explanation is in terms of the functioning of the system. If, on the other hand, society . . . emerges from, and is maintained or changed only by what people do, then individuals are autonomous agents and systems are consequences of their actions and, in the last instances, explicable by them.'

4   Greenhouse effect

1 See note 2, Chapter 2.

2 I am aware that such phrasing lifted out of context could seem offensive to proprietors who, of course, run their own homes and enjoy family life. Perhaps this is a point at which again to make explicit my own concern with imagery. The way in which the image of the 'home' is presented to the paying visitor is not isomorphic with such 'home' as the residents may also construct for themselves. The proprietor's home is, of course, likely to bear more resemblance to the homes their visitors have left 'at home'. I should also make explicit that in a number of places I write with affection, indeed have gone out of my way to select for consideration cultural imagery that comes from areas of life I value, as well as those I do not.

3 The remark should be juxtaposed to what I take to be very different Melanesian assumptions. Two examples which show the facility to keep scale between analogies may help. (1) If the tree growing on clan land that will be cut into a canoe is for the people of Gawa simultaneously the mother and the child she carries, that idea is suggested by colour marking and by verbal reference, as Munn (1986) describes, but the image itself is allowed to form in the mind. You do not go and *carve* the tree into a likeness of a mother: it remains with these images 'inside'. Consequently the tree is a tree while it is also a canoe, a mother, a descent group or whatever is being drawn from it. Any one of these possibilities may be hidden again. (2) The men of Mt Hagen show inner wealth by decorating their outer persons: that inner capacity brought outside, made visible, is then hidden again in the recesses of the house, underneath the dirty apparel of everyday work: what is exposed returns to an original position within. Inside and outside can be seen as equivalent analogies or reciprocal inversions of each other. Much Melanesian ceremonial concerns the momentary nature of revelation, for revelation can never be a permanent state of affairs.

4 The image of the penetrating eye has been much discussed; with respect to anthropological knowledge, see Fabian (1983), to its gender connotations, see Jordanova (1989). (Perhaps it is of no surprise that such perspectival imagery is nowadays displaced by other imaginings, for example in 'visuals' which do not represent what can be seen (such as fractal graphics) or through 'measurements' conceived as 1,000 times smaller than the micron (*The Coming Era of Nanotechnology* is the title of a work by K. E. Drexler, Fourth Estate, 1990).)

5 Thus an attempt by Fortes to describe the analogous fields of politico-jural and domestic domains in a non-Western context is understood merographically in one recent commentary: Goldthorpe (1987: 7) takes Fortes' 'domestic field, viewed from within as an internal system' to be 'the psycho-social interior of the family'.

6 Rapport (n.d.2) develops an intriguing contrast between British 'social pluralism' and American 'cultural pluralism'.

7 The English habitually contrasted themselves with Americans here, of whom they supposed that money provided a single scale of measurement.

8 For example, Barrett and McIntosh (1982: 91): 'An analysis couched in terms of contradictions is certainly more satisfactory than a complacent evocation of tidy functional relationships. We need to ask, however, whether such contradictions are generated within the dynamic of capitalist production relations or whether they are a consequence of perceiving the family as a unified category.'

9 Note that Darwin had to work from a situation in which civilisation – rank and class – was already in place. His concern was to extend an ancestry that would reveal common origins lying beyond the inequalities of social worth. The contrast Ingold (1986: 59f) draws between him and Morgan is suggestive. Their evolutionary perspectives, he says, took off from quite different vantage points. Darwin was concerned to 'downgrade' man while Morgan wanted to 'upgrade' animals. Ingold cites what Morgan was supposed to have learnt from Darwin (but misunderstood), a view of man as commencing at the bottom of the scale and working himself up to his present status, whereas Darwin's scale was in fact bottomless, extending back into the lower animal kingdoms. Darwin talks about natural forces; Morgan talks about the purposeful 'working up' of man's present position as the result of 'the struggles, the sufferings, the heroic exertions and the patient toil' of his ancestors (quoted 1986: 62). Of course, one cannot match this difference with a simple contrast between England and America, even though one *English* view of Americans is that they are all 'self-made'. After all, Morgan's view was also close to Tylor's, that the development of the arts takes place by skill and effort. In the English case, however, any claim to privilege must negotiate pre-existing class identity – whether of the aristocracy or the masses.

10 Not having a communicable view on events has 'always' been true of minority groups. The difference is that we have vastly multiplied the number of such minorities – ethnicising this or that characteristic into a special case. A phenomenon of the last decade has been the appearance of public advertisements by charitable organisations that bring particular physical and mental disabilities to people's attention, simultaneously creating a minority perception of the deaf or rheumatic and appealing to the public to treat them 'as persons'. But a further difference lies in the prevalent value given to communication. Jencks (1987: 44) refers to the new para-class as the cognitariat, those who live on passing on information.

11 One of the forms in which the quotations appeared, purportedly in a BBC interview. A version quoted in a New Right debate on television in mid-1988 went:

'Who is society? There is no such thing. There are individuals and families.' On this programme the opinion was also offered that individualism was our tradition and there was no single national community. A further note is in order: with the change of regime in late 1990 appears to have come a reinstatement of society. But Major's 'society of opportunity' has nothing *social* about it. As I note, the backpedalling began almost as soon as Thatcher finished her utterance. That it should have been uttered at all is what interests me.

12 I say 'we' because Thatcher was simply speeding up a common devolution of ideas. Anthropological conceptualisations of society are also implicated, as in the following statement, from an American but in the tradition of the Englishman Spencer. The subject is Kluckhohn's 1949 distinction between society and culture. 'Since culture is an abstraction, it is important not to confuse culture with society. A "society" refers to a group of people who interact more with each other than they do with other individuals – who co-operate with each other for the attainment of certain ends. *You can see and indeed count the individuals* who make up a society. A "culture" refers to the distinctive ways of life of such a group of people' (quoted in Ingold 1986: 236, my emphasis). Note that what emerges as visible and concrete is not society but the individuals who make it up.

13 This has been a sore point with apologists for the New Right: what meaning can be given to the idea of active citizenship when there is no *corresponding* promulgation of an idea of community or body to which the citizen, so-called, belongs? The anti-monarchical connotations of 'citizen' have not been lost on the Opposition (e.g. David Marquand of the SLDP writing in *The Guardian*, 2 January 1989).

14 As their argument about the bourgeois 'right to choose' shows, what makes the exercise of alternatives desirable in the above case is the fact that the family is already in place: 'the family' is an ideological construct and when we consider debates on '"its place in society", "its historical development" and "its relationship to capitalism" we have to look at the extent to which the analyses are themselves constituted in political and ideological terms' (Barrett and McIntosh 1982: 85).

15 Suppose, he says (1985: 114), 'modern art and modernism – far from being a kind of specialized aesthetic curiosity – actually anticipated social developments along these lines; suppos[e] that in the decades since the emergence of the great modern styles society has itself begun to fragment in this way, each group coming to speak a curious private language of its own, each profession developing its private code or idiolect, and finally each individual coming to be a kind of linguistic island'.

16 '[A] signifier that has lost its signified has thereby been transformed into an image' (Jameson 1985: 120).

17 And thus 'logical' and 'rational' (for that domain). The constructions are in this sense figurative (Ch. 2, note 21). On the rhetoric of rationality in self-referential models, see Mirowski (1990). In animating the concepts referred to in this paragraph, I am of course pointing to their effects, that is, the conventional understanding of (other) phenomena entailed in their usage.

18 The 1830s cholera epidemics that forced people to take account of the interrelationships between different aspects of life had a similar effect in France (Rabinow 1989: 15): 'medical commissions produced a detailed statistical analysis of the relationships of social class, housing, and disease'. The increased use of numbers in solving social problems, as he says, led eventually to the concept of statistical norms, that is, norms intrinsic or 'natural' to the society in question. (Rabinow (1989: 66) describes Quetelet's precocious insistence in 1833 that the

only way to study individuals was to take them as indications of general population characteristics; hence his formula of the 'average man'.)

19 Thus Douglas Hurd, then Home Secretary, allegedly first used the phrase 'active citizen' in a speech in February 1988 in the context of urging people to take an interest in 'the community' and restore 'the amazing social cohesion' (!) of Victorian England. But whatever community or cohesion might exist, the Government does not symbolise it. 'The first instinct of the active citizen', said Hurd, 'should *not* be to apply for a Government grant' (*The Guardian*, 9 November 1988, original emphasis).

20 A phrase used by the Nuer of the Sudan to underline their own insignificance in God's eye (Evans-Pritchard 1940: 12).

21 Lord Young of Graffham, then Secretary of State for Trade and Industry and head of the Enterprise Policy Unit, was speaking in 1989 at a conference on 'The Values of the Enterprise Culture' (see Heelas and Morris 1991). In his own view, the present mandate is to restore 'the Age of the Individual' that between 1870–1970 has been overshadowed by the state. As he put it, private enterprise should subsume public responsibility.

22 The elision between role and property – both involving 'rights' that persons exercise *vis-à-vis* others – should be understood in the context of a changing series of conceptualisations about property and propriety that extends back beyond the compass I have chosen for myself here. I note just one notable English contribution to the Enlightenment: Locke's idea that no man could be proprietor of another. Then the reason lay in neither Society nor Nature but God. Only God as the Supreme Proprietor owned men, and he owned all men. Men only 'owned' one another's labour as a service bought and sold: the products of work are separate from the will to work, and that will could only be exercised by the individual before God.

23 It is unlikely that Thatcher meant family in terms of a ramifying set of networks or anything like a 'family of man' between people across the globe; the statement has been taken as obviously referring to nuclear families of the English type.

24 Hence perhaps the topsy-turvy status of public funding in Britain in the late 1980s. There is an unprecedented central intervention in the conduct ('accountability') of those who receive public funds. The person visibly dependent on public funding (and I include employees of state institutions as well as recipients of public benefit) is compromised in a way that one dependent on private funding is not. Those who receive public funds in effect lose individuality.

25 Cf. Haraway (1985: 88). The new communications eradicate public life: modern society produces 'private life'. But what is public and what is private has itself become problematic.

26 That idea, that people make relations/people make society, is itself the precondition for this move. (It is the same idea as that peculiar notion that people have a relationship with society.) In Melanesia, people make people; people do not 'make relations'. Relations, already in place, are made to appear.

27 He was interested in how essentially identical facilities provided by the local council had been differently utilised by the occupants (1988: 356), and in how as consumers people appropriated commodities to create an inalienable sense of 'being at home'.

28 He writes (1988: 64) that this has consequences for social policy: 'social policy should be related to the *actual needs* of people in their lives as lived and that their lives should be conceived of as *unities* not disparate segments of education, health, income or social work needs' (original emphasis).

29 One such collectivity of purpose is acted out in Norwegian working-class families
    through constant attention to 'doing up [decorating] the home [house]' (Gullestad
    1984: Ch. 5). Home seems to have a self-defining emphasis in Scandinavian culture
    that goes beyond the English: see for instance Frykman and Löfgren (1987: Ch. 3).
30 A similar contrast is made by Bauman who notes the shift from the (modern) idea
    of state society as the environment for goal-achievement to the (postmodern)
    concept of community. The old setting 'derived its solidity from the presence of
    mutually reinforcing, coordinated and overlapping agencies [domains] of integ-
    ration' (such as economic system, body politic) while communities are 'grounded in
    their activities only' (1988: 800).
31 BBC 2, *Horizon*, 'Signs of Life', 11 June 1990 (film by John Wyver). It noted that
    artificial life researchers have turned traditional biology on its head. 'Instead of
    analysing living things by taking them apart, they are using computers to simulate
    simple organisms' (from accompanying booklet). The new metaphor builders!
32 Ulmer is discussing Derrida's concept of mime ('mimicry imitating nothing').
33 It is not that we did not 'consume' nature in the past, but that the image of the
    consumer has come to dominate late twentieth-century representations of the
    relationship between nature and its social or cultural despoliation.
34 For me the date is precise: between writing the first and second drafts of this book.
    What was initially in circulation as a doomsday image, hardly to be taken seriously,
    turned into the language of public discussion over the course of 18 months.
35 Another, related, answer is given by Franklin (n.d.) who locates the desire of
    infertile couples to procreate in what she calls a modern and 'very British'
    narrative: the scientific discovery of the facts of nature. Couples are invited to
    understand their experience as a contribution to scientific progress.
36 The context for this statement is admirable (a critique of the insufficiencies of
    provisions for the disabled): it is the utterability of the sentiment that is intriguing.
    Hicks says that the choice should not be between dependency and being
    independent, but for interdependence. From where, then, do we find the language
    for interdependence?
37 Gallagher, concerned to restore a balance to the debate about embryo rights and
    the new technologies, comments that as feminists we 'have to learn better to avoid
    the media caricature of feminism that ignores our carefully wrought and balanced
    agendas. We need to project a vision that addresses the whole range of women's
    reproductive experiences, to publicly associate ourselves with affirmative proposals
    and demands supportive of a woman's choice to become a mother' (1987: 145). I
    simply draw attention to how the debate is constituted by the problematic status of
    'choice' as one of its key terms. No wonder the sperm bank established by Robert
    Graham in the States was called 'Repository for Germinal Choice' (Spallone 1987:
    31).
38 Rapp (1988; 1989) reports on the new responsibility taken on themselves by
    members of the medical profession to ensure that mothers *do* exercise choice. She
    refers to the process as one of privatisation: such choice is supposed to be
    something one can exercise in isolation, with only counsellors to help.
39 Rowland continues (original emphasis, 1987: 70): 'with the intensification of male
    power inside the home comes the greater demand for a father's *rights* but not
    necessarily a parallel increase in his *responsibilities*'.
40 Helman points to the imagery of difference mediated through the englobing and
    rejecting processes of a body in relation to the 'foreign bodies' that invade it. The
    language of xenophobia and transplant surgery mix. Emily Martin (n.d.) examines

a similar range of metaphors concerning the militaristic representation of the immune system.

41 Thus when Rapport (n.d.l) defines the multiplicity of viewpoints which E. M. Forster sustains in *Howards End*, he points out that 'Forster foresaw connectedness in the form of an intermediary (a participant–observer) making repeated excursions between separate realms, domains or entities, and drawing comparisons by coming to terms with *the regularities of life* practised by each as he interprets them' (my emphasis). This is the merographic amalgam of pluralism. A postplural world has 'lost' this mathematics insofar as it can no longer enumerate such different domains. What looks like a breach of outworn dichotomies ('the old oppositions – science versus art, fact versus fiction, Left versus Right, high culture versus low culture, mass culture versus "progressive" modern art and so on – no longer hold' (Hebdige 1989: 49)) in fact breaches the facility to perceive social life as made up of countless (i.e. potentially countable) discrete logics and 'separate realms'.

42 Petchesky (1987: 63, reference omitted) quotes an article by Sofia in *Diacritics* (1984): '"In science fiction culture particularly, technologies are perceived as modes of reproduction in themselves" ... The 'Star Child' of *2001* is not a living organic being but "a biomechanism ... a cyborg capable of living unaided in space". This "child" poses as the symbol of fertility and life but in fact is the creature of the same technologies that bring cosmic extermination, which it alone survives.'

43 One feminist–anthropological critique (Kirby 1989: 13–14) refers to Derrida's economy of *différance*, the transference onto an other of all that is residual to the One/Referent, as the solution to difference in a binary mode. 'It is this flickering "in-between" ... of content and form, interiority and exteriority, surface and depth, an oscillation that urges a continual revaluation of each against the other until the disjunctions become blurred and ambiguous, that discovers a "third term" that escapes and somehow betrays the system.' But such a vision also contains its own nostalgia for plurality, for it encourages 'the proliferation of a multiplicity of readings/meanings such that the "truth" of any one perspective might be rendered ambiguous, parasitic, relational'. A postplural world does not deal in perspectives. It knowingly appropriates alterity: 'We do not sell; we make people want to buy' (John Hegarty, Advertiser, interview with Michael Ignatieff, BBC 2, 8 January 1988 (programme: *Three Minute Culture*)).

Recapitulation: nostalgia from a postplural world

1 His qualification should be entered.

> When I say 'American' I do not mean ... the type of social American who lives in New York or Paris. I am not thinking either of the lonely, home-sick American whom we encounter on his travels abroad, and who is apt from lack of self-assurance to render his manners too emphatic. I am not referring to American big business which is to me wearisome and incomprehensible. Still less do I have in mind the political manager who encourages the fiction that it is unprofitable to differ from the average; that it is un-American to manifest intellectual or aesthetic distinction or to be interested in thoughts or feelings that are beyond the range of the common man. The best heads America possesses have always been her egg-heads. The type that I esteem is ... the calm scholar who preserves all that is most venerable in the tradition of the founding fathers. (1955: 285)

2 I owe these remarks to another gift, Ottesen's book, and thank Mary McConnell.

The reference here is to the Introduction that Frank Waugh from the Massachusetts Agricultural College wrote to a volume on *Foundation Planting* (1927). One of his own works (1917) was called *The Natural Style in Landscape Gardening*.

3 It follows that whatever model of 'private industry' America might offer, it cannot provide a model for the present and radical English spate of 'privatisation', simply because American private industry is already there. If we have produced a version of American individualism, we have produced it English-style.

4 And individuals as containing unique personalities and emotions (1975: 79).

5 'When the actor's intention is focused upon "relating", he will perceive his action as a transformation of discrete phenomenal entities into a consistent relational pattern' (Wagner 1977b: 391). All human activity may be analysed into both literal and figurative (non-referential) components, each of which acts as a context for the other, Wagner argues, but different world views support different modalities of the conventional. For Westerners, convention is a relational exercise. In this view, '[t]he morality of convention lies in the fact that it is seen to accommodate and control [innate] difference' (J. Weiner 1988: 8).

6 One may think of an epoch as an event that is also a relation, for each event assimilates what has preceded it into its own 'now' (Wagner 1986: 81).

7 Thus all obviational sequences of a temporal kind will end just before a 'final' obviation (as Wagner's double sequence ends before its own closure).

8 Choice has also changed: no longer the exercise of discrimination and thus revelation of social or natural (good) breeding, but a preference on a par with opinion and decision-making, to be exercised no matter how trivial or momentous the occasion, and to be seen to be exercised. I enter the qualification here noted earlier *apropos* home furnishings (Chapter Four), and in Sandra Wallman's (pers. comm.) words, that in advertising parlance there is no mass market these days; every individual is perceived to be a market of one – and 'customised' thereby.

9 Hence their differentiating function in keeping apart the 'domains' of social life.

10 In his argument, a new concept of nature is the first revelation of the turn between Medieval to Modern times; it displaced human responsibility to God by human responsibility for God, and thus for an elucidation of the world that had to explain not only God but humankind's place in it. This displacement obviated earlier assumptions. In Medieval Europe, humankind had always been placed in an order beyond itself, but insofar as that order was personified in God, the question of the individual person's relationship to it was a question of personal responsibility to God. The world was full of divine presence, of which natural manifestations constituted signs for the faithful. When the context or ground of being then became apprehended as nature, God was internalised: people became responsible for the conventions by which they apprehended divinity. As a consequence, what appeared at issue for individual persons was their relationship to the conventional order. The world was seen to contain both creations and inventions, facts of nature and people's interpretations of them. The connection between the apparatus for discovering the world (reason) and its internal autonomy (nature) became understood not as a matter of decoding signs but as a matter of unravelling relations. Hence, throughout the subsequent Modern cycle, what is being refashioned at each moment is the nature of relations, namely, humankind's relationship to a world conceived in the abstract as the work of a Creator, or the hand of Nature or eventually Society itself, but always posing the question of how one 'does' the relationship.

11 Thus Rabinow (e.g. 1989: 18–19), after Foucault's *The Order of Things*. Modernity

was not distinguished by the attempt to study humankind with objective methods but with the appearance of what Foucault calls a doublet: 'Man appears as an object of knowledge and as a subject that knows.'

12 Might Culture finally be seen as 'added' to Technology? 'Modernists and Late-Modernists tend to emphasise technical and economic solutions to problems, whereas Post-Modernists tend to emphasise contextual and cultural *additions* to their inventions' (Jencks and Keswick 1987: 22, my emphasis). But, then, this only refers to architecture!

13 Werner Sperschneider brings to my attention an observation by Brian Hale (from Fokkema and Bertens, eds., *Approaching Postmodernism*, 1986) that the dominant theme of modern writing is epistemological (how do we know knowledge) by contrast with what he identifies as the ontological stance of postmodern writing (what kinds of worlds are there?). Ontological here carries the connotation not of grounding but of being.

14 The 'cannibalism' is literal for chickens that eat recycled chicken/feed. Some of the outrage expressed in the popular press may stem from the 'familial' association of domestic farmyard animals. Wild carnivores quite properly eat other animal species, as may carnivorous house pets.

15 It is alleged that the BSE disease was transmitted when, in the interests of financial economy, the Government allowed a drop in the minimum standard for the temperatures at which cattle feeds were sterilised.

16 *The Guardian*, 7 June 1990, carried a double spread on multimedia as 'new products which offer combinations of text, sound, animation and images' and on the computer virus as the possible 'harbinger of a new form of life, able to spread uncontrolled through the world's network'.

17 'The development of a genetic and physical map followed by a complete sequencing of the estimated 3,500 million base pairs making up the human genome are now technically feasible: all that is required is the will and the money (about 50 pence per base pair)' (Ferguson 1990: 8). E. P. Thompson's novel *The Sykaos Papers* (Bloomsbury 1988) depicts a 'human' species without kinship.

References

Anderson, Michael, 1980, *Approaches to the History of the Western Family 1500–1914*, London: Macmillan.

Apffel-Marglin. Fredrique, n.d. 'Woman's Blood: Life Rhythm and Work Discipline'. Paper presented to WIDER conference. *Systems of knowledge or systems of domination*, Karachi, 1988.

Austen, Jane, 1917 [1811], *Sense and Sensibility*, London: Macmillan and Co. Ltd.

Barnard, Alan and Anthony Good, 1984, *Research Practices in the Study of Kinship*, London: Academic Press.

Barnes, Fancourt, 1898 [1843], *Chavasse's Advice to a Wife on the Management of Her Own Health, etc.* (Revised: 14th Edn), London: J. and A. Churchill.

Barnett, Steve and Martin G. Silverman, 1979, *Ideology and Everyday Life: Anthropology, Neomarxist Thought, and the Problem of Ideology and the Social Whole*, Ann Arbor: University of Michigan Press.

Barnett, Steve and JoAnn Magdoff, 1986, 'Beyond Narcissism in American Culture of the 1980s', *Culture Anthropology*, 1: 413–24.

Barrett, Michèle and Mary McIntosh, 1982, *The Anti-Social Family*, London: Verso.

Battaglia, Debbora, 1985, '"We Feed our Father": Paternal Nurture among the Sabarl of Papua New Guinea', *American Ethnologist*, 12: 427–41.

1990, *On the Bones of the Serpent: Person, Memory and Mortality in Sabarl Island Society*, Chicago: University of Chicago Press.

Bauman, Zygmunt, 1988, 'Viewpoint: Sociology and Postmodernity', *The Sociological Review*, 36: 790–813.

1990, 'Philosophical Affinities of Postmodern Sociology', *The Sociological Review*, 38: 411–44.

Beer, Gillian, 1983, *Darwin's Plots. Evolutionary Narrative in Darwin, George Eliot and Nineteenth Century Fiction*, London: Routledge and Kegan Paul.

1986, '"The Face of Nature": Anthropomorphic Elements in the Language of *The Origin of Species*.' In L. Jordanova (ed.), *Languages of Nature*, London: Free Association Books.

Bell, Clive, 1928 [1914], *Art*, London: Chatto and Windus.

Bernardes, Jon, 1988, 'Founding the *New* "Family Studies"', *The Sociological Review*, 36: 57–86.

Bloch, Maurice, 1971, *Placing the Dead: Tombs, Ancestral Villages and Kinship Organization in Madagascar*, London: Seminar (Academic) Press.

1986, *From Blessing to Violence. History and Ideology in the Circumcision Ritual of the Merina of Madagascar*, Cambridge: Cambridge University Press.

1987, 'Descent and Sources of Contradiction in the Representation of Women and Kinship.' In J. Collier and S. Yanagisako (eds.), *Gender and Kinship*, Stanford: Stanford University Press.

Boon, James A., 1982, *Other Tribes, Other Scribes. Symbolic Anthropology in the Comparative Study of Cultures, Histories, Religions, and Texts*, Cambridge: Cambridge University Press.

Bouquet, Mary, 1985, *Family, Servants and Visitors. The Farm Household in Nineteenth and Twentieth Century Devon*, Norwich: Geo Books.

1986, '"You Cannot be a Brahmin in the English Countryside". The Partitioning of Status, and its Representation within the Family Farm in Devon.' In A. P. Cohen (ed.), *Symbolising Boundaries*, Manchester: Manchester University Press.

1988, 'All Modern Conveniences: Properties of Home Comfort in English Farmhouse Accommodation.' Paper presented at Conference *Anthropology of Tourism*, London.

Bouquet, Mary and Henk de Haan, 1987, 'Kinship as an Analytical Category in Rural Sociology: An Introduction', *Sociologica Ruralis*, 27: 243–62.

Brooker, Peter and Peter Widdowson, 1986, 'A Literature for England.' In R. Colls and P. Dodd (eds.), *Englishness*, London: Croom Helm.

Carrithers, Michael, 1985, 'An Alternative History of the Self'. In M. Carrithers, S. Collins and S. Lukes (eds.), *The Category of the Person*, Cambridge: Cambridge University Press.

Carsten, Janet, 1990, 'Women, Men, and the Long and Short Term of Inheritance in Pulau Langkawi, Malaysia', *Bijdragen*, 146: 270–88.

n.d., 'Women, Kinship and Community in a Malay Fishing Village on Pulau Langkawi, Malaysia', Ph.D Thesis, University of London, 1987.

Cheal, David, 1988, *The Gift Economy*, London: Routledge.

Chowning, Ann, 1989, 'Death and Kinship in Molima.' In F. Damon and R. Wagner (eds.), *Death Rituals and Life in the Societies of the Kula Ring*, deKalb: Northern Illinois University Press.

Cohen, Anthony P., 1985, *The Symbolic Construction of Community*, London: Tavistock Publications.

1986, 'Of Symbols and Boundaries, or, Does Ertie's Greatcoat Hold the Key.' In A. P. Cohen (ed.), *Symbolising Boundaries*, Manchester: Manchester University Press.

1987, *Whalsay. Symbol, Segment and Boundary in a Shetland Island Community*, Manchester: Manchester University Press.

Colls, Robert and Philip Dodd, 1987, *Englishness. Politics and Culture 1880–1920*, London: Croom Helm.

Corrigan, Philip and Derek Sayer, 1985, *The Great Arch. English State Formation as Cultural Revolution*, Oxford: Basil Blackwell.

Culler, Jonathan, 1979, 'Jacques Derrida.' In J. Sturrock (ed.) *Structuralism and Since: From Lévi-Strauss to Derrida*, Oxford: Oxford University Press.

Damon, Frederick, 1989, 'The Muyuw *Lo'un* and the End of Marriage.' In F. Damon and R. Wagner (eds.), *Death Rituals and Life in the Societies of the Kula Ring*, deKalb: Northern Illinois University Press.

Damon, Frederick and Roy Wagner (eds.), 1989, *Death Rituals and Life in the Societies of the Kula Ring*, deKalb: Northern Illinois University Press.

Davidoff, Leonore and Catherine Hall, 1987, *Family Fortunes. Men and Women of the English Middle Class, 1780–1850*, London: Hutchinson.

Dixon, W. Macneile, 1938 (1931), *The Englishman*, London: Hodder and Stoughton.

Dodd, Philip, 1987, 'Englishness and the National Culture.' In R. Colls and P. Dodd (eds.), *Englishness*, London: Croom Helm.

Douglas, Mary, 1978, *Cultural Bias*, Occasional Paper 35, London: Royal Anthropological Institute.

Doyal, Lesley, 1987, 'Infertility – A Life Sentence? Women and the National Health Service.' In M. Stanworth (ed.). *Reproductive Technologies: Gender, Motherhood and Medicine*, Cambridge: Polity Press.

Doyle, Brian, 1986, 'The Invention of English.' In R. Colls and P. Dodd (eds.), *Englishness*, London: Croom Helm.

Dreyfus, Hubert, L. and Paul Rabinow, 1982, *Michel Foucault: Beyond Structuralism and Hermeneutics*, Chicago: University of Chicago Press.

Dyson, Anthony and John Harris, 1990, *Experiments on Embryos*, London: Routledge.

Elliot, Faith R., 1986, *The Family: Change or Continuity?*, London: Macmillan Education Ltd.

Ennew, Judith, n.d., 'Desire and the Anecdote: The Ethnographic Present of Research on Children and Childhood.' Presented at ASA Conference, *Autobiography and Anthropology*, York, 1989.

Evans-Pritchard, E. E., 1940, *The Nuer. A Description of the Modes of Livelihood and Political Institutions of a Nilotic People*, Oxford: Clarendon Press.

Fabian, Johannes, 1983, *Time and the Other. How Anthropology Makes it Object*, New York: Columbia University Press.

Ferguson, Mark, 1990, 'Contemporary and Future Possibilities for Human Embryonic Manipulation.' In A. Dyson and J. Harris (eds.), *Experiments on Embryos*, London: Routledge.

Fernandez, James W., 1971, 'Persuasions and Performances.' In C. Geertz (ed.) *Myth, Symbol and Culture*, New York: Norton and Co. Inc.

Finch, Janet, 1989, *Family Obligations and Social Change*, Cambridge: Polity Press with Basil Blackwell.

Firth, Raymond (ed.), 1956, Introduction to *Two Studies of Kinship in London*, University of London: The Athlone Press.

Firth, Raymond and Judith Djamour, 1956, 'Kinship in South Borough.' In R. Firth (ed.), *Two Studies of Kinship in London*, London: Athlone Press.

Firth, Raymond, Jane Hubert and Anthony Forge, 1969, *Families and Their Relatives. Kinship in a Middle-Class Sector of London*, London: Routledge and Kegan Paul.

Fletcher, Ronald, 1962, *The Family and Marriage in Britain*, Harmondsworth: Penguin.

Fortes, Meyer, 1958, Introduction to *The Developmental Cycle in Domestic Groups*, Cambridge: Cambridge University Press.

1969, *Kinship and the Social Order*, Chicago: Aldine Pub. Co.

Foster, Hal, 1985, 'Postmodernism: A Preface.' In H. Foster (ed.), *Postmodern Culture*, London: Pluto Press.

Fox, Robin, 1967, *Kinship and Marriage. An Anthropological Perspective*, Harmondsworth: Penguin Books.

Franklin, Sarah, 1988, '"Life Story": The New Gene as Fetish Object', *Science as Culture*, 3: 92–101.

n.d., 'The Changing Cultural Construction of Reproduction in the Context of New Reproductive Technologies: Redefining Reproductive Choice.' Paper delivered at BSA/PSA Conference, London, 1990.

Frykman, Jonas and Orvar Löfgren, 1987, *Culture Builders. A Historical Anthropology of Middle Class Life* (trans. Alan Crozier), New Brunswick: Rutgers University Press.

Gallagher, Janet, 1987, 'Eggs, Embryos and Foetuses: Anxiety and the Law.' In M. Stanworth (ed.), *Reproductive Technologies: Gender, Motherhood and Medicine*, Cambridge: Polity Press.

Geertz, Hildred and Clifford, 1964, 'Teknonymy in Bali: Parenthood, Age-grading and Genealogical Amnesia', *Journal of the Royal Anthropological Institute*, 94: 94–108.

Gellner, Ernest, 1964, *Thought and Change*, Chicago: Chicago University Press.

1987, *The Concept of Kinship and Other Essays*, Oxford: Basil Blackwell.

Gillison, Gillian, 1987, 'Incest and the Atom of Kinship: The Role of the Mother's Brother in a New Guinea Highlands Society', *Ethos*, 15: 166–202.

1991, 'The Flute Myth and the Law of Equivalence: Origins of a Principle of Exchange.' In M. Godelier and M. Strathern (eds.), *Big Men and Great Men: Personifications of Power in Melanesia*, Cambridge: Cambridge University Press.

Glover, Jonathan *et al.*, 1989, *Fertility and the Family The Glover Report on Reproductive Technologies to the European Commission*, London: Fourth Estate.

Godelier, Maurice, 1986 (1982), *The Making of Great Men. Male Domination and Power among the New Guinea Baruya* (trans. R. Swyer), Cambridge: Cambridge University Press.

Goldthorpe, J. E., 1987, *Family Life in Western Societies. A Historical Sociology of Family Relationships in Britain and North America*, Cambridge: Cambridge University Press.

Goody, Esther and Christine Groothues, 1982, 'The Quest for Education.' In E. N. Goody, *Parenthood and Social Reproduction*, Cambridge: Cambridge University Press.

Goody, Jack R., 1962, *Death, Property and the Ancestors*, London: Tavistock Publications.

1976, *Production and Reproduction. A Comparative Study of the Domestic Domain*, Cambridge: Cambridge University Press.

1983, *The Development of the Family and Marriage in Europe*, Cambridge: Cambridge University Press.

Gullestad, Marianne, 1984, *Kitchen-table Society. A Case Study of the Family Life and Friendships of Young Working-Class Mothers in Urban Norway*, Oslo: Universitetsforlaget.

in press, 'The Transformation of the Norwegian Notion of Everyday Life', *American Ethnologist*.

Handler, Richard and Daniel A. Segal, 1985, 'Hierarchies of Choice: The Social Construction of Rank in Jane Austen', *American Ethnologist*, 12: 691–706.

1990, *Jane Austen and the Fiction of Culture: An Essay on the Narration of Social Realities*, Tucson: University of Arizona Press.

Haraway, Donna, 1985, 'A Manifesto for Cyborgs: Science, Technology, and Socialist Feminism in the 1980s', *Socialist Review*, 80: 65–107.

1988, 'Situated Knowledge: The Science Question in Feminism and the Privilege of Partial Perspective', *Feminist Studies*, 14: 575–99.

Harris, John, 1990, 'Embryos and Hedgehogs: On the Moral Status of the Embryo.' In A. Dyson and J. Harris (eds.), *Experiments on Embryos*, London: Routledge.

Hastrup, Kirsten, n.d., 'Writing Ethnography: State of the Art.' Presented at ASA Conference, *Autobiography and Anthropology*, York, 1989.

Hebdige, Dick, 1989, 'After the Masses', *Marxism Today*, January 1989: 48–53.

Heelas, Paul and Paul Morris, 1991, *The Values of the Enterprise Culture: The Moral Debate*, London: Unwin Hyman.

Helmann, Cecil, 1988, 'Dr. Frankenstein and the Industrial Body: Reflections on "Spare Part" Surgery', *Anthropology Today*, 4: 14–16.

Herdt, Gilbert H., 1981, *Guardians of the Flute: Idioms of Masculinity*, New York: McGraw Hill Book Co.

   1987, *The Sambia. Ritual and Gender in New Guinea*, New York: Holt, Rinehart and Winston.

Hicks, Cherrill, 1988, *Who Cares: Looking After People at Home*, London: Virago Press.

Hobsbawm, Eric and Terence Ranger (eds.), 1983, *The Invention of Tradition*, Cambridge: Cambridge University Press.

Hockey, Jennifer and Allison James, n.d., 'Growing Up and Growing Old: Metaphors of Ageing in Contemporary Britain.' Presented at ASA Conference, *The Social Construction of Youth, Maturation and Ageing*, London, 1988.

Holy, Ladislav and Milan Stuchlik, 1983, *Actions, Norms and Representations. Foundations of Anthropological Inquiry*, Cambridge: Cambridge University Press.

Howkins, Alun, 1987, 'The Discovery of Rural England.' In R. Colls and P. Dodd (eds.), *Englishness*, London: Croom Helm.

Ingold, Tim, 1986, *Evolution and Social Life*, Cambridge: Cambridge University Press.

Jackson, Michael, 1987, 'On Ethnographic Truth', *Canberra Anthropology*, 10: 1–31.

Jameson, Frederic, 1985, 'Postmodernism and Consumer Society.' In H. Foster (ed.), *Postmodern Culture*, London: Pluto Press.

Jencks, Charles and Maggie Keswick, 1987, *What is Post Modernism?*, London: Academy Editions/New York: St Martin's Press (2nd ed).

Jenkins, Richard, 1990, 'Dimensions of Adulthood in Britain: Long Term Unemployment and Mental Handicap.' In P. Spencer ed., *Anthropology and the Riddle of the Sphinx: Paradoxes of Change in the Life Course*, London: Routledge.

Jerrome, Dorothy, 1989, 'Age Relations in an English Church', *The Sociological Review*, 37: 761–84.

Johnson, Colleen Leahy, 1989, 'In-law Relationships in the American Kinship System: The Impact of Divorce and Remarriage', *American Ethnologist*, 16: 87–99.

Jordanova, Ludmilla, 1986, Introduction to L. Jordanova (ed.), *Languages of Nature*, London: Free Association Books.

   1989, *Sexual Visions. Images of Gender in Science and Medicine between Eighteenth and Nineteenth Centuries*, London: Harvester Wheatsheaf.

Keat, Russell, 1990, 'Starship Britain or Universal Enterprise?' In R. Keat and N. Abercrombie (eds.), *Enterprise Culture*, London: Routledge.

Kirby, Vicki, 1989, 'Capitalising Difference: Feminism and Anthropology', *Australian Feminist Studies*, 9: 1–23.

Kuper, Adam, 1988, *The Invention of Primitive Society. Transformations of an Illusion*, London: Routledge.

La Fontaine, Jean S., 1985, 'Anthropological Perspectives on the Family and Social Change', *Quarterly Journal of Social Affairs*, 1: 29–56.

   1988, 'Public or Private? The Constitution of the Family in Anthropological Perspective', *International Journal of Moral and Social Studies*, 3: 267–89.

Lancaster, Osbert, 1953 (1939), *Homes Sweet Homes*, London: John Murray. (Revised 1975, *A Cartoon History of Architecture*).

Langham, I., 1981, *The Building of British Social Anthropology. W. H. R. Rivers and his Cambridge Disciples in the Development of Kinship Studies, 1898–1931*, Dordrecht, Holland: D. Reidel Pub. Co.

Laslett, Peter and Richard Wall, 1972, *Household and Family in Past Time*, Cambridge: Cambridge University Press.

Lévi-Strauss, Claude, 1966 (1962), *The Savage Mind* (trans.), London: Weidenfeld and Nicolson.

Lewis, Charlie, 1986, *Becoming a Father*, Milton Keynes: Open University Press.

Lewis, Charlie and Margaret O'Brien, 1987, *Reassessing Fatherhood. New Observations on Fathers and the Modern Family*, London: Sage.

Lowenthal, David, 1990, 'Awareness of Human Impacts: Changing Attitudes and Emphases.' In B. Turner *et al.* (eds.), *Earth Transformed*, Cambridge: Cambridge University Press.

Lutz, Catherine, 1986, 'Emotion, Thought and Estrangement: Emotion as a Cultural Category', *Cultural Anthropology*, 1: 287–309.

Macfarlane, Alan, 1978, *The Origins of English Individualism. The Family, Property and Social Transition*, Oxford: Basil Blackwell.

1986, *Marriage and Love in England. Modes of Reproduction 1300–1840*, Oxford: Basil Blackwell.

1987, *The Culture of Capitalism*, Oxford: Blackwell.

Magarey, Susan, 1985, 'Women and Technological Change', *Australian Feminist Studies*, 1: 91–103.

Maine, Henry S. 1870 (1861), *Ancient Law, its Connection with the Early History of Society and its Relation to Modern Ideas*, London: John Murray.

Martin, Emily, 1987, *The Woman in the Body. A Cultural Analysis of Reproduction*, Boston: Beacon Press.

n.d., 'The Cultural Construction of Gendered Bodies.' Paper at invited session, *Reproductive Technology, Medical Practice, Public Expectations and New Representations of the Human Body*, AAA Meetings, Phoenix, 1988.

McNeil, Maureen, 1986, 'The Scientific Muse: The Poetry of Erasmus Darwin.' In L. Jordanova (ed.), *Language of Nature*, London: Free Association Books.

Metcalfe, Andrew, 1987, 'The Ghosts that Walk: A Critique of Objectivism in Marxism', *Mankind*, 17: 78–91.

Miller, Daniel, 1987, *Material Culture and Mass Consumption*, Oxford: Basil Blackwell.

1988, 'Appropriating the State on the Council Estate', *Man* (n.s.), 23: 353–72.

Mingay, Gordon, 1981, see Sperling.

Mirowski, Philip, 1990, 'The Rhetoric of Modern Economics', *History of the Human Sciences*, 3: 241–87.

Morgan, David H. J., 1985, *The Family, Politics and Social Theory*, London: Routledge and Kegan Paul.

Mosko, Mark, 1983, 'Conception, De-conception and Social Structure in Bush Mekeo Culture', *Mankind*, Special Issue, *Concepts of Conception: Procreation Ideologies in Papua New Guinea*, D. Jorgensen (ed.).

1985, *Quadripartite Structure. Categories, Relations and Homologies in Bush Mekeo Culture*, Cambridge: Cambridge University Press.

Munn, Nancy D., 1986, *The Fame of Gawa. A Symbolic Study of Value Transformation in a Massim (Papua New Guinea) Society*, Cambridge: Cambridge University Press.

1990, 'Constructing Regional Worlds in Experience: Kula Exchange, Witchcraft and Gawan Local Events', *Man* (n.s.), 25: 1–17.

Nicolson, Harold, 1955, *Good Behaviour, Being a Study of Certain Types of Civility*, London: Constable and Co.

Oakley, Ann, 1987, 'From Walking Wombs to Test-Tube Babies.' In M. Stanworth (ed.), *Reproductive Technologies: Gender, Motherhood and Medicine*, Cambridge: Polity Press.

Ottesen, Carole, 1987, *The New American Garden*, New York: Macmillan.

Paul, Robert, 1987, 'The Individual and Society in Biological and Cultural Anthropology', *Cultural Anthropology*, 2: 80–93.

Petchesky, Rosalind Pollack, 1980, 'Reproductive Freedom: Beyond "A Woman's Right to Choose"', *Signs*, 5: 661–85.

1987, 'Foetal Images: The Power of Visual Culture in the Politics of Reproduction.' In M. Stanworth (ed.), *Reproductive Technologies: Gender, Motherhood and Medicine*, Cambridge: Polity Press.

Pfeffer, Naomi, 1987, 'Artificial Insemination, In-vitro Fertilization and the Stigma of Infertility.' In M. Stanworth (ed.), *Reproductive Technologies: Gender, Motherhood and Medicine*, Cambridge: Polity Press.

Price, Frances, V., 1990, 'The Management of Uncertainty in Obstetric Practice: Ultrasonography and In Vitro Fertilisation and Embryo Transfer.' In M. McNeil and S. Franklin (eds.), *The New Reproductive Technologies*, London: Macmillan.

Rabinow, Paul, 1989, *French Modern. Norms and Forms of the Social Environment*, Cambridge, Mass.: MIT Press.

Radcliffe-Brown, A. R., 1950, Introduction. In A. R. Radcliffe-Brown and D. Forde (eds.), *African Systems of Kinship and Marriage*, London: Oxford University Press.

1952, *Structure and Function in Primitive Society*, London: Cohen and West.

1964 (1922), *The Andaman Islanders*, New York: Free Press.

Rapp, Rayna, 1988, 'Constructing Amniocentesis: Maternal and Medical Discourses.' In F. Ginsburg and A. Tsing (eds.), *Negotiating Gender in American Culture*, Boston: Beacon Press.

1989, 'Chromosomes and Communication: The Discourse of Genetic Counselling', *Medical Anthropology Quarterly*, 143–57.

Rapport, Nigel, n.d.1, 'From Forster's England to Newfoundland Academics: A New Image of the Comparative Anthropologist', University of Manchester: manuscript.

n.d.2, 'Passage to Britain: A Stereotypical View of Coming Home from the Old World to the New', University of Manchester: manuscript.

Rathbone, Eleanor, 1927 (1924), *The Disinherited Family. A Plea for Direct Provision for the Costs of Child Maintenance through Family Allowance*, London: George Allen and Unwin Ltd.

Raymond, Janice G., 1987, 'Fetalists and Feminists: They are not the same.' In P. Spallone and D. L. Steinberg (eds.), *Made to Order*, London: Pergamon Press.

Rheubottom, David, 1988, '"Sisters First": Betrothal Order and Age of Marriage in Fifteenth-Century Ragusa', *Journal of Family History*, 13: 359–76.

Rivière, Peter, 1985, 'Unscrambling Parenthood: The Warnock Report', *Anthropology Today*, 4: 2–7.

Rose, Hilary, 1987, 'Victorian Values in the Test-Tube: the Politics of Reproductive Science and Technology, in M. Stanworth (ed.), *Reproductive Technologies: Gender, Motherhood and Medicine*, Cambridge: Polity Press.

Rosser, Colin and Christopher Harris, 1965, *The Family and Social Change. A Study of Family and Kinship in a South Wales Town*, London: Routledge and Kegan Paul.

Rothman, Barbara K., 1984, 'The Meaning of Choice in Reproductive Technology.' In R. Arditti *et al.* (eds.), *Test-Tube Women*, London: Pandora Press.

1986, *The Tentative Pregnancy*, New York: Viking.

Rowland, Robyn, 1987, 'Of Women Born, but for how long? The Relationship of Women to the New Reproductive Technologies and the Issue of Choice.' In P. Spallone and D. C. Steinberg (eds.), *Made to Order*, London: Pergamon Press.

Ruskin, John, 1906 (1858–9), *The Two Paths. Being Lectures on Art and its Application to Decoration and Manufacture*, London: Geo Allen.

Sahlins, Marshall, 1976, *Culture and Practical Reason*, Chicago: Chicago University Press.

1985, *Islands of History*, Chicago: Chicago University Press.

Schapera, Isaac, 1977, *Kinship Terminology in Jane Austen's Novels*, London: Royal Anthropological Institute, Occasional Paper 33.

Schneider, David M., 1968, *American Kinship: A Cultural Account*, Englewood Cliffs: Prentice-Hall.

1969, 'Kinship, Religion and Nationality.' In V. Turner (ed.), *Forms of Symbolic Action*, Proc. American Ethnol. Society, 1969, Seattle: University of Washington Press.

1984, *A Critique of the Study of Kinship*, Ann Arbor: University of Michigan Press.

Schneider, David M. and Raymond T. Smith, 1973, *Class Differences and Sex Roles in American Kinship and Family Structures*, Englewood Cliffs: Prentice-Hall.

Scott, Peter, 1988, 'The Case for an Aristocratic State?' Article in series *Matthew Arnold and Modern Education*, *THES*, 12 August 1988.

Segalen, Martine, 1986, *Historical Anthropology of the Family* (trans. J. C. Whitehouse and S. Matthews), Cambridge: Cambridge University Press.

Sharrock W. W., 1987, 'Individual and Society.' In R. J. Anderson, J. A. Hughes and W. W. Sharrock (eds.), *Classic Disputes in Sociology*, London: Allen and Unwin.

Simons, Peter, 1987, *Parts: A Study in Ontology*, Oxford: Clarendon Press.

Smart, Carol, 1987, 'There is of course the Distinction Created by Nature: Law and the Problem of Paternity.' In M. Stanworth (ed.), *Reproductive Technologies*, Cambridge: Polity Press.

Smith, Gavin, 1987, 'The Crisis of Fatherhood', *Free Associations*, 9: 72–90.

Smith, Raymond T., 1973, 'The Matrifocal Family.' In J. R. Goody (ed.), *The Character of Kinship*, Cambridge: Cambridge University Press.

Spallone, Patricia, 1987, 'Reproductive Technology and the State: The Warnock Report and its Clones.' In P. Spallone and D. L. Steinberg (eds.), *Made to Order*, London: Pergamon Press.

Spallone, Patricia and Deborah L. Steinberg (eds.), 1987, *Made to Order: The Myth of Reproductive and Genetic Progress*, Oxford: Pergamon Press.

Spallone, Patricia and Deborah L. Steinberg, 1987, 'International Report.' In P. Spallone and D. L. Steinberg (eds.), *Made to Order*, London: Pergamon Press.

Sperling, Diana, 1981, *Mrs. Hurst Dancing: And Other Scenes from Regency Life, 1812–1823*, with text by G. Mingay, London: Victor Gollancz Ltd.

Stanworth, Michelle (ed.), 1987, *Reproductive Technologies: Gender, Motherhood and Medicine*, Cambridge: Polity Press.

Stanworth, Michelle, 1987, 'Reproductive Technologies and the Deconstruction of Motherhood.' In M. Stanworth (ed.), *Reproductive Technologies: Gender, Motherhood and Medicine*, Cambridge: Polity Press.

Stocking, George W., 1968, *Race, Culture and Evolution*, New York: The Free Press.

1987, *Victorian Anthropology*, New York: The Free Press.

Stolcke, Verena, 1986, 'New Reproductive Technologies – Same Old Fatherhood', *Critique of Anthropology*, 6: 5–31.

Strathern, Marilyn, 1972, *Women in Between: Female Roles in a Male World*, London: Seminar (Academic) Press.

1980, 'No Nature, No Culture: the Hagen Case.' In C. MacCormack and M. Strathern (eds.), *Nature, Culture and Gender*, Cambridge: Cambridge University Press.

1981, *Kinship at the Core: An Anthropology of Elmdon, A Village in North-West Essex, in the 1960s*, Cambridge: Cambridge University Press.

1982, 'The Place of Kinship: Kin, Class and Village Status in Elmdon, Essex'. In A. P. Cohen (ed.), *Belonging: Identity and Social Organisation in British Rural Cultures*, Manchester: Manchester University Press.

1984, 'Localism Displaced: A "Vanishing Village" in Rural England', *Ethnos*, 49: 43–60.

1988, *The Gender of the Gift. Problems with Women and Problems with Society in Melanesia*, Berkeley and Los Angeles: University of California Press.

1991, *Partial Connections*, ASAO Special Publication 3, Savage, Maryland: Rowman and Littlefield.

Thomas, Keith, 1984, *Man and the Natural World. Changing Attitudes in England 1500–1800*, Harmondsworth: Penguin Books.

Thompson, E. P., 1978 (1965), 'The Peculiarities of the English.' In *The Poverty of Theory and Other Essays*, London: Merlin Press.

Thorne, Barrie and Marilyn Yalom, 1982, *Rethinking the Family: Some Feminist Questions*, London: Longman.

Thorns, David, 1973. *Suburbia*, St. Albans: Paladin.

Thornton, Robert, 1988, 'The Rhetoric of Ethnographic Holism', *Cultural Anthropology*, 3: 285–303.

Trautmann, Thomas R., 1987, *Lewis Henry Morgan and the Invention of Kinship*, Berkeley and Los Angeles: University of California Press.

Ulmer, Gregory, 1985, 'The Object of Post-Criticism.' In H. Foster (ed.), *Postmodern Culture*, London: Pluto Press.

Ungerson, Clare, 1983, 'Women and Caring: Skills, Tasks and Taboos.' In E. Gamarnikov *et al.* (eds.), *The Public and the Private*, London: Heinemann.

1987, 'The Life Course and Informal Caring: Towards a Typology.' In G. Cohen (ed.), *Social Change and the Life Course*, London: Tavistock.

Urry, John, 1987, 'Nature and Society: The Organisation of Space.' In R. Anderson, J. A. Hughes and W. W. Sharrock (eds.), *Classic Disputes in Sociology*, London: Allen and Unwin.

Varenne, Hervé, 1977, *Americans Together: Structured Diversity in a Midwestern Town*, New York: Teachers College Press.

Verdon, Michel, 1980, 'Descent: An Operational View', *Man* (n.s.), 15: 129–50.

Wagner, Roy, 1975, *The Invention of Culture*, Englewood Cliffs: Prentice-Hall.

1977a, 'Analogic Kinship: A Daribi Example', *American Ethnologist*, 4: 623–42.

1977b, 'Scientific and Indigenous Papuan Conceptualizations of the Innate: A Semiotic Critique of the Ecological Perspective.' In T. Bayliss-Smith and R. Feachem (eds.), *Subsistence and Survival*, London: Academic Press.

1986, *Symbols that Stand for Themselves*, Chicago: University of Chicago Press.

Warnock, Mary, 1985, *A Question of Life: The Warnock Report on Human Fertilisation and Embryology*, Oxford: Basil Blackwell.

Weiner, Annette B., 1976, *Women of Value, Men of Renown: New Perspectives in Trobriand Exchange*, Austin: University of Texas Press.

1983, '"A World of Made is not a World of Born": Doing *kula* in Kiriwina.' In J. W. Leach and E. R. Leach (eds.), *The Kula. New Perspectives on Massim Exchange*, Cambridge: Cambridge University Press.

Weiner, James F., 1988, *The Heart of the Pearlshell: The Mythological Dimension of Foi Socially*, Los Angeles and Berkeley: University of California Press.

Werbner, Richard P., 1989, *Ritual Passage, Sacred Journey. The Process and Organisation of Religious Movement*, Washington: Smithsonian Institution Press.

1990, 'On Cultural Bias and the Cosmos: Home Universes in Southern Africa.' In M. Jackson and I. Karp (eds.), *Personhood and Agency: the Experience of Self and other in African Cultures*, Washington: Smithsonian Institution Press.

Williams, Raymond, 1961 (1958), *Culture and Society, 1780–1950*, London: Penguin Books.

1985 [1973], *The Country and the City*, London: The Hogarth Press.

Willmott, Peter and M. Young, 1960, *Family and Class in a London Suburb*, London: Routledge and Kegan Paul.

Wilson, Patricia and Ray Pahl, 1988, 'The Changing Sociological Construct of the Family', *Sociological Review*, 36: 233–66.

Wolf, Eric, 1988, 'Inventing Society', *American Ethnologist*, 15: 752–61.

Wolfram, Sybil, 1987, *In-Laws and Out-Laws. Kinship and Marriage in England*, London: Croom Helm.

Yanagisako, Sylvia J., 1978, 'Variance in American Kinship: Implications for Cultural Analysis', *American Ethnologist*, 5: 15–29.

1985, *Transforming the Past. Tradition and Kinship among Japanese Americans*, Stanford: Stanford University Press.

Yeatman, Anne, 1983, 'The Procreative Model: The Social Ontological Bases of the Gender–Kinship System', *Social Analysis*, 14: 3–30.

Young, Edward D. K., 1986, 'Where the Daffodils Blow: Elements of Communal Imagery in a Northern Suburb.' In A. P. Cohen (ed.), *Symbolising Boundaries*, Manchester: Manchester University Press.

Young, Michael and Peter Willmott, 1957, *Family and Kinship in East London*, London: Routledge and Kegan Paul.

1973, *The Symmetrical Family*, London: Routledge and Kegan Paul.

Zipper, Juliette and Selma Sevenhuijsen, 1987, 'Surrogacy: Feminist Notions of Motherhood Reconsidered.' In M. Stanworth (ed.), *Reproductive Technologies: Gender, Motherhood and Medicine*, Cambridge: Polity Press.

Index